Education
Equality and
Society

Education
Equality and
Society

EDITED BY BRYAN WILSON

Reader in Sociology, University of Oxford

London

GEORGE ALLEN & UNWIN LTD

Ruskin House   Museum Street

First published in 1975

© George Allen & Unwin Ltd, 1975

ISBN 0 04 370058 6

Printed in Great Britain
in 10 point Times Roman type
by Clarke, Doble & Brendon Ltd
Plymouth

Contents

This book owes its existence to the late Tibor Szamuely. Although Dr Szamuely's long illness and tragic death meant that he could never make his own contribution to the collection he had initiated, it is the hope of the authors that this volume will be a worthy statement of the case for the standards he maintained and advocated throughout his life.

1

Introduction

BRYAN WILSON

Equality has become one of the touchstones of advanced industrial democratic societies. In common with a number of other
abstract concepts, equality is enshrined in the real or imaginary
political charters of these modern nation states. Any new institutionalisation of inequality is regarded as in some sense an
affront to human dignity; the continuance of past arrangements
in which inequality is entrenched is scarcely tolerated. Eventually
all political parties, whether purporting to be conservative (and so
nominally committed to the maintenance of past traditions)
socialist, or progressive, have all found it expedient to brandish
the idea of equality as one of their explicit goals. Inequality is
scarcely to be justified, and political argument proceeds as if man
had no past, no differential inheritance, as if a received culture
should be regarded as disposable if in any respect its continuance
might imply the continuance of inequalities in the treatment, or
even in the capacities, of men.

It is not enough to declare the concept of equality 'doctrinaire'
and impractical, and it is necessary to recognise that in its name
social arrangements have been changed in ways which few would
now wish to challenge. Beginning with the extension of religious,
political, and social freedom, a conception of the equality of men
has clearly been entrenched in the British way of life. Freedom of
worship; universal franchise (for adults); equality before the law;
the equal and impartial operation of fiscal arrangements; have all
become firmly established in a society under the rule of law, in
which human dignity is recognised. Equality is a highly abstract
concept which is often given concrete application only contro-
versially and with difficulty, but—in the abstract—equality pre-

vails in respect of all our fundamental social arrangements. But the establishment of such equalities is, of course, merely a conventional and hypothetical base-line in terms of which to deal with individuals within a complex social context in which they are constantly exhibiting their capacities for cultivating profound inequalities. And these inequalities relate not only to inherent capacities, such as native intelligence, physical endowment, and temperament, but to much more ineluctible items, such as moral dispositions, the strength of motivation, bigness (or meanness) of spirit, will-power, a sense of realism, suggestibility, and so on, the specific social or biological sources of which remain obscure. Inequalities in all of these respects profoundly affect not only the life-chances of individuals, but also the extent to which they can utilise equal opportunities.

Equality of basic rights in the various departments of life alluded to above are capable either of rather mechanical application, or are a statement of the rights that the individual should enjoy in respect to what he himself might wish to do. Thus in political matters, the establishment of the vote has gradually come to conform to a simple quantitative assumption about the worth of each individual's opinions in respect of political arrangements. Equality in respect to the fiscal requirements of the state is a highly impersonal operation, concerned more with wealth than with the individual himself; freedom of worship and freedom of opinion, are facilitating rights rather than actual social provision; and equality before the law is a guarantee for the individual that certain basic arrangements will be made in an impersonal way, and, as far as possible, that the law will be applied impersonally to his particular case.

All of these developments of the principle of equality, although not without some inherent difficulties, differ significantly from the application of such a principle in any instance in which the impersonal agency—the State—is to take a less mechanical and less impersonal role. In respect of those forms of provision which, in their intrinsic nature, cannot be reduced to an impersonal agency (money), the application of an egalitarian ideal becomes difficult. This is so precisely because in such cases, provision must necessarily take into account, not merely the fact of the individual as a unit, but also, at least in some particular respects, his quality. In such cases individuals cannot be dealt with as homogenous units, and regard must be paid to their specific personality endowments and dispositions. Nor is the case similar to that of a particular equal freedom, such as freedom to worship, where the individual's dispositions are passive items—and the state merely 'licenses' the individual for particular purposes, which he can seek to implement according to a range of existing facilities, or, if he will, by providing new ones. In cases, such as education, where active relationships are involved, and where, one may safely say, irreversibly the state is involved, equality must always be compromised by differentials of quality.

If the issue were merely the equal right to education; if men were equally endowed; and if the educational process in respect of all individuals were itself mechanical, sequential, and passive—then the egalitarian ideal would find few opponents, and its realisation would present few difficulties. Self-evidently, and most would say, blissfully, the reality is otherwise. Nor is the issue made less complex by the fact that education has been progressively transformed into a political weapon, and the school into an arena about which—if not as yet within which—ideological contention rages. While freedom of belief and freedom of assembly, and other basic freedoms have steadily been established as fundamental aspects of democracy, in respect of education freedom has increasingly been made—by egalitarians—into a controversial issue. Democratic polity, at this point, puts equality, however artificial the concept becomes in the process of its application, before freedom. As democratic states experience internal polarisation between socialist and laissez-faire modes of organisation (and as the conservative legitimations of traditional patterns of social order are further eroded), the conflict between these two concepts must become intensified.

Each of the essays in this volume explores a particular level at which the concept of equality must be applied if educational equality is to be realised, and whilst each stands independently of the others, inevitably there are many points of convergence and even of overlap in the perspectives of the writers, each of whom represents a different discipline. At every level false assumptions are revealed. Mr Lucas illustrates the looseness of arguments about equality; Dr Burt points to basic misunderstanding, even among psychologists, of the findings of intelligence tests; Professor Bantock makes clear the cultural coinage in which the high cost of egalitarian effort must be paid; and Dr Boyson illustrates the manifold administrative difficulties in trying to operate an educational system in which egalitarian assumptions have been entrenched. Equality is revealed as a superficially attractive, indeed seductive, notion. Its seductiveness in argument is exposed by Mr Lucas, who traces its relationship with unity, uniformity, and justice, and examines the face it presents when disguised as equality of opportunity.

The philosopher's concern with the meaning of terms is complemented by the psychologist's attempts to discover the extent to which men are unequal in natural intellectual endowment, and Dr Burt's essay covers the history of attempts to measure differential intelligence, itself a basic item in the arguments of those who canvass absolute equality in education on the assumption that environment and experience really determine the level of human intelligence. Indeed, the frequency with which those who are politically committed to equal provision are also strongly disinclined to believe in the possibility of significant differences in inherited intelligence, must itself provoke the thought that only an emotionally powerful ideological position could persuade people of such a convenient convergence. If the fullest development of intellectual potential is one of our educational goals, then marked differences in innate intelligence must be a basic limitation on the equality of the outcome—a conclusion which ideological egalitarians would be loathe to accept. It is in this respect that Dr Burt's paper is of importance to an appreciation of the extent to which equality in education (whatever the concept might mean) would fail to bring about (supposing that all the difficulties in 'administrating equality' could be overcome) anything approaching equality among men.

Intelligence is not, of course, the only respect in which individuals differ. Nor is the fullest development of intellectual potential our only—or necessarily our most important—educational goal. Apart from intelligence individual temperaments and dispositions are further items in which the differences are wholly recalcitrant to egalitarian treatment. And these differences have of course played their part in the creation of western civilisation. A large part of our cultural inheritance has depended on the operation of social inequalities, and without those inequalities in the past a great many of what are now very widely regarded as the finest among human achievements would not have been possible. No one would perhaps wish to justify a cultural and civilisational profit and loss account in terms of human misery, but equally, few would wish to suggest that the world's self-acclaimed egalitarian societies had made really important creative contributions to the arts, to the growth of human sensitivity, decency, and justice (excepting always the occasional Solzhenitsyn). Professor Bantock looks at the relationship of human culture and social equality, and demonstrates the extent to which any mechanical application of the idea of equality would suffer the mainsprings of human creativity to fail. Dr Boyson reviews the actual operation of the educational system in which egalitarian ideals have, since the end of the Second World War, steadily gained dominance. He examines the way in which a variety of administrative devices introduced to promote equality have had somewhat unintended consequences. As a practising headmaster, Dr Boyson is in an excellent position to reveal deficiencies in the day-to-day implementation of the abstract concept of equality. In recent decades, the schools system has been constantly under threat of transformation, but, as Dr Boyson illustrates, this has arisen less from a concern with the actual transmission of knowledge, the sharing of culture, and the socialisation of children, than from the new role of education as an ideological and political issue.

In view of the many difficulties which surround the notion of equality it is a matter of sociological interest that the concept persists as a widely-endorsed goal among public figures in, or interested in, the world of education. Some politicians discuss equality as if, by decree, egalitarian principles could be quickly implemented in education. But equality in education cannot be established as if it were analogous to equal freedom in, say, religion. Education is not, after all, a mere matter of license. It depends upon complex provision, and its immediately distributive character compromises any assumption of mechanical equality. No one can ensure equality of performance for many role players performing their roles under widely different circumstances, all with different individual personalities, motivations, and differently endowed with energy, enthusiasm, social skill, intellect, and pedagogic competence. Indeed, the equality of physical plant, equipment, or even of local choice cannot even be approximated although these items are more easily adjustable than are role performances. All that an educational agency can do is to prescribe minimum standards for those elements in the educational situation that can be objectively assessed and effectively controlled. By no means everything can be assessed or controlled. In so far as items can be reduced to monetary terms some degree of measurement and control obtains, but perhaps more than in any other profession the skills of teachers are diffuse, personalised, expressive, and dependent on affective dispositions—principally towards pupils, but in a measure also towards learning as a process—all of which elude the formulations of a precise professional code of ethics.[1]

[1] On the teacher's role and its dependence on affectivity and diffuseness,

Clearly teachers perform unevenly. Not only are some better than others, but individuals have better and less-good days, and may very well have different capacities for teaching at different stages of the life-cycle. It is a mark of the uncertainties in measuring teaching skills that we do not even know how to balance the benefits of experience against those of energy and enthusiasm. Even where certain objective tests are imposed—the attainment of certain examination standards—we have no real means of knowing how warranted they are: they may satisfy the bureaucratic requirements of a government ministry, or the unduly intellectual aspirations which institutes of education entertain for the teaching profession, but they may have little to do with actual effective teaching. Good uncertificated teachers have, before now, been ousted from their posts for the sake of bureaucratic uniformity, and may have been succeeded by inferior but certificated replacements.

Nor are pupils' results in examinations a completely reliable guide to teaching competence. Individual cases certainly are not, and long-term statistical comparisons, whilst they undoubtedly tell one something about teaching abilities, are undoubtedly also influenced by local traditions, the prevailing ethos of study, which may be both collective and continuing phenomena but little dependent on any one teacher's contribution. Teachers' motivations are stimulated in specific concrete situations, in the atmosphere of particular schools, perhaps by the guidance of a particular headmaster, by the inspiration of the schools' record, even by the congeniality of the local culture and life-style. In so far as teacher mobility plays a part, these factors are undoubtedly elements both in teacher mobility and perhaps also in bringing competent teachers to able pupils.

What can be offered in education is a guaranteed minimum, in the assessed competence of teachers in their subjects; in the exposure of intending teachers to courses in which the art of teaching is itself expounded; in the physical standards of school buildings; and in the provision of equipment, ancillary services, and facilities. Even these items are not easily made equal, as a casual acquaintance with school buildings makes evident. Since schools cannot all be of an age—any more than teachers can be of an age—some pupils must be catered for in buildings that are nearing the end of their service, as must also be the case in respect

see Bryan R. Wilson, 'The Teacher's Role', British Journal of Sociology, Vol. XIII, No. 1, March 1962, pp. 15–32; and for a discussion of role-conflicts, see Gerald Grace, Role Conflict and the Teacher (London: Routledge), 1972.

of their teachers. (It does not follow that either buildings or teachers that are nearing the end of their service are necessarily worse than others: indeed, with contemporary standards of building, it is arguable that the reverse might be the case, and some might wish to argue the same about contemporary standards of teacher training.)

Thus attempts to secure a basic and guaranteed minimum of school facilities and teacher competences, is as near as any flat provision of equality can go in education. Obviously, since modern society relies on elaborate procedures of social selection in the allocation of individuals to specific roles, a hierarchy of educational establishments must arise above such a minimal provision. The manifest inequality of such diversified provision is met, by those in favour of abstract justice, by the concept of equal opportunity. The concept accommodates the fact of diverse capacities in pupils, the inevitably varied relations established between teachers and pupils, and also the needs of society for men of highly diverse skills. Thus the system built on equality of opportunity implies ultimate inequalities of provision as well as inequalities in capacity to utilise such diverse facilities. The principle of equality of opportunity demands that unequal endowments should be matched by facilities of varying sorts, while the diversity of social roles for which people are being prepared requires that we capitalise on inequalities and accommodate our institutions to them.

Equality of opportunity is one of our contemporary shibboleths, and political capital is recurrently made from the measures that are proposed to realise this principle more completely. The more fully this particular equality is attained, the more directly will background inequalities—of genetic inheritance, family culture, parental influence, and a variety of haphazard factors—come to manifest themselves in the subsequent inequality of performance. Equality of opportunity in itself—were it ever to be fully attained —would not of course result in anything approaching an equal society, it could at best only ensure that differences in actual intelligence, motivation, examination capacity, cultural and genetic endowment would find appropriate levels for their realisation in actual educational attainment.[2]

Absolute equality of opportunity would demand that all provision of education should be in the same hands, in particular in the contemporary context, that inequalities other than those which

[2] This point was made long ago by the sociologist, T. H. Marshall, *Citizenship and Social Class* (Cambridge: University Press), 1950, pp. 65–6.

were intrinsic to the individual pupils themselves should be eliminated. It demands that for pupils whose level of antecedent attainment is similar, like institutional provision should be made; that no individual's education should be monetarily more heavily subsidised than another's at the same level of competence. The implication of the principle is emphatically meritocratic, even though there is, as Dr Burt makes plain, no way in which (in a democratic society in which the family remains a private institution, at any rate) the very considerable inequalities deriving from the family ethos can themselves be eliminated. Whatever else, then, the equality of opportunity, has to take the randomly disparate 'given' qualities of individuals as its own base line for operation. It justifies the hierarchy of very unequal education institutions by reference to the inequalities among individuals stemming from innate qualities, family culture and a welter of happenstance factors (such as illness, death of one or both parents, birth-order and its effects on individual dispositions and intelligence, pre-natal influences, random but impressive experiences in childhood, and so on).[3] Many of these items are, of course, quite beyond individual choice. Nor can they be eliminated by legislative measures, social planning, nor even by an act of national will, were, say the whole nation to dedicate itself to the attainment of the goal of total equality.

The principle, then admits inequalities that are intrinsic and involuntary, and reinforces them, but would, were it rigorously applied, exclude inequalities that stem from choice and are extrinsic. Influence, wealth, and social standing, are all inadmissible items if equality of opportunity is to be provided. But in fact, the very items which the principle selects are often items that are very much influenced by differences in precisely these areas. A richer child is given equal opportunity with a poorer, but if the relative wealth of his family has been transformed into the maintenance of cultural interests, or permits parents to give more personal attention to children, or leads to the cultivation of a wider and better educated acquaintance, then it is the effects of exactly these differences that equality of opportunity will enhance in the immediate and subsequent selection of the child for further, better, or more, education.

This point is made not to derogate the principle of the equality of opportunity, but only to make apparent the effects of its

[3] The impossibility of dealing with these items is dealt with by John Charvet, 'The Idea of Equality as a Substantive Principle of Society', *Political Studies*, March 1969, pp. 1–15.

operation. And this must raise the question of whether it is in any sense more fair, or socially more advantageous (since in socialist and semi-socialist society this particular concept is the one usually applied in judging social arrangements) to permit inequalities that may ultimately derive from differences in wealth to become effective in the educational system (indeed to become part of its *raison d'etre*) while excluding inequality of treatment which could be obtained directly by means of money. The irony of such an arrangement is that it favours those whose wealth has been longer in the family where it may have been more effectively transmuted into high standards of civilised life, into a cultural inheritance of good talk, informed opinions and the accumulation of cultural appurtances—of which books and musical instruments are perhaps the most conspicuous—which are regarded as essential sources for the enrichment of the individual's private life. The man who has worked hard to produce wealth, however, may not have had time also to acquire a cultural inheritance to pass on to his children, and a system demanding complete equality of opportunity will deny him the right to 'buy' one, in so far as it may be purchased by paying for their better education. It can scarcely be surprising that, as was long ago pointed out, the effect of the 1944 Education Act, which was intended as a measure enhancing the equality of opportunity, was in many ways to advantage those with middle-class backgrounds against those with working-class backgrounds, even in a period when a considerable redistribution of income was occurring between those classes.[4]

There is, of course, a more widely recognised and perhaps more important implication to the operation of the principle, and that is the diminution of diversity in education (other than that which prevails by virtue of its hierarchic structure). The rigorous application of the concept might demand not only the elimination of all educational choice, but also the endeavour to make uniform all educational institutions. Elements that have been important in the creation of the national style in Britain, and which have influenced the history of various national institutions, would certainly be lost. We should lose, in particular, the useful co-existence of the educated man of less intelligence and the less educated man of more intelligence. The former may—although one speculates without more than impressionistic evidence—have been a considerable influence in British public life, and this not for the worse. Less intelligent people with a certain cultural style, with some

---

[4] This point emerged clearly in Jean Floud, A. H. Halsey and F. M. Martin, *Social Class and Educational Opportunity* (London: Heinemann), 1957.

B

acquaintance of what education is, and what its intentions are, may play important social roles in supporting, socially, financially, and politically, institutions devoted to the training of the mind, and ensuring them of a respected place within a social system which has never been dominated by intellectuals as such—ensuring therefore that intellectual institutions are not socially and culturally isolated. They may, too, from a position of some social advantage, make evident the importance of cultivating virtues other than those which depend too closely on intelligence *per se*. It is not always easy, so intellectualised has our thinking become, and so much of it is done (for the rest of society) by people who operate almost exclusively in intellectual milieux, and who evaluate intelligence perhaps more highly than is socially warranted, to make apparent the importance of other social virtues. But intellectuals are by no means conspicuous as those who do most to maintain social and civic standards, and it may be that in an age of easy vandalism of impersonal urban contexts, we shall come to appreciate the civic concern, social responsibility, and cultural goodwill of individuals who may not count among the highest bracket of intelligence, but who have—often from their selective schooling (private, public, or grammar)—learned some of the qualities that life, even in a highly rational and technologised social system, still demands.

It may seem difficult to justify the importance of the less-educated, more intelligent individuals of the world. Yet in some respects it is only because we have rather easily accepted the assumption that high intelligence should mean more education (and therefore the likelihood of considerable upward social mobility) that obscures the fact that there have been, and perhaps still are, many such people about in the world. They have been significant in the past in the role that they have played in, for example, the voluntary societies of Victorian England, indeed in England until the Second World War perhaps. They were the people of character and ability who in many ways were capable of getting their own education by one means or another, and who became in consequence men of genuine culture, without the overlay of sophistication which has sometimes been a handicap to their social 'betters'. What they gained they appreciated, and in many respects made more from it than has been the case with their automatically educated grandchildren. The paradox of institutionalisation applies to just such generations of people as it does to new religious movements or voluntary societies. There are creators and receivers, and in many ways we continue to recognise the singular virtues of those who have made their own way against the odds, not just because they have made their own way, but also because of the particular qualities of tenacity, integrity, and loyalty which that process has demanded and elicited. They have often built up intense commitment to the local institutions—libraries, mechanics institutes, trades unions, chapels, evening institutes, friendly societies, workers educational groups, co-operatives—in which they have forged their character and to which they have given their time and energy. Our society still depends on the qualities and the loyalties shaped by that sort of experience, not least for the maintenance of our national inheritance of voluntary agencies and local welfare activities (those agencies recently rediscovered by the contemporary left and inappropriately politicised in the concept of 'community politics'). The significance, in the face of global principles and concepts such as equality, of commitment to the local and parochial as a necessary element in the maintenance of civilised standards is often overlooked.

It might be said against this point, that it is easy for an academic to argue the virtue of such less-educated men, depriving them as it were, by argument, of the need for better provision of education (for which of course, many of them themselves fought politically and socially). Clearly, one does not make the point with reference to specific individuals or in particular cases, but one does make a general point that since absolute fairness is in itself impossible, and since in many ways diversity has proved to have unexpected and important benefits for society at large (which, for socialists, is so often the decisive criterion of policy), then one must recognise that inequalities, at least within the measure that we have known in the recent past, do not result in universally evil consequences. Indeed they may result in many happier consequences than the rigid enforcement of an abstract conception of equality. 'Happier' is, of course, a question-begging word, and inter-personal comparisons cannot be made, but one might note incidentally that the under-educated intelligent men of the past (one thinks of working men, but one must remember that they were not the only ones in this circumstance) were not conspicuously unhappy, and may have taken greater pleasure in the results of their own achievements and efforts than has commonly been the case for those who have merely passed through the educational system of advanced society as a matter of course.

The foregoing considerations are, however, only marginal items that arise as consequences of seeking to implement the idea of equality in educational opportunity. There are others which make manifest the impossibility of attaining this ideal, and the extraordinarily high costs of pressing it beyond that point where 'rough justice' is attained. It scarcely needs be said, that we have no means of knowing whether the distribution of intelligence among men even remotely approximates the requirements of differential intelligence and education for the performance of social roles. It might be that men are much more equal in intelligence than are the demands of the diverse role-performances of industrial society. If that were so, the corollary of equality of opportunity, namely the provision for everyone of the full 'amount' and quality of education which they could manage, might result in a general public the level of whose education exceeded the opportunities for its use.

Of course, if education were geared for leisure pursuits, for the enrichment of the individual personality, for high cultural appreciation, the acquisition of a keen civic sense, and personal creativity—and if society could afford to allow the mass of men the time to indulge these capacities—then an 'over-educated' society in the sense described above would present no problems: few would find any grounds on which to oppose it. But this hypothetical arrangement fails to correspond with reality in a number of important respects. Whatever the distribution of intelligence, personal motivation is an extremely important element in educability, and one which does not vary directly with intelligence. It may be that the very diversity of social roles in our society, and the very different requirements in duration of effort and application of intelligence, and the complex pattern of rewards attached to different roles, are themselves important items which affect motivational patterns in individuals, but do so in many diverse ways. Our society cannot, apparently, afford to educate people primarily for their personal creativity and cultural enrichment, and the emphasis on vocational education has—in part because of the expense of mass education into the middle and late teens—grown rather than diminished.

Clearly if education is predominantly vocational, serious dislocations between educational training and society's need for a particular distribution of jobs, must be expected as a persisting feature of modern economies. Such is the pace of social change, and such the complexity of factors involved, that it is impossible to plan accurately for replacement requirements in all except a very few professions, and those the ones which are themselves least affected by change. In considerable measure a market mechanism has to operate, and there must be a considerable range of people whose trained skills are either sufficiently unspecific to allow them to change occupations (occupations which are, in consequence, at a relatively low level of expertise) or who are prepared to forego the use of their trained skills, either because they find some other work more attractive, or because they have no opportunity to find a job which allows the exercise of their skills. The last eventuality, if relatively highly trained people are involved, entails both personal frustrations and social waste, and might, if extensive, be a potent source of social disruption.

Such is the pace of social and technical change, of course, that there are likely also to be counter-vailing scarcities in other areas, and to meet these re-training or 'recurrent education' is clearly necessary. The more a society comes to rely on recurrent education, the more it must be sure that what it provides in the earliest education is itself not unduly specific, that it provides a basis for the acquisition of specific skills later, a basis of fundamental competences established in early life. This in itself—although it is not the point at issue here—suggests that academic discipline, those disciplines in which the mind is trained, rather than 'disciplines' in which a subject is taught, must still be the hard core of education for the future. Specialisation and vocationalism must be held in check in the education which an individual receives in the first sixteen to twenty years of life: otherwise we shall produce an extensive range of trained incapacities, individuals who are not basically able to adapt to new life requirements.

It is perfectly conceivable that despite technological progress even advanced industrial societies will continue to rely for many of their work-needs on labour of relatively little skill. This is apparent more than anywhere else in the realm of family life. Whatever progress is made by the Women's so-called Liberation movement, as long as the present arrangement of family life continues (and some of the imperative items are biological and do not appear to allow for very radical variation) there will of necessity be a large section of the adult population involved in what might be called simple maintenance activities—shopping, cooking, cleaning, and caring for others. Even though this work role has been simplified and made less onerous by a variety of 'modern conveniences', it remains a time-taking set of activities calling for relatively low skills but high degrees of commitment and devotion. Those engaged primarily in this work are likely to be less frustrated if they are not, in so spending their time, ignoring expert skills and technical competences which they are prevented from exercising. They are more likely to enjoy this role if their educational background has prepared them for it, and has given them personal creative and cultural interests which harmonise rather than conflict with it. Since male and female roles are, in the main, likely to continue to be different for the vast majority, it is perhaps worth asking again whether most boys and girls ought to receive the same education, and whether there is not a case to be made out on these (and perhaps also on other grounds, to do with the sexual impressionability of teenage children) for some degree of educational specialisation by sex.

Housewives are of course not the only section of the population whose roles require low specificity of skill. There are others, and in these cases there may be no compensatory requirement of a high degree of dedication. Rapidly changing industrial societies have—to their own inconvenience and at considerable cost to the general quality of life—made the cost of low-skilled work, and social maintenance work (in particular in the public sector, from the defence and police forces, medical ancillary services, catering, institutional maintenance, postal communication and transport work, and civic cleansing services) so high that breakdown appears to be not infrequently threatened. If to this problem is increasingly added the need to recruit the inappropriately educated who can find no work better suited to their skills, the problem will be considerably intensified. It is by no means agreeable to make the point that some there must be who fulfil these functions if society is to continue at all, but it is a truism which even the most embattled socialist must acknowledge. The problem does not admit of *Brave New World* solutions, and even committed social planners might not care to assign individuals to the more menial of these jobs. They, too, would prefer to hide this unpleasant face of social selection behind the market mechanism, a mechanism which itself relies on, by no means always equitable, assumptions that an able boy or girl will make his own way to a better education and therefore to a better job. The canvass of equality of opportunity cannot be pressed too vigorously in case the result turns out to be some type of Dodo race in which everybody wins and vital services are left to be done by those too over-educated to undertake them. But all of this, of course, on the assumption that our education must be as heavily vocational in character as—under strong political pressure—we have in recent years seen it become.

For a long time we have assumed that the course of social progress would itself iron out some of our difficulties in these respects: boredom and labour-intensive jobs were assumed to be doomed by successive technological advances, from steam to electronics and computers. Development has not gone as far and as fast as idealists might have hoped, and it may be that an irreducible minimum of low-skilled, manual, and menial tasks will always remain. No one wants society to breed *Untermenschen* for their performance.[5] Indeed one wishes to see this type of labour dignified and esteemed, and one wants those engaged in it to have a sense of their social worth. That result will not be attained by vocational over-education. It might be attained by providing new types of education for leisure and creativity, particularly for those whose work offers no intellectual challenge, and who may themselves be temperamentally, motivationally, or intellectually unequal to, or ready for, such challenge.

Even if the distribution of natural intelligence were eventually shown to be more or less equal among men, would it follow that at the behest of the principle of equality, every effort should be made to allow each individual to realise that intelligence through courses of vocational education? As long as society itself has a highly diversified role structure, with highly divergent demands for intelligence in different roles, the consequences of giving an affirmative answer to the question can hardly be left out of account. We are already seeing the consequences of our high-principled and well-intentioned efforts to reduce every form of disease, and to foster and maintain all human life. The policy was utterly unexceptionable and few could ever have doubted its moral rightness. But the over-population that has resulted now makes apparent the fact that we were not solving problems, we were only shifting them. That in eliminating processes that might be called natural selection, we were cultivating a situation in which serious consequences would ensue. Were we to eliminate social and educational selection, an analogous result might follow: a society the continuance of which was jeopardised because insufficient people were prepared to undertake menial social roles because

---

[5] Perhaps one makes such a point over-confidently. Referring to the limits to which the social environment might be altered to achieve greater equality of opportunity, Bernard Williams ('The Idea of Equality', in Peter Laslett and W. G. Runciman, *Philosophy, Politics and Society*, 2nd Series (Oxford: Blackwell), 1962, pp. 128–9) asks whether brain operations to eliminate hereditary differences in intelligence might not be thought justifiable. The question is asked hypothetically and in the context of social science fiction, but if such a thought occurs to those who are keen to promote the absolute equality of men, it might also occur to others who wish to ensure the orderly allocation of individuals to social roles—horrific as such a prospect is.

they had been educated beyond them, and could find no joy in them.

As yet, of course, we have not approached solutions to the conundrum that people of apparently equal native intelligence experience very different courses of intellectual development. We have not discovered how to control motivation, and we are still at the mercy of differences of temperament which vary randomly in respect of intelligence. And although we know a good deal about some aspects of personality development we are by no means in a position to eradicate the factors and events which promote one sort of development, nor to stimulate those which cause another. We can, however, scarcely be happy that it is our ignorance which prevents us from embarking on a course of social self-destruction.

Social selection and placement are problems for sociologists and economists, rather than an issue of direct concern to educationalists, and it is conceivable that social need and economic arrangements might easily differ from the range of educated competences which emerge from the schools. The ideology of equality of opportunity, and the demand for equal facilities have, of course, been implemented by new arrangements and new methods in teaching, and new structures in school organisation. The social consequences of these changes have not, however, been the straight-forward realisation of greater educational equality. Perhaps the most disturbing trend in the egalitarian thrust has arisen with respect to discipline. Social control in school, the means of ensuring that certain necessary preconditions for teaching and study are met, has come to be increasingly represented as a form of undue interference with the rights of pupils. In the contemporary climate any exercise of authority is easily represented as 'authoritarian'. The charge comes not from parents, but from educationalists, self-appointed advisers on education, and some sociologists. In general, parents appear to complain that teachers are no longer exercising sufficient discipline in schools.

The exercise of discipline by teachers is, of course, fundamentally inegalitarian: pupils are treated as having fewer rights, of being subject to obedience, of being under instruction, open to correction, and, in cases of recalcitrance and defiance, of meriting punishment, which may include corporal punishment. The opponents of a system which includes these characteristics regard it as operating in defiance of the principles of natural justice. Differences in age and experience between teachers and pupils are regarded as irrelevant items. A statement that motivation to learn needs encouragement, is regarded as a demand that teachers should engage in a form of manipulation of their pupils. The demand of society to have its young people socialised, is seen as no more than a form of brain-washing of the young to make them conform to 'the rat race', to 'bourgeois society', or to 'the system' —the 'reified', 'objectivated', construct of society which authoritarians promote in order to exploit 'the people'. These are the responses of some contemporary educational theorists.

The notion of equality, once introduced into any particular area of social operation, knows no easy boundaries: from equality of opportunity for pupils, the ideology of the equality of all participants in the social aspects of the education process has now acquired wider acceptance. The idea that education can occur only in unconstrained contexts, that play, free expression, and individual discovery are the basis for learning are all ideas that feed the demand for equality among all classes of participant in the educational process. At the most extreme and strident, though as yet less dignified by solemn academic theorising, are the demands for student power and pupil power. Fortunately, and particularly in respect to pupils, the inherent and biologically-determined capacities of the young militates rather strongly against any significant accumulation of power in well-sustained pupil organisations. But these, most extreme, formulations of egalitarian ideology derive their support from precisely the same arguments, and gain their victories in precisely the same ways, as the more reasonable demands that stem from the call for equality of opportunity.

There are of course many strands to the arguments in support of the new methods of learning; the assumption that differences in ability are largely the consequence of environmental factors is one of them. The process of socialisation is charged not only with impairing man's native intelligence, but also of crippling him with a burden of guilt (in the Freudian variants of the argument); of conditioning him in a way which is fundamentally alienating (in the Marxian versions); of rendering him 'insane' in order to fit into the insane requirements of society (in the Laingian twist of the case). The canvass for the new methods of learning is thus quickly involved not in merely seeking ways to educate children as an end in itself, but in seeking ways to alter society through the education of children. This implication is not, of course, always readily perceived by those who have uncritically espoused the new techniques and the new theories.

All but the ideologically-committed votaries of the new theories of learning, would probably regard education as itself a process preparing individuals to play a part in society—society constituted not radically differently, and in essential evolutionary continuity with society as we know it and have known it in the past. The business of teaching, the building of schools, and the provision of books, equipment, and experience has grown up on the assumption that each generation was involved in preparing its successors to assume their appropriate responsibilities, to undertake social roles, and to contribute to the general welfare by the acquisition of transmitted skills and accumulated wisdom. In no society has the effort and expenditure of resources been made for the young simply to let them develop 'as they liked', or in essential alienation and hostility to the society into which they have been born. Almost all of us, except for a small number of (none the less not un-influential) theorists, expect schools to equip young people to take a place in our on-going social system. The intention is to cultivate lively and enquiring minds in responsiveness, sensitivity, the ability to criticise constructively, an appreciation of culture, and, with all, a sense of civic and social responsibility (which means, since radical theorists quickly distort common sense understandings, an awareness of the needs of others, and a willingness to share in collective effort as well as in social benefits).

It is neither materialistic, manipulative, nor unduly calculating to take into account, as we have done in the foregoing paragraphs, social need for a particular distribution of roles, and for the allocation of proven ability to particular roles. The more complex our technological organisation grows, and the more specialised professional services become, the less we can ignore the need for an effective transmission of skills, and the cultivation of that disinterested goodwill, civic concern, and adjustment of the individual ego to social constraints, on which all the benefits of civilisation depend. Nor need the choice of educational method be seen as a simple conflict of the demands of society against the individual in the manner of nineteenth-century social theorists (or their twentieth-century psychiatrist followers). Education for social purposes is not a way of 'crippling' or 'brain-washing' the individual psyche in adjustment to an exploitative capitalist system, as naïve conspiracy theories of social organisation suggest. No one in the past has ever been in a position to organise such a conspiracy, nor have they been aware of the requirements to produce the results that they might have wanted. Any process of maturation involves the moulding of the individual and his exposure to influences and persuasions. Men, even when they endorse radical egalitarian theories about the inviolability of the individual psyche, not only impinge on each other, but are inextricably involved in interpersonal and social concerns. The duration of a society of nature's children, untouched by a socialisation process, would undoubtedly be nasty, brutish, and short. We have no choice but to transmit knowledge, and to pass on accumulated insights and sensitivities, and to inculcate civic responsiveness and disinterested goodwill—a process in which, until perhaps two or three decades ago we were steadily becoming more expert and effective.

This being so, we must accept that effort, constraint, and discipline are involved in the process of teaching children. Clearly, over time the goal is that effort should be self-induced, that social control should become self-control, and that external sanctions should become unnecessary as self-discipline is acquired. With sensitivity, affection, and sustained relationships between teaching and learning individuals, there is no reason why the process should be painful, and at its best it can occur as an undisturbed accompaniment of biological and intellectual growth. The individual learns, as society must teach him, that the denial of mere instantaneous gratifications is essential for the attainment of all but the simplest goals. Slowly the individual learns that the restraint of impulse-ridden and instinctive behaviour is as vital to long-term personal satisfaction as it has been to the development of human culture, the evolution of technology, and the creation and maintenance of civilised habits of mind, body, and society.

Learning these things involves the experience of inequalities. It involves superordination and subordination; authority and obedience; the graduation of attainments, and the privileged status of mastery. Clearly, the lessons can be ill-learnt. Status can become a false god; privilege can become disproportionate to effort; privileged positions can be sought before the appropriate disciplined techniques for attaining them have been mastered. Without affection, personal concern, care for others, and a sense of mission, education can be reduced to mere training, and training to dessicated routines of boredom mixed with petty tyranny. Restraint can be made into repression; discipline can be turned into brutality, punishment can become sadism. But all this is merely to refer to distortions of the system: the very existence of words to express these differences indicates the way in which they must be viewed, and the distinctions that must be made between a form and its pathological counterpart. (It is, of course, a subtle device of those attacking traditional educational methods that they contrive to make neutral terms into negatively-loaded emotive language: words like *discrimination, discipline, loyalty, patriotism, duty,* have, with many others, undergone this process to a point where in some circles their use is tabooed, and the realities which they describe are derided as *passé*.)

To suppose that education can take place without discipline, authority, restraint, and postponement of gratifications is to engage in a mode of Utopian theorising which has never been realised in the working arrangements of any human society. Even those miniscule so-called Utopian societies that were successfully established and maintained, ordered their way of life under strong authoritarian controls. This is true of the Oneida Community, the Bruderhof, the segregated sects or Rappites, Hutterians, and Shakers. Whilst those Utopian communities which took freedom and equality as their slogans—Owen's New Harmony for example —simply could not survive. Those which did continue for any length of time became immensely more totalitarian, exacted more obedience, and imposed far more discipline than do any of the western nation states.

THE ASSAULT ON CATEGORIES

The principal structural form in which the ideal of equality has found expression, is the comprehensive school. There, it was initially argued, equal facilities would be provided for each of the three levels of competence which were recognised by the 1944 Education Act, and which were to be distinguished at the eleven-plus examination. At first the idea of distinguishing competences was one which aroused only the vaguest sense that this was in some way socially invidious. A common school for all abilities was the way to mitigate any attendant social implications of intellectual discrimination. Subsequently, the assessment of distinctive types of ability itself came under increasing attack. *Streaming,* which was an attempt to teach pupils in accordance with their actual differences in ability, came to be attacked for the same ideological reasons: *setting* now suffers the same ideological assault. No matter what the actual differences in ability among children, in an egalitarian age it becomes increasingly heretical to mention them, and worse to provide names and categories to note these actual divergences.

This rejection of categories is itself an important element in the contemporary campaign for equality. It is an assault which is being mounted in many other departments of life, and particularly in those areas affected by the social and psychological sciences. To categorise is to stigmatise—so it is thought. In public and political life, it is noticeable how frequently accepted designations have nowadays to be replaced by new ones, as if words became worn out. All that happens in fact is that they become loaded with a false emotional charge, become offensive to egalitarians who wish to destroy the whole social apparatus of order, gradation, status, distinction and categorisation. In the psychiatry of R. D. Laing and his associates, which has had a particular appeal among left-wing intellectuals and fringe communities, the categories of *sick patient* and *sane society* are reversed—it is society with its role-systems which is schizophrenic.[6] The central dogma of the *new criminology* is to challenge the 'validity' of the concept of crime. An over-blown and pretentious neologism, 'labelling theory' is the sociological contribution to the assault on categories. The ethnomethodologists wish (in this remarkably like the Church of Scientology) to stand you on your head and see how then you 'construct reality'. In this widespread celebration of the re-discovery of a rather prosaic and ancient truth, namely that man invents categories and employs them for his own purposes, it would be surprising were education to be immune. For a long time education has been the principal playground of social scientists, an area where they can influence policy, where their mistakes are not visible, and where theoretical advances, such as the demand for 'destructuration', can be put into operation with a captive public.

The hostility to categorisation was pre-echoed in the designation 'comprehensive' for the new 'all-in' schools. Categories, discrimination, assessment were all implicitly under attack in the very idea of 'comprehensive' schooling. The categories which it has seemed useful to construct, which corresponded to observable and testable differences, and to which sensitive and discriminate facilities could be matched, were now to be seen as nothing more than an artificial pre-structuring of reality, with the implication that any attempt to structure the world was to do so for some conspiratorial purpose. 'People,' the new credo implied, 'or at least children, are not significantly different.' Categories were a product of false consciousness, and were themselves a means of perpetuating that consciousness. In the mass society, the bourgeois distinctions of

[6] *See* R. D. Laing, *The Politics of Experience* (London: Penguin), 1967, and idem., *The Politics of Reality* (London: Tavistock), 1971. For a trenchant sociological critique, *see* David Martin, *Tracts Against the Times* (London: Lutterworth Press), 1973, pp. 65–103.

earlier periods were not only to be eschewed but also exorcised. Fine discriminations and interpersonal differences which had been steadily elaborated and which had been employed in the attempt to make more appropriate the treatment and facilities for individuals were now to be eliminated in favour of mass provision.

This excursus into the contemporary rejection of categories and boundaries is not merely of theoretical consequence. It is evident in a wider range of contemporary institutions, and in the practical organisation of education. Schools without walls, with large windows (whatever the practical inconvenience to those working in such rooms), with 'open plan' arrangements, are a manifestation of the same phenomenon. Dr Boyson comments on the practical difficulties of these changed physical arrangements. But the destruction of categories applies to the curriculum, to school assemblies, to relationships, which have now lost their old structure and stability. The boundaries may, in the past, often have been too rigid, and the communication between units may have been poor, but to abandon all boundaries, to reduce all studies to the 'inter-disciplinary' and the 'humanistic', is to lose a sense of order and a range of distinctions that have proved of value in teaching and learning. What now occurs is an increase in the amorphous quality of subject matter, and a growing sloppiness in method.[7] The unwillingness to make distinctions, to assess, and to judge becomes a permanent feature of education as practised, and this process is associated with the idea of the individual's primary integrity as an equal, whose mind should be unsullied by any prejudicial pre-structuring of reality. Teaching children how to think (which is often and quite falsely juxtaposed to teaching them what they need to know) is, of course, desirable, and the best schools have always done it. Teaching the fragility of our categories is, at the appropriate stage—perhaps in university—also highly desirable. But this is a long way short of the contemporary celebration of uncertainty, the deliberate destruction of categories, and the emphasis on everyone being equally 'valid' as an individual.

SOME IMPLICATIONS OF COMPREHENSIVE EDUCATION

The purpose of creating comprehensive schools was explicitly political rather than educational, to diminish differentials in

[7] For a balanced discussion of some of these issues, *see* Robin Richardson and John Chapman, *Images of Life: Problems of Religious Belief and Human Relations in Schools* (London: SCM Press), 1973.

social status. In so far as an educational goal was espoused, it was to equalise facilities (not at that stage to provide the same instruction) for children of what were then admitted to be of unequal intellectual endowments. Since that time the idea that differences in individual competences were not educationally significant (except at the extreme lower end of the scale) has steadily gained ground. And as we have seen, any emphasis on individual differences is now regarded by some advanced theorists as being no more than an artefact of false perceptions of society (a false reconstruction of social reality) which was to be attributed to a grossly unequal social system. Of course, the ideal of comprehensive education was espoused by many without malice (or social theory) aforethought. Many who favoured comprehensive schooling have not been drawn into the further implications of the egalitarian argument; many of them are perhaps unaware of the 'de-structuration' of education which is occurring; but some are probably being borne into this stream of educational theorising without any serious reflections about the terms in which much contemporary discussion is conducted or the subtly shifting assumptions on which it rests.

The attempt to create equality in schooling by comprehensive education has produced in many of these schools several associated features which cannot but be said to have had deleterious results. These features are the consequences of large size, the loss of distinctive school identity, and the difficulty, in multi-purpose establishments with diversely-endowed clientele, of creating and maintaining a positive ethos for learning. Clearly, not all that is amiss in contemporary education arises from the change to comprehensives. The breakdown in discipline which is now frequently given as a reason why teachers leave big-city schools; the growing problem of truancy, which has now reached proportions unthinkable in the days of the old 'board-school man'; and the alarming reports of inability to spell and to do simple mental arithmetic, and ignorance of basic geography and general knowledge—all arise from a complex set of contemporary circumstances.[8] But comprehensive schooling has contributed to all of them.

[8] There are frequent complaints, from headmasters, inspectors, psychologists and others, often published in the daily press, about truancy, the poor quality of teacher training, the squalid conditions and impersonal atmosphere of schools, and bullying. A report published in February 1974, on bullying in a Southampton school which had led to a girl's suicide, commented that the amount of bullying at the school was quite unacceptable, but by no means

Just at a time when the problem of controlling large collectivities of people has been growing (witness the relative orderliness of football crowds in the 1930s, compared with today; or cinema audiences in pre-war years and those, especially in suburban cinemas, in the 1950s and 1960s) we have introduced educational changes that have concentrated much larger numbers of young people in single establishments. The change was made to equalise benefits, and to take advantage of supposed economies of scale. Unfortunately, the attempt to equalise facilities failed to allow for the wastage that occurs when communities become impersonal and when facilities cease to be regarded as *belonging* to a known group. Carelessness, indifference, waste, and ultimately vandalism occur in impersonal social contexts. Such contexts arise when too many people are expected to use the same facilities which, in consequence, cease to be regarded as 'ours' and instead become mere public provision. The advocates of economies of scale—which works well enough in purely technical operation—do not appear to have realised the differences that arise when they apply their principles

exceptional. The point is a serious comment on our large, impersonal, comprehensive schools, where teacher mobility, and a permissive ethos destroy the quality of civilised human relations. This particular case drew a comment from Louise F. W. Eickhoff, Consultant Child Psychiatrist, of Birmingham, who wrote: 'Southampton is not alone. In the Midlands we too have girls truanting, wandering in a state of despair and attempting suicide because they cannot stand the bullying, cannot face the demands with menaces for money, goodies, or the food brought for dinner, and the jibes and physical attacks exercised upon the innocent by the sexually knowledgeable and experienced. Girls in the mass always have been catty, but only towards their contemporaries. Bullying, that tormenting of the younger and weaker, is not an attribute of the female sex. Weakness, frailty and smallness automatically call out the protective maternal instinct in the normal girl. The suicide of the schoolgirl in Southampton is a warning of the destructive process at work that is changing the female to being the very opposite of her natural self. Present-day secondary education is the denial of every adolescent girl's due rights and needs—respect for her physiology, protection from the excitements of the opposite sex, time and peace in which to dream in preparation for her important womanly role, restfulness and relaxation of the body, mind and spirit to accustom her to her femininity, preservation of her innocence and natural modesty, and opportunity to use and extend her gifts of intuition and sympathetic understanding. An ever-increasing number of girls give up the struggle and give in to the régime that makes them more masculine than the male, more destructive, more disgusting and, indeed, more deadly. It is not one Southampton school that should be reviewed, but a whole education system if we would preserve the woman in our society and protect the adolescent girl from disaster.' Dr Eickhoff raises a consequence of equality barely touched upon in this paper, equality between the sexes. Co-education may itself be another way in which human relationships are coarsened by treating manifestly different people as if they were the same.

to human situations. The economists' assumption that other things will remain equal when they multiply factors simply does not work where human beings are concerned. Goodwill may thrive fairly naturally among face-to-face groups where the boundaries of a community are known. It deteriorates rapidly in situations which, because of sheer size, become completely impersonal, and in which individuals become anonymous. Only by continuous conscientious commitment can it be re-evoked where large numbers are involved, and this, in the comprehensive teaching situation, is precisely what is also diminishing.

These points are particularly relevant where young people are concerned, since they themselves are not fully socialised; they have few responsibilities to the wider society; and they are as yet ignorant of the way in which facilities are provided, what they cost, and what sort of human effort and conscientious care are involved. (The cliché that the taxpayer's money is at stake is not the less true for being so hackneyed a comment: it must also be seen as a symbol which stands for more than money—namely, the accumulated sense of responsibility, care, goodwill, and community effort—all of which is loosely referred to in money terms.) Large numbers cause a breakdown in the personal methods of social control of individuals, and thus permit a wider range of behaviour (and misbehaviour) to occur. Control, because of size, becomes impersonal and therefore may become apparently mechanical, intolerant, and even brutal. Cautions can no longer be sounded in a context of well-manifested and well-understood human concern. Formal injunctions cease to be cushioned and tempered by personal knowledge of individual dispositions and individual circumstances. The objective rules become alien. The individuals who live under them see them as entirely hostile, rather than as sensible working arrangements that protect the interests of all members of the community. Can one then wonder that in large schools—and comprehensive schools are large schools—discipline deteriorates, and the benefits of personal involvement, that once characterised so many schools, disappear.

This argument has nothing to do with the actual type of school, the intelligence levels of its clientele, or their class situation. There were many elementary schools and technical schools which were characterised by these qualities of personal involvement on the part of teachers and pupils, and in some measure also of parents: the benefit was not confined to grammar schools. It was simply a function of size, the knowledge of secure boundaries, and the stability of commitment which could be elicited in those circumstances. In equalising facilities, and in making schools larger, the comprehensive programme has succeeded in destroying the basic conditions for constructive attitudes to education. Equality *may* have been achieved in some marginal respects, but a reduction of quality in the actual circumstances of education, and in the attitudes towards it, has certainly been accomplished.

The impersonality and anonymity that occur as a function of size, arises essentially because in large communities the great majority of interpersonal contacts are likely to be of shorter duration and of less depth. Beyond a certain size (and the actual magnitude must depend on the specific type of activities) the extent to which repeated contact leads to an increase in the knowledge of other individuals declines. Beyond that size, a community becomes impersonal, a context in which the accumulation of personal knowledge is no longer expected, in which new attitudes, new modes of address, new presentations of the self, and new expectations of others, come into being. Up to a certain size there will be a process at work in a community in which everyone will acquire personal knowledge of, and acquaintance with, all other members. Beyond a certain size, the impersonal ethos just described will become increasingly evident, mitigated only by the persistence of small groups of closer acquaintances within the wider collectivity. The tendency is then for such closer relationships to develop only within particular groupings of people, so that, in a university for example, the associations would be among dons, or among students, with diminished contact between those within each of these groups. The basis is prepared for the emergence of 'us' and 'them'.

Size of school also has its effects on the use which is made of facilities. American research has established that reduced participation in activities, and more limited accumulation in extra-curricula experience, occurs in larger schools.[9] Thus, although comprehensive schools were intended to equalise facilities among pupils of different ability, ironically—if we may assume that the American evidence might hold for Britain—they may in fact have led to less use of facilities and less participation than would have been the case had the facilities been made available in smaller schools.

[9] Roger G. Barker and Paul V. Gump, *Big School, Small School* (Stanford: Stanford University Press), 1964. Size of school and its consequences—despite the many new problems that have arisen on a large scale with the growth in average size of school in Britain—appears to be a problem that has received very little attention from sociologists and educationalists. The impression cannot be avoided that the research which is supported is overwhelmingly committed to an egalitarian ideology.

The search for identity is today a common theme in sociology. It is used in particular reference to the myriads of young people who run away from home, who set up communes, who seek mystical experiences by drugs or in new religions, or who simply express profound boredom with most of modern life. The identity of a school was something which was very much taken for granted in the past, when schools enjoyed the long-term service of the same teachers, served a persisting local community and not infrequently the successive generations of the same families. The identity of corporate bodies, of which schools are one type, is clearly under threat in a highly mobile society, in which the pursuit of wealth and the continual supersession of skills and technical procedures have become commonplace. As we have seen, there are many who wish to destroy such identity, regarding it as a type of captivity. Yet it is clear that the security of knowing one's place, one's relationships, one's role, and the rules of the situation, are not only indispensable for social order, but also for personal stability and security. Yet our new schools have become places with which it is harder to identify than were schools in the past. The process of privatisation—as sociologists describe the development of personal isolation and concern only for one's own affairs and the making of one's own choices—has affected our schools too. This is largely because they have lost their distinctive character, in seeking to merge all abilities and all social classes; in being transformed into impersonal contexts which elicit very little personal allegiance. Schools, which pupils could once regard very easily as an extension of their own personal world, and think of as 'ours', have become increasingly mere public spaces where a certain provision is made. We know from studies of high-rise housing that the intersticial spaces between individual front-doors are not regarded with the same sense of responsibility that occurs when people live in conventional dwellings, sharing the space between, defending it, and regarding it in a significant way as their own.[10] We know that in such anonymous contexts, rates of delinquency and crime are higher, and we observe that dirt is tolerated in the intersticial public spaces much more readily than it would once have been; that vandalism flourishes; and that outside each man's island there is an impersonal and anonymous concrete jungle, the laws of which grow steadily more savage. Our new, large schools appear to follow in the same pattern. As the sense of identity diminishes, so control of pupils will become more

[10] Oscar Newman, *Defensible Space* (New York: Macmillan), 1972.

difficult, and truancy, indiscipline, assault on teachers will increase, and the ethos of involvement in a process of learning will be more and more difficult to sustain. Clearly many contemporary social processes promote this process, but comprehensive schooling has also made its own contribution.

HIGHER EDUCATIONAL EQUALITY

In Britain, the principle of radical equality has not yet been rigorously applied in institutions of higher education. Unlike continental peoples, who take principles seriously, the British prefer *ad hoc* solutions, compromise, improvisation, and interim arrangements. For once there may be some benefit in this national foible, if it at least allows us to see the consequences of the policy of others (and if we can bring ourselves to learn from them, rather than assuming that our way of life must conform to European patterns).

The concept of equality has been applied at various points in continental universities. In particular, the idea that all who qualify for higher education must be admitted to the university is now widely accepted. The result has been not so much to enlarge the community of well-educated and socially useful people, as to jeopardise not only educational standards but the university system itself. In Italy, large numbers enrol in universities not to be seen again until the time of their final examination. Since, in some faculties, junior lecturers are too ideologically committed to equality to allow anyone to fail, the result is a great Dodo race. The education of these graduates is dubious and their examination is a travesty. The general public may not notice or may not very much care if this occurs in literature and political science, but if this occurs in the social sciences (the faculty where, inevitably, this ideological stance has been most readily adopted) might it not follow in engineering, medicine, and physics? Since lecturers refuse to be involved in the bourgeois activity of giving what they regard as spuriously objective marks to candidates who, as men and women must be equal, so all candidates pass.

The same abandonment of the principle of competitive merit in the admission of candidates to universities has occurred in Holland and Germany, where some universities are now faced with sustained disruption as students increasingly decide on the content of courses, insist on playing an equal part with professors in administration, and use mob tactics to exert their will. In Denmark, students reject the hierarchy of teaching and learning, of mastery and apprenticeship, and even enjoy places on those committees which make new professorial appointments. They systematically reject applicants for posts whose political thinking does not conform to their own egalitarian ideologies. Similarly, in some cases left-wing graduate students duplicate the actual courses of their professors, so that an ideologically acceptable slant can be introduced even into such apparently non-controversial subjects as oriental languages. (Of course, to suppose that any body of knowledge is free from ideological biases, is itself a bourgeois prejudice, until class itself is eliminated by the development of true proletarian consciousness. Even after Lysencko's genetics, the lesson is not learned.)

A rather different consequence has arisen in the name of equality in the United States, and one which operates on a much more mechanical application of the concept. Because, statistically, various vociferous social groups—women, blacks, chicanos, most conspicuously—have been represented in the undergraduate, graduate, and professorial strata of universities in lower propor-tions than in the general population—so, in the name of equality, it is demanded that a quota system should operate to ensure that universities take their due proportion of each group whether there are enough qualified people in the group or not. Thus the principle of abstract equality not in respect of achievement, but by virtue of certain primary biological data, triumphs over what thus far have been thought to be relevant objective data. The fact of being a woman or black transcends the question of comparability in terms of merit.

Higher education is not the burden of the discussion in the following pages of this book, but the foregoing brief comments may serve to indicate some of the consequences which have arisen from the application of the ideal of equality in that branch of education. They reveal the extent to which doctrinaire egalitarian-ism is fundamentally opposed to educational standards and attainments. In the essays which follow, the case for complete equality in education is shown to rely on inherent weaknesses of philosophical argument, to depend on fallacious psychological assumptions, to have unintended and deleterious cultural conse-quences, and to face insuperable problems to its practical realisa-tion. All of this is not to campaign for, or even to defend, a policy of deliberate inequality simply for its own sake; it is to acknowledge the importance and the ineradicability of certain inequalities. It is to recognise that there are other values which may be esteemed dearer than the abstract principle of radical equality. In some earlier age it is conceivable that all the writers in this volume might have campaigned for a greater measure of equality in education, and that all might have supported a variety of educational reforms. Looking back, all of the contributors could readily endorse many enactments which have extended educational opportunities and developments which have promoted cultural appreciation and scientific knowledge among widening sections of the people. There is a profound difference, however, between this desire to extend facilities and advantages to more people and the abstract doctrine of equality which now dominates educational thinking. The contributors seek to make apparent this distinction, and to indicate the threat which egalitarianism poses to educational and social diversity, the maintenance of excellence, and the persistence of climates within which sensitivity, creativity, civic concern and the intellect can flourish.

2

Equality in Education

J. R. LUCAS

I

To speak of equality in education is rather like speaking of equality in love. Young men sometimes wax indignant about the unfairness of their lot, and say there ought to be arrangements whereby the available girls should be shared out equally, so that everyone should get his whack; or, more sophisticatedly, that the most desirable girls should be made to bestow their favours on egalitarian principles, so that the total female talent be fairly distributed and nobody be deprived of his rightful meed of femininity. We smile; not only at the ludicrous incongruity of bureaucrats in the Ministry of Love issuing ration cards to students giving them 2·7 date-points per week, but because the very vehemence of the young men's protestations shows that they do not understand the nature of love or what personal relations really are like. It is the same with education. Learning or teaching are like loving and friendship in being primarily a matter of personal initiatives and personal responses. I learnt because my teachers talked to me and listened to me, often told me things and often tried to see what my difficulties were and help me overcome them, and occasionally inspired me or enraged me or led me to have new insights entirely of my own. And so it is with all pupils and all teachers. In so far as anybody is educated by anyone else at all it is by personal contact and personal commitment. Institutions and syllabuses, examinations and educational authorities may have their part to play, but what makes education a reality is a personal relationship between teacher and pupil, and with personal relationships no questions of equality can arise. Educationalists can ask whether one child has as many books or as many footballs as another child, or whether his teachers have as many 'A' levels or as many Certificates or Diplomas of Education. They can also ask whether a certain selection-procedure is fair, or whether, in some specified sense, it gives all candidates equal opportunity of success. But if they become obsessed with these questions or if they make grandiloquent demands for educational equality of every sort, they raise the suspicion that they do not know what education is. For education is essentially the sort of thing to which the concept of equality does not apply.

It is easy, and proper, to counter the demand for equality in education with the question 'Do you know what education really is?' It is a fair rejoinder, but an ineffective one, because those most vulnerable to this attack are least aware of their own ignorance. And whereas time often tames adolescent anger and teaches young men what love is like and why it cannot be had as of right or assigned on egalitarian principle, educationalists seldom come to know by further experience what education is really about, and continue to talk about it and apply inappropriate concepts to it with a confidence that increases with the passage of time and the distance from the class-room. And, unfortunately, they have great influence. The educational world is a grey one in which those who can, teach, and those who cannot, administrate or pontificate, and the administrators and pontificators are allowed to tell the teachers what to do. In this book, therefore, we address ourselves not to education, but to arguments, often bad arguments, about the periphery of education, not in order to elucidate the concept or give hints about its practice, but to prevent its being prevented by the mistaken pursuit of illusory and inappropriate ideals.

II

If we cannot usefully put questions about education, we can about equality. Equality has its original *locus* in the mathematical sciences. We can say that the number of children in this class is equal to the number in that, or that the two children have got an equal number of marks, or that the amount of money per pupil spent by this educational authority is equal to that spent by the neighbouring one, or that the average weight of a Lancashire lass is equal to that of a Yorkshire lad of the same age. We may go further and apply equality to variables which are not metrical but only ordinal, as when we say that these stones are equally hard, or these two boys are equally intelligent. We mean that neither stone is harder than the other, neither boy is more intelligent than the other. Such usages may be intelligible, but may conceal hidden assumptions which may be false. In the language of the mathematicians an ordering may, or may not, be complete. In our ordinary understanding of time any event is either before some other given event, or after it, or else at the same time as it: but in relativity theory we have to contemplate events which are neither before nor after each other nor contemporaneous with each other. So too we may say of two boys that neither is more intelligent than the other without implying that they are equally intelligent, because one is better than the other at Latin and modern languages, but worse at mathematics and the natural sciences. Psychologists used to make out that there was a single factor, called intelligence, which could be measured by intelligence tests, and expressed as an intelligence quotient. We cannot rule out such a possibility *a priori*, but only remark that it runs counter to the facts as most people experience them, and that too often under pressure intelligence was covertly defined as the ability to do intelligence tests, which is indeed a magnitude that is completely ordered. Psychologists apart, we believe that different people have different intellectual gifts and that a boy who is worse than his fellows at some subjects may still be better at others. People who press for precise assessments of intelligence are like those who argue whether Plato was a greater philosopher than Aristotle or Kant, or the Parthenon more beautiful than Santa Sophia or the Dome of the Rock. It is not that we cannot ever make comparisons of philosophical profundity or aesthetic perfection, but that we cannot always. Plato is a greater philosopher than Plotinus or Porphyry, the Parthenon is more beautiful than the temples at Bassae or Agrigento: and by the same token it may be true that one boy is more intelligent than another. But from the fact that we can make comparisons it does not follow, although it is often believed to follow, that we can usefully apply the concept of equality. In some cases we can, as with hardness or with age: in others we cannot, as with relativistic time, and, as I believe, intelligence.

It is the same with social equality. I habitually pay respect to the Warden, the Vice-Chancellor, the Archbishop of Canterbury, and the Queen, and undergraduates and scouts like to call me 'Sir', and shop-keepers and parents listen to my opinions with deference. But if an American Congressman or a rising journalist or a successful pop-singer were to come across me, he would be as little likely to feel respect towards me as I towards him: yet it would be an unwarranted conclusion that we were, therefore, social equals. Social equality is something much more positive than a mere absence of an ordering relation, and may, indeed, be compatible with a definitely defined order. The situation is further complicated by the fortunate fact that in most societies there is no single all-embracing hierarchy of status, but a multiplicity of conflicting ones. As a College tutor I give authoritative advice to an undergraduate on what subjects to study or books to read for our next tutorial, but down on the river as a member of the dons' eight I endeavour to manoeuvre my oar in accordance with the instructions of our undergraduate coach; and there is no incongruity in my being represented on the town council by a scout, or following the lead of a shopkeeper in Church, a boys' club, or a folk-dancing group. This is not to say that the concept of social position is useless; but except in strict status societies, like Russia or large business firms, it is a fairly imprecise concept, and one that cannot give us a useful, negative, definition of social equality.

Equality can be characterised in mathematics not only negatively in terms of ordering relations, but positively in terms of equivalence relations. An ordering relation is one that is transitive and asymmetrical: if I am taller than you and you than James, then I am taller than James; and if I am taller than you, then you are not taller than me. An equivalence relation is likewise transitive, but symmetrical, not asymmetrical: if my weight is equal to yours, and yours to James', then mine is equal to James, but also if mine is equal to yours, then yours is equal to mine, not unequal. Ordering relations and equivalence relations are the two most important types of relation. Ordering relations are often expressed in English by the form 'er than' (with the one exception of 'other than'): equivalence relations are often expressed by some phrase using the word 'same', e.g. 'the same weight as'; an equivalence relation relates together all those things which have the same property. In fact, we often use equivalence relations to introduce, or even to define, properties. The concept of weight depends on our having balances, together with the facts, vindicated in experience, that if two objects exactly balance when placed in the scales, they will still balance if we interchange them, and that if two objects each exactly balance when weighed against a third, they will balance also when weighed against each other. Balancing is a symmetrical and transitive relation, which therefore enables us to pick out all those things that balance with one another, and say that they are all in some respect the same, namely in respect of weight. Weight is just the property with the respect to which each equivalence class is the same. Frege and Russell used a similar strategy in defining the concept of number. They were able to define a 'similarity relation' which could hold between classes (in the logician's sense of the word, often now called sets) and which was transitive and symmetrical: if one class is similar to another, and that other to a third, then the first class is similar to the third; and if one class is similar to another, then that other is similar to the first. All those classes which are similar to one another are said to be equinumerous, and a natural number is then defined as what a class of equinumerous classes have in common. Twelve is what the class of the apostles, the class of calendar months, the class of the sons of Jacob, the class of inches in a foot, etc., etc., all have in common. It may seem a very artificial way of defining number, and, indeed, all sorts of logical objections have been discovered. Nevertheless, the approach is a common one. When we were first introduced to the concept of a fraction at school, we were taught to cancel out, and write 9/12 as 3/4, 14/63 as 2/9 etc. More formally, we could have been told that any pair of natural numbers constituted a ratio, but that two ratios, a/b and c/d were equal to one another if $ad = bc$, and then that a fraction was to be defined as an equivalence class of ratios that were, according to this definition, equal to one another. Equal ratios constitute one and the same fraction. Once we have defined a relation that is an equivalence relation, we can use it to specify, define or introduce a further, higher-order, concept which is what is common to all those entities between which the given relation holds. In politics we often argue the other way, and represent the fact that a number of men all have some property in common as their being all equal in this respect. Instead of saying that we all shall die—which is true but not very grandiloquent—we talk of death being the great equaliser. Equality before the Law does not mean that the Law metes out the same sentence to us all, innocent and guilty alike, but only that we are all under the law and all answerable for our illegal acts. Many egalitarian arguments rest upon a pompous and misleading reformulation of undeniable and important truths. All men are men—nobody would deny it, and few would doubt that important consequences flow from the fact of our common humanity. But if we reformulate this truth and say that all men are equal in respect of their humanity, it is easy to forget that this is a mere tautology, misleadingly expressed, and to take it as meaning, among other things, that all men have an equal right to go to grammar schools. That this is a fallacious argument can be best demonstrated by replacing the word 'men' by the word 'numbers', when we have:

> All numbers are numbers.
> ∴ All numbers are equal in respect of numberhood.
> ∴ All numbers are equal.

Although fertile of fallacies and confusions, the connection between equality, sameness and unity is of fundamental importance in their applications of these concepts in social, legal and political contexts. Often we have good reasons for meting out the same treatment to different people, and often we are wanting to pick out some pervasive principle of unity, and in either case it may seem more economical or down-to-earth to talk in terms of the relevant equivalence relation. Countries are remote entities of abstract political theorising, but fellow-countrymen are real. The ideal of justice is difficult to understand, difficult to realise, but we can easily tell if others are being treated differently from ourselves, and sense that it violates our fundamental equality before the law. Hence we often express in egalitarian terms demands which are at bottom demands for unity or uniformity; and egalitarianism becomes the vehicle by means of which a large number of different, and not always compatible, aspirations are voiced. Egalitarians wax righteously indignant if any one dares to gainsay them, but the fervour of their denunciation is not matched by any corresponding clarity of discrimination. We know that there is great moral passion in the demands, but not what exactly is being demanded. And it is this latter point on which the whole question turns. Unity and uniformity are manifold, and there are many unities and many uniformities we might reasonably desire: but we cannot hope to have them all, and if we are wise we shall recognise that there are also many unities and many uniformities we ought not to, and usually do not, want. We must discriminate. Some similarities are important and ought to be taken into account, others are irrelevant and ought to be discounted. Some uniformities are desirable and ought to be encouraged or enforced, others are of no particular value or even positively unjust. Whenever equality is spoken of, we need to know in respect of what people are said to be equal, or in respect of what the treatment accorded to them is supposed to be equal. And nearly always we shall find it a great aid to clarity if we re-phrase the contention

in terms not of equality but of the underlying features and
properties in respect of which the relevant sort of equality is
alleged to hold.

Equal opp

III

Opportunity, like Equality, is a treacherous concept, and Equality
of Opportunity doubly so. To have an opportunity of doing
something is not to be able to do it, but to be able to try, though
without any certainty of success. As I consider what course to
take, I have to recognise that many courses are not open to me
and that I had better put them out of my mind at once. I have no
opportunity of becoming President of the United States or Pope;
these doors are closed to me, and I cannot set about making my
way in the direction of those goals; but I do have the opportunity
of becoming a city councillor or a member of the diocesan synod;
if I wanted to, I could set about getting myself elected. I might not
be successful, but for all I know now I might be successful, and
at least I could try. The door is open—the relevant door that I can
see from my present situation—although if I go through it, I may
find other doors which are barred, or may lose my way in the maze
of rooms and passages beyond. But for all I know, I may succeed.
And therefore if I do not decide to make the attempt, it is because
I do not want to, not because I cannot.

It follows that whether I have an opportunity or not depends
very much on the context in which I am speaking. Although I have
no opportunity of being President of the United States or Pope,
I do, in a sense, have an opportunity of being Prime Minister. I
am eligible, in the sense of not being disqualified on the score of
nationality or religion, as I am disqualified from being President
or Pope. But although I am eligible in this sense, I am not eligible
in another. I am not a Member of Parliament, and therefore the
Queen could not even consider sending for me. And although in
one sense I should have an opportunity of becoming an MP next
time there is an election—I am not a peer or a lunatic, and so can
stand—in another sense I have no opportunity at all—nobody
will vote for me on the strength of my personal characteristics, and
I cannot get a party to put me forward as their candidate. Thus
whether I have an opportunity or not depends on how I see the
situation in which I am making the choice. So far as formal
eligibility goes, I have an opportunity—I am not formally disqualified: but so far as practical politics go, I am entirely out of
the running. If I were a citizen of Boston, Massachusetts, but a

Protestant, I should have an opportunity in the formal sense of being Mayor, but not in any substantial sense. One of Scott Fitzgerald's heroes worked out that undergraduates at Princeton invariably elected blond men with blue eyes as their leader; in which case I, whatever formal opportunities I might possess, would never have any real opportunity of leading Princeton's youth. Although the formal door is open, yet if I look through it I can see that the next door, one of the practical ones, is shut, and so I reckon that that way is effectively closed to me. It depends on how far I can see ahead and how far I look, what opportunities I can reasonably reckon I have.

Equality of opportunity implies comparison. My opportunities are being compared with yours. We must therefore be aiming at the same sort of goals, or our opportunities would clearly be non-comparable—how could we compare my opportunity of getting on the town council with yours of making friends? We must also be assessing the situation from the same vantage point, or again we shall be talking at cross-purposes—had I the same opportunity of getting to the University in the 1940s as you in the 1970s? I may say that I had less of an opportunity because far fewer places were available, but you may say I had far more of an opportunity because there were fewer people trying for them. Unless we define the situations in which our respective opportunities are being assessed, comparisons become impossible. Hence equality of opportunity tends to be applicable only in the context of a competition where a number of people are competing for the same goal in accordance with rules, which can be assessed as being equal or unequal. We can say of bridge or football or monopoly that the players have all an equal opportunity of winning. This does not mean that they all will win; nor necessarily that they all have the same chance of winning—skilled bridge-players or footballers tend to win more often than their opponents; but it does mean that the rules of the game do not themselves favour any one competitor rather than any other. And where the rules do introduce some asymmetry—as between the Surrey and Middlesex banks in the Oxford and Cambridge boat-race, or the choice between batting and fielding in cricket, or having the first turn in Monopoly, it is felt to be a blemish, requiring a preliminary toss of the coin or shake of the dice to allocate advantageous asymmetries impartially. Games lose their point if the outcome is a foregone conclusion, and if from the mere rules of the game it is clear that one competitor has a significant advantage, we do not think much of it as a game. We require of games that they shall, so far as their rules are concerned, give each competitor an equal opportunity of winning.

The distinction between rules and other factors is difficult to maintain. However they start, games (other than cricket) tend to end in victory for one competitor and defeat for the rivals. And in so far as we can account for the outcome it will be in terms of some antecedent asymmetry between the players which may in turn be stigmatised as unequal and unfair. Even in games of chance it depends very much on how we describe the situation whether we assign equal or unequal chances to the players: given the disposition of the cards or the dice, I have no chance whatever of winning; it is only under another, and not obviously more applicable, description that I can be said to have an equal chance; and considerable philosophical argument is required to assure us that the latter is both applicable and relevant.[1] The difficulty strikes us more forcibly in games of skill, and often we arrange the competitors in 'leagues' where they will be more or less evenly matched, or impose handicaps on the stronger, in order that the result may still be open.

Games are played only for fun, and there is no very strong reason why one set of rules should be preferred to another. We may think that the result of the boat-race should depend on the muscles of the oarsmen and not on skilful coxing, but we may not; just as some people think that players should not handle the ball in football, and different people have different conventions for playing bridge. But life is not a game, and when we assess competitive situations in which real goods are at stake, we can criticise the rules not merely for formal inequalities but substantial ones. We often decide disputes by some form of competition—as when we put a public contract out to tender, or award scholarships by an examination, or hold an election—and essentially we require the parties to the dispute to conduct a rule-governed exercise on the basis of which the dispute will be decided. We can therefore criticise either the exercise or the rules whereby it is interpreted, as being irrelevant to the dispute in issue. Ordeal by combat has fallen into desuetude because ability to fight is irrelevant to the justice of one's case. If we are going to award contracts by competitive tender, we must advertise the fact, so that contractors have an opportunity of tendering, and should take into account not only the price they ask but the quality of their workmanship. If we are going to have an examination, we should not tell

---

[1] For a fuller account, *see* J. R. Lucas, *The Concept of Probability* (Oxford), 1970, Ch. VI and VII.

some candidates but not others what questions are going to be asked.

Although the structure of any real-life competition is inherently open to criticism, it is inherent also in the nature of a competition that not all such criticisms be accepted. For competitions are artifices whereby we deem one exercise, fairly easy to evaluate, to be the decision also of another more difficult dispute. Hence it is bound to be somewhat crude, placing a premium on some features that are irrelevant and neglecting other relevant ones. The large well-known firm that can undercut its rivals has an advantage in securing public contracts. The undergraduate with a quick facile mind does better in university examinations than one with a more profound but slower-moving intellect. The scion of an ancient family has a better chance of achieving public office than his opponent whose name is entirely unknown. We should be always prepared to admit the force of such criticisms, and sometimes to alter the rules so as to meet them—as when one consulship at Rome was reserved for plebeians, or when some places in the Civil Service were given without a written examination: but we cannot meet them all, or we shall no longer be having a rule-governed way of deciding the dispute at all. In this, as in many other aspects of political life, we have to forgo the best in order to ensure that we do not end up with the worst. Examinations, we should concede, are often an evil. But they are less of an evil than any alternative might become. If we have an examination, there are certain rules, not totally irrelevant to the awards in issue, and everyone has an equal opportunity under those rules of winning the awards in question. It does not give everyone everything he wants: in particular, it does not and cannot give everyone a guarantee of success, or even an equal chance of success. But it does mean that nobody starts off at a formal disadvantage by reason of the rules. And this is something.

We can make sense of Equality of Opportunity in particular games or particular competitions, but life is not a game, nor should it be viewed as a continuing race. Convention can determine what counts as a goal in soccer but not what should be regarded as the goals in life, and therefore we cannot lay down what factors should be relevant, and what ought not to be allowed to count. We are equally uncertain when the race begins and where the finishing post is. Every contest ends in some contender winning and others not. But if every contest is succeeded by another contest, the strict egalitarian may object to the result of the first contest being allowed to have any influence on the outcome of the second. Those who pass the eleven-plus have an advantage over those who fail, when they come to compete for places at the university. So egalitarians, who were loudest in their support of the eleven-plus in the 1940s, on the ground that it gave children equality of opportunity, clamour for its abolition, on the ground that it denies children equality of opportunity.[2] Even at the outset of their school career, the children of middle-class parents have an advantage by reason of their home environment, and equality of opportunity seems to require that all children should from birth be brought up in state *crêches* in order to ensure that none should obtain any adventitious advantage over his peers. But even birth is too late. Ability is partly inherited, and genetic inheritance is fixed from the moment of conception. And therefore the egalitarian finds himself unwillingly toying with the unwelcome conclusion that only in a Brave New World where we are all clones shall we have secured true equality of opportunity.[3]

It is clear what has gone wrong. As we have generalised from a game or an isolated competition to the whole of life, both the purposes and the temporal limits of the competitive situation have become indefinite, and therefore the crucial distinction between asymmetries in the rules—which are open to objection as denying equality of opportunity—and differences in skill and luck is obliterated, and it becomes easy to argue the toss. Every competition must result in some being successful and others not: and therefore, if the competition proceeds on a rational basis, it not only creates a new inequality, but reveals an antecedent one. A competition in which there is equality of opportunity is one in which the best man wins, and therefore one in which the winner is deemed to have been the best man, and in that crucial respect, unequal. Many educational statisticians have laboriously amassed figures to show that children of professional people obtain proportionately more places at the university than children from the working classes, and have concluded that this shows up the unfairness of the system. But what these figures reveal is not that children from the working classes have less opportunity of getting into the university, but only that they are less likely to. We can say that there is a smaller probability of a child of working-class

---

[2] 'The central and irresistible argument against the eleven-plus lies in the denial of social justice and equal opportunity which this implies.'—Mr Crosland at Harrogate, 7 January 1966.

[3] *See*, for example, B. A. O. Williams, 'The Idea of Equality' in Peter Laslett and W. G. Runciman (Eds.), *Philosophy, Politics and Society* (Oxford), 1962, pp. 125–9.

parents getting into the university than of a child of middle-class or upper-class parents; and it is tempting, but fallacious to re-phrase this as that a child of working-class parents has a smaller chance of getting into the university, and then construe that as meaning that he has less opportunity, or that there is discrimina-tion against working-class children. For although the low propor-tion of children from the working classes could be due to their not having had the same opportunities, it could also be due to their not having wanted to go to the university or to th... ...having been as academically gifted as their competitors, ... having been quite fairly turned down in a compe... tion. Only if we make the two assumptions that ... to go to the university and that all people a... academically can we infer any unfairness from ... these assumptions are not only unwarranted b... all that we know about young people's moti... human heredity.

But even so the egalitarian will not be cont... equality of opportunity, it only serves to reve... other inequalities. If there is any selection at ... sense, discrimination, to which the egalitaria... still takes exception, and demands that ... 'Discrimination against working-class ch'... most elementary requirement of justice ... equality, not equality of opportunit... reflects neither dishonesty nor outstan... egalitarians, but the ambiguity of the ... the internal inconsistency of that of ... we talk of opportunities we shoul... talking about is whether it is *wor*... sure of success: and whenever v... to be able to say *in respect of wh*... to remember that although w... respects between members of ... and under certain conditions ... equality in all respects betwee... all conditions.

[4] Mr Brian Simon, Reader in Education, in Leicester University, addressing the Confederation for the Advancement of State Education, as reported in *The Times*, 27 September 1965.

IV

Equality of opportunity is a treacherous concept, but has seemed a natural one with which to express a certain requirement of justice we wish to maintain in our society. We believe in justice, and one of the tenets of distributive justice is that benefits at the disposal of the state should be apportioned fairly. And therefore education, which is generally reckoned to be a good, and which is largely financed by public funds, should be made available according to some just principle of distribution. But justice is many-faceted, and may, as Aristotle observed, be taken as requiring that each be given an equal share or that each be given a share proportional to his deserts. Much of the present debate is a re-play of that which went on in Athens in the fourth century BC; in particular, the egalitarian feeling which is current now is to be seen historically as a natural reaction against the meritocratic argument fashionable in the forties and fifties of this century, and shares with it the mistaken assumptions that education is a good that can be distributed according to formula and that life is a competitive exercise in which those competitors who have a good education have an advantage over those who do not. These are both profound untruths, but contain enough truth to be very plausible and widely believed. Education is not a good to be doled out by civil servants like petrol rations: but since it is institutionalised in schools and universities, admission to these is naturally regarded as a good for which people may reasonably compete. Again, although education should be aimed at enabling each individual to fulfil himself, fulfilment depends on his relations with society as well as with himself, and for some people depends very much on being successful according to various external, public criteria. Since the Middle Ages England has been a country in which clever boys 'get on' by climbing the educational ladder. Education has been for them a way up to the top, and has been represented in this light to many others. One source of our present discontents has been the over-extension of this concept. So long as only a few schoolboys regarded education as a race, no great harm was done. Their own view of themselves and their potentialities may have been needlessly narrowed, but other people were free to develop their abilities uncompetitively, and those who failed to get full marks were under no pressure to regard themselves as failures for life. The meritocrats thought this wrong. In the name of equality of opportunity, they made every one compete, and made out that the only way of doing well in life was to go from school to University and thence into the higher reaches of the Civil Service or some other suitable setting for Top People. Most people, however, do not want to wear bowler hats or read *The Times*. They feel that although life has its competitive aspects, it is not to be construed *itself* as a competition; and if other people insist on so construing it, those who can would rather not compete, and those who cannot, feel themselves unfairly done by. There are great virtues in learning Latin—to have read Catullus will forewarn a young man and enable him to know in advance what love can be like—and in order to overcome individual idleness we may add the argument that only by learning Latin will some necessary examination be passed. But if the overarching justification for learning Latin, or anything else, is solely in terms of clearing examination hurdles in order to stay in the field for a further examination still, the whole activity is, and is seen to be, a pointless exercise. The meritocratic view of education, like the meritocratic view of life, is tolerable only so long as it is not generally accepted. A generation ago, reactionary schoolmasters and dons were being criticised by educationalists for not showing adequate enthusiasm for competitive examinations, intelligence tests and the like. Now that our educational system has been strait-jacketed by competitive examinations, it is being discovered, as a new truth, that examinations are not everything, and that competition is not necessarily the criterion of justice.

It is too easy, however, simply to say that competition is bad. Education is a good, both in itself and as a means to other ends, and although it largely depends on one's own attitude and efforts, it does depend on other things too, some of which can be assessed in a reasonably impersonal way. Some schools are better than others, and although often it is no kindness to a boy to send him to a school where the pace is too hot for him, nevertheless there are many boys who would benefit but who cannot all go. The meritocrats recognised the problem, and offered a solution: good things in education were to be assigned not on the basis of parental pull or wealth but by innate merit as measured by intelligence test or examination. The egalitarians think this is a bad solution, and would rather that there were no problem, and seek to achieve this by ensuring that there are no good things in short supply. In each case, the negative argument seems stronger than the positive. It seems right that facts about the child rather than facts about his parents should be the basis of decisions about him: but the belief that each child has an innate ability which is the sole criterion of educational merit is itself open to serious criticism. For one thing, as we have seen, the concept of intelligence as a single factor which can be assessed by intelligence tests, is based on dubious assumptions and runs counter to the facts of everyday life. More seriously, even granted that we can make some crude comparisons of intellectual ability, it would be wrong to make this the sole grounds on which to allot the good things of life. Justice is many-faceted, and we fail to do justice to our ideal of justice if we altogether overlook the claims not only of promise but of actual performance, or altogether discount claims based on parental or childhood choice, or on need. Schoolmasters and dons are entitled to devise examinations to show up natural ability rather than industriously acquired knowledge, but they are unfair (as well as extremely unwise) if they make it a rule always to prefer the man who is intelligent but idle to the virtuous but unbrilliant slogger. A willingness actually to work does constitute a claim on scarce educational resources as strong as imputed, but as yet unrealised, potentiality. So too the fact of being willing to forgo other goods in order to devote time or money to scholarly pursuits. Nor are we entitled to rule out the willingness of parents to pay as absolutely irrelevant to whether a child should go to a particular school or not: no man is an island, and no child ought to be regarded as a mere atom in complete isolation from his parents. For better or worse we are our parents' children, and our parents' attitudes are, as much as their genes, deeply relevant facts about us. This is not to say that we are merely our parents' children, and that their inability or unwillingness to pay should be an absolute bar to their children's being educated; but from the fact that a child is not merely its parents' offspring, it does not follow that it is not their child at all, and the valid insight that it was wrong to deny schooling to the children of the poor needs to be distinguished from the fashionable illiberalism which would forbid parents to spend any money whatever on their children's education. If we deny people the right to do the best they can for their children, not only do we infringe one of the fundamental freedoms of family life, but we are being unfair to both parents and children in failing to accord to them that liberty which is their due of deciding their priorities for themselves.

The argument from need is less unfashionable, but no less cogent. The Plowden Report maintained that the country should devote extra resources to depressed areas, and even ardent egalitarians seldom complain at additional attention being given to backward pupils. But remedial teaching for the dull is as clear a breach of the principle of equality as streaming or setting or any sort of special attention for the clever. But justice is not equality, and what justice requires is not that we treat all children the same, but that we give proper regard to their many and various claims, claims not only of need but of desert, not only of ability but of justice. Justice is not a one-dimensional concept, as both the meritocrats and the egalitarians have wrongly assumed, and is not to be identified either with merit or with equality, or with any of the strands of which it is composed, but rather is to be seen as a web of different guide-lines, each affording some indication of what ought in some circumstances to be done, but none constituting a sole and sufficient criterion for all cases. It is an untidy concept, and can never be completely realised in any actual society. Aristotle realised this, but educational idealists are unwilling to recognise any limitation to their idealism, and, rather than balance the claims of one sort of justice against another, seek to redefine justice in terms of only one aspect of it, and to the neglect of all its other facets; and having reconstructed justice, have little compunction in strait-jacketing education to fit. But if we are wise, and if we value justice and education for their own sakes, we shall take a humbler view of our powers, and see our duty not as that of aspiring to an ideal best, but of avoiding the many actual injustices to which all educational systems—like all other systems—are prone. We cannot hope to have an educational system that is absolutely just, because we cannot hope to have *any* system that is; and if we delude ourselves by too much talk about ideals, we shall probably overlook glaring injustices under our eyes. What we should do in our concern for education is to take care not to neglect the many different claims based on many different aspects of justice—on merit, on need, on promise, on freedom of choice—and to ensure that, while they cannot all be entirely satisfied, none of them is altogether ignored.

v

The argument for equality in education is not only founded on a claim for justice. It is often now contended that any difference of schooling is in itself divisive, and that if we want to have a society that is at one with itself and united by strong bonds of fellow-feeling, we must abolish all separation and *apartheid* between different sorts of school, and educate our young in one homogenised mass.

Fellow-feeling is a powerful sentiment. We could not use the first person plural at all unless we had something in common whereby we all could be referred to by the one word 'we', and we could not do things together unless we shared some understanding whereby we could concert our activities. Even barely to communicate requires, as the word witnesses, that we have something in common, a common language and all the subtle, tacit presuppositions of mutual talk. Not only are we bound to admit a common humanity, but often we want to. Shylock speaks to us all when he says

'I am a Jew! Hath not a Jew eyes? hath not a Jew hands, organs, dimensions, senses, affections, passions? fed with the same food, hurt with the same weapons, subject to the same diseases, healed by the same means, warmed and cooled by the same winter and summer as a Christian is? If you prick us, do we not bleed? if you tickle us, do we not laugh? if you poison us, do we not die? and if you wrong us, shall we not revenge? If we are like you in the rest, we will resemble you in that.'

If we did not share at least these values in common, and did not all eschew pain and seek ease, we could hardly understand one another, or discuss our other values, at all. Yet it is scarcely enough to recognise in another a bare sentient being, and although some great religions and philosophies have proclaimed the common humanity of man, the sympathies that have moved us most have been more limited ones, restricted to one's countrymen, co-religionists, members of the family, or wearers of the old school tie. Not only are such sentiments of social solidarity often intense, but often too they are exquisitely delectable. Middle-aged men look back nostalgically to the days of Dunkirk, because then we all were equal in the face of Hitler's threat, and even Britons talked to one another in trains, knowing that we were all in it together, and that defeat could be averted only if we sank all our differences, and all strained our utmost to preserve everything we held most dear. Family sorrows are often also occasions of great happiness, because in the face of great sorrow members of the family are drawn together, and rediscover how close they are to one another. Friends hark back to hard times they have been through together, and the best days of an undergraduate's life often appear in retrospect to be those when with his contemporaries he walked in the shadow of their final examinations. These moments of stress seem moments of truth, in which we strip away the adventitious artificialities of our normal existence, and know ourselves as we really are, and how much we are at one with one another. We lose the normal sense of alienation from our fellows, of isolation in private little insulated cells, of insincerity and *mauvaise foi*, and realise ourselves as part of a whole, which is greater than our puny insignificant efforts can ever be, as a manifestation of an objective fact which is of serious moral worth, in contradistinction to our subjective whims and selfish efforts to have everything just as we happen to please. And so it is that students start demonstrations, and existentialists write books about the moral purity of mob rule.

Plato was the first to be disenchanted with individual autonomy, and seek to replace it by selfless absorption in the pursuit of the common good. In his *Republic* we read of an ideal society in which individuals no longer seek to maximise their own separate goods, but believing that they all are of one common blood and fashioned from the same clay as their fellow-citizens, are so much of one mind with them that they no longer have any use for the possessive pronouns 'mine' and 'yours', and even have their wives and children in common. We feel the fascination of Plato's dream. It strikes a chord, especially with those newly come to man's estate, who are finding the burden of making their own decisions heavy, and are yearning for the support that total membership of a group seems to offer. But although drawn, we are also repelled. It is unrealistic to suppose that we could be as selfless as Plato would require us to be, and undesirable that we should be. To be totally of one mind with someone else is to be the same person as he. Of all the different marks of personal identity, the crucial one is the ability to make up one's mind for oneself. Unless one has a mind of one's own, and can take decisions which are at variance with those of other people, one is not a person at all, but only a cypher or a robot. We are conscious of ourselves as autonomous agents, and unless we are free to think for ourselves and form our own intentions, we should not use the first person of ourselves, but only an impersonal third; and our fundamental complaint with Plato is that in his effort to replace 'I' by 'we', he has succeeded in only replacing it by 'one'. True though it is that each one of us can discover his identity only as a member of a group, it is likewise true that each can be himself only also in contrast to everybody else. We need individuality as well as solidarity, liberty as well as equality, the right to be different as well as the recognition that we all are, in some respects, the same.

Social equality obtains its emotional appeal from our sense of social solidarity. I like the company of my equals because I feel at one with them, and can feel at ease and speak my mind freely in their presence. I do not have to mind my step, as when I am among my social superiors, or to maintain my position, as among my social inferiors; nor am I shy, as among strangers. I am accepted as one of them, and am at home among them, and can be myself, naturally and without strain. We are quite right to value this relationship, and to be anxious to foster it: our only error is in our analysis of its essential nature, and of the conditions under which it can flourish. Although it requires that we be the same in some respects, it cannot, as we have seen, require that we be the same in all respects, nor does it, in fact, require that we be the same in many respects to which egalitarians attach importance. We congregate naturally with those who speak the same language, are the same age, share the same genes, have the same intellectual, aesthetic or athletic interests: but any one of these bonds granted, we do not demand that all the others should be too, but positively welcome some sorts of diversity: young people feel kinship with other young people of different lands, and can communicate in spite of a diversity of tongues; members of the same family have different hobbies and different interests; the rowing fraternity links Old Blues and young oars irrespective of age, nationality or economic status. Although every group presupposes something held in common by its members, it presupposes differences between them too. With large groups we boast that they transcend the barriers of religion, race and residence, and that people are welcome 'irrespective of creed, colour or nationality', whereas with small groups we reckon that each member is enabled to make his own individual contribution, and is accepted and valued for himself alone.

The interplay between uniformity and diversity is complex, and may be resolved in a number of different ways. The two paradigm examples are found in marriage and the peer-group. In marriage the different contributions of the two partners are emphasised, in the peer-group the similar backgrounds, tastes and interests. Husband and wife are essentially different, as the etymology of the word 'sex' shows, but it is because they are different and lack what the other has, that the bond is so strong, and enables the individuality of each to find its most intimate expression. It is because husband and wife complement each other that it matters intensely exactly what sort of person each of them is, so much so that each is to the other irreplaceable and unique. It is in love and in marriage that most people discover their individuality most fully: it is no accident that as Plato works out his programme of total collectivism, it is his treatment of sex and family life that we most immediately find repugnant. Women and children are subversive of communal life, as the monasteries realised and the *kibbutzim* have discovered. Although there is intense togetherness between husband and wife, and they have more things in common than any other two people, the relationship is exclusive, and its effect individualistic, and if we want always to be using the first person plural rather than the first person dual, we must have our main institution not marriage but the peer-group—as in the gang, the club, the college, the regiment, the union, the old comrades' associations, the pub and perhaps the Women's Institute and Mothers' Union. The obsessive concern with sex in Anglo-Saxon countries since the War has led to a general neglect of institutions based on the peer-group, and this may, in turn, be responsible for the yearning for group solidarity that many people now feel. It is a less demanding relationship than marriage, and emotionally at a lower temperature. It is not exclusive, and one is not indispensable. Whereas my girl-friend's boy-friend is very much not my friend but my rival, my 'good friend's good friend' (to borrow a useful American phrase) is for that very reason my good friend. It is easy to enter a circle of friends on the introduction of any one of them, and correspondingly easy to move away without repine or recrimination. Particularly when growing up, we need this relationship, as an easy one not too demanding or constricting, in which we can try out different possible personalities and develop the one that is going to be our own. But, just as marriages although founded on the principle of difference need also a large measure of similarity in outlook, assumptions and interests, so peer-groups, although founded on the principle of similarity, need also to admit many differences in attitude, circumstance and aspiration. If a peer-group becomes too demanding in its requirements of conformity, it loses its liberating effect and is felt as a tyranny. We are happy to wear the same clothes as our fellows, have our hair the same length, and rave about the same pop-stars: but cannot long abide having all our thoughts and all our likes dictated by theirs. If we value social equality because we value peer-groups, we shall need to act very sensitively in establishing similarities of circumstance. It is quite possible to have a strong sense of solidarity even though there is an established hierarchy according to which orders are given and taken—as in an Officers' Mess: and it is quite possible to have no sense of community in spite of the fact that no orders are given or obeyed—as in a railway waiting-room. If we throw people together by virtue of some common circumstance we may succeed in establishing a peer-group; or we may not. It is often assumed by educationalists that by sending everybody to the same school, they will get to know one another and all feel equal. But knowledge does not always breed respect. It can breed informed dislike, and will if the wrong similarities are too much insisted upon. An age-group will not mean much to those who believe athletic prowess more important than age, or truth more important than youth, and if in the name of social equality we force them to congregate with uncongenial contemporaries, we shall only find them asserting their superiority with their fists, or by opting out and saying '*Odi profanum vulgus et arceo*'. Comprehensive schools could be far more divisive than public or grammar schools were ever even alleged to be, because enforced juxtaposition in accordance with an egalitarian ideology which denies the right of people to be different is liable to breed in those who are or who want to be different a far more intense resentment than an enforced differentiation among those who want to be the same. If we go to different schools, we can still do things together in the evenings, at the week-ends or in the holidays: but if I am subject to pressure to be like everybody else at school in every respect, to dislike Latin and to like boxing, to dislike art and to like television, I am likely to become very rebellious indeed. A peer-group will be an effective focus of loyalty only if it is not too demanding, and allows individuals to be themselves, and only if it is based on similarities that are felt to be relevant. It is difficult to fashion institutions which will unite men by the bonds of a common love. Some schools have done it—often because of the love that certain school-masters have poured into their work—but larger groups (age-groups or nationality groups) are united less easily by love than by hate or fear or hardship, and in the absence of sweet uses of adversity, are likely to generate an adventitious antagonism merely as a means of mass unification. The final result of forcing equality on the young could be that they found a sort of unity in a universal hostility to the middle-aged who had, in the name of equality, insisted on treating them not as individuals but as units.

We have distinguished two senses of social equality which may be the concern of education. Education is concerned, among other things, to promote the unity of a country, of a culture, or of mankind, and in so far as it succeeds, we may be said to be recognising one another as equals. But the sense of solidarity which we feel with other men does not require that we should have received exactly the same education, any more than it requires that we should have the same tastes or the same hobbies. Rather, especially in England, there is built into our fellow-feeling for our fellow-countrymen a considerable measure of 'live and let live': differences, provided they are not felt to be unfair, are acceptable, and strengthen rather than weaken the sense of unity. Liberty and justice, rather than equality, are what bind the different members of society together, and there is no overriding need for education to be the same for every one without regard to individual needs and capacities. Education is also concerned with social equality in a second sense in that each person needs to have the experience of being a social equal, not necessarily with every one, but at least with some other people. In order to secure this we may need to establish suitable institutions or lay down certain rules—school uniforms have sometimes been defended on the grounds that they prevent rich children having visibly better clothes than poor ones can afford. Exactly what rules are required will depend very much on time and circumstance, and is a matter for practical judgement on the part of schoolmasters rather than abstract theorising on the part of educationalists. Schoolmasters have a strong sense of the importance of corporate activities at school, and seldom fail to convey to their pupils the importance of getting on with their equals.

VI

It is difficult to fight equality. Egalitarianism is not so much a doctrine as a temper of mind, which is ready to wax indignant at particular inequalities it dislikes, but is not prepared to think through the alternative and submit it for rational assessment and criticism. In so far as any articulate doctrine is propounded, it is expressed in terms of such cloudy indeterminacy that it is difficult to know what is being maintained. Under attack, it withdraws into a set of morally innocuous truisms, but in application it is extended to make highly questionable claims. Under attack, equality collapses into some principle of similarity or uniformity, treat like cases alike, or some principle of solidarity or unity, e.g. that we all should recognise one another as our fellows and live on a basis of reciprocity with them. These are valid principles, which can scarcely be gainsaid. But they are not the only principles, nor is their application automatic. I should treat like cases alike—true: but it does not at all follow that we should therefore send all children, who are all alike inasmuch as they are children, to the same school, or that the mere existence of direct grant schools is a flagrant violation of natural justice. I should, within limits, encourage patriotism and *esprit de corps*—true: but it does not at all follow that this is best done by enabling children to learn at close quarters how unlovable their fellow-countrymen are, or by making social solidarity seem a suffocating ideal from which any sensitive individual will be seeking to escape. We must balance different ends against one another, and choose those ways and means that will achieve them with the least encroachment on other ideals we ought also to cherish. But this is just what the doctrinaire egalitarian will not do. Acutely aware of some sorts of inequality, he is quite oblivious of the many other differences and difficulties which are relevant to the schoolmaster's job. If only his eyes could be opened and he could be enabled to see the complexities of the considerations which have to be borne in mind, we could discuss his points, and see how far they could be met without sacrificing other goods we value. *If only.* . . . It is difficult to be patient, difficult to listen, to appreciate, and then to point out the woolliness and the *non sequiturs* without betraying irritation. It is easy to lose one's temper, and to match the shrill stupidity of egalitarian propaganda by equally shrill counterblasts, and if less stupid, equally unattractive. It is tempting, but both wrong and ineffective: wrong, because although egalitarians are in error, the points they are expressing in a muddled and confused fashion often have some validity, and in trying to preserve education from their procrustean propensities, we should not say that we have no regard for justice or the other concerns of society; and ineffective, because silliness is seldom silenced by denunciation. We shall not succeed in saving our schools by shouting down the egalitarians, but by arguing with them, understanding what they say, and why it is wrong, and being able to show them where their terms are equivocal, where their arguments are invalid, or where relevant factors have been overlooked; not by decrying the fashionable feeling for equality in education, but by educating our educationalists and teaching even egalitarians to think.

3

The Inheritance
of Mental Differences[1]

SIR CYRIL BURT

HISTORY OF THE PROBLEM

Popular Theories

'Men differ in their capacities and character even more than in
their faces, voices, and bodily strength: the important thing is to
pick the best—if you can!'[2] It is a truism echoed again and again
by industrialists and organisers of big business. And for two
thousand years or more philosophers, biographers, men of letters,
and men of affairs have aired their speculative notions about the
nature, causes, and the best means of detecting these all-important
differences.

The first to state the problem clearly and suggest a plausible
solution was Plato. In outlining his blueprint for an ideal state he
begins by discussing the rich variety of human nature. 'No two
persons,' he declares, 'are born exactly alike; each differs from
each in natural endowment, one being suited for one type of
occupation, another for a different. . . . Our rulers, therefore, so

---

[1] Much of the substance of this chapter is taken from earlier articles in
various technical journals, where more detailed evidence will be found. I am
specially indebted to the editors of the *British Journal of Educational Psychology*, the *British Journal of Statistical Psychology*, and the *American Psychologist* for permission to incorporate material which appeared in their publications.

[2] Dr C. S. Myers, *Symposium on Selection in School and Industry* (1929); he
attributed the quotation to an interview with Andrew Carnegie ('From
Bobbin-Boy to Millionaire') during which Carnegie explained the advice he
regularly gave to the managers of his various companies.

the citizens of our republic must be told, have received this all-important duty—to scrutinise every child, and ascertain what metal (so to speak) has gone to the making of his mind and character, since an oracle has foretold that the State will perish if ever its control falls into the hands of men of inferior quality.' Plato's ideas were revived and developed by several social writers of the Renaissance, notably Campanella in proposing a constitution for his utopian *City of the Sun*.[3]

Most social reformers, however, have placed chief stress on the effects of the environment, particularly the material and social conditions in the home and the training and education each child receives or fails to receive. The influence of heredity they belittle or deny. Of this alternative view the most lucid and emphatic expression is to be found in the writings of the so-called *philosophes* who paved the way for the French Revolution. In a treatise entitled *De l'esprit* (1758) Helvétius argued that 'all men are born equal in mental capacity; the manifold differences that seem so conspicuous result from nothing but the inequalities in men's social conditions and opportunities'. The book was formally condemned by the Sorbonne, and publicly burned. Fifteen years later Helvétius published an impassioned sequel entitled *De l'homme*, containing a plea for universal education: 'l'éducation peut tout' was now his watchword.

These revolutionary doctrines exercised a profound influence on Jeremy Bentham and the British 'utilitarians' or, as the historians of psychology usually style them, the 'associationist school'. 'If education cannot do everything', said James Mill, 'there is little that it cannot do.' Individual differences were attributed to the diverse associations formed by each man or woman as a result of personal experience and the influence of pleasure and pain—the sole source of human motivation. Twentieth-century behaviourism was essentially a revival of nineteenth-century associationism, reformulated in terms of Pavlov's theory of conditioned reflexes. Its arch-apostle, Professor J. B. Watson, was equally uncompromising in his rejection of all hereditarian theories. 'Give me', he cried, 'a dozen healthy infants, and my own world to bring them up in, and I'll guarantee to take any one at random and train him to become any type of specialist you like to select—doctor, lawyer, merchant, soldier, sailor, beggar-man or thief.' (*Behaviorism*, 1921, p. 104.)

As to methods of assessing a man's mental characteristics a yet

[3] Plato, *Republic*, II, 370A, III, 415 A-C (abridged). T. Campanella, *Civitas Solis* (1623).

wider variety of suggestions have been proposed. Galen, physician to Marcus Aurelius, and a writer whose authority lasted until well into the nineteenth century, took the Hippocratic doctrine of 'temperaments' and applied it to explain human differences in both character and capacity. This remained one of the most popular theories with the champions of heredity. There are, it was believed, four main body-fluids (or 'humours')—blood, lymph (or 'phlegm'), yellow bile, and black bile. These form the basis of all physiological activity. Health, intellect, and character all depend on the equable proportions in which they are mixed and tempered. Four special types were accordingly distinguished, due to an undue preponderance of each—the sanguine, the phlegmatic, the choleric, and the melancholic, recognisable from their physical appearance. The sanguine tended to be corpulent rather than slim, usually fair, with rosy complexions; the choleric were lean and muscular, often broad-shouldered, with a 'jaundiced' (i.e. yellowish) complexion and brownish hair tinged with yellow or red; the melancholic, dark-haired, dark-eyed, cadaverous, of an olive complexion; and the phlegmatic fat and puffy, pale, and mouse-coloured hair. The sanguine and phlegmatic were easy-going optimists, the choleric and melancholic serious and pessimistic; the sanguine and choleric were active and intelligent, the phlegmatic and melancholic passive, and relatively dull.

> Let me have men about me that are fat—
> Sleek-headed men, and such as sleep o'nights;
> Yond Cassius has a lean and hungry look;
> He thinks too much: such men are dangerous.

The words that Shakespeare puts into the mouth of Julius Caesar are almost a word-for-word translation from Plutarch s *Life*; and Plutarch got his notions of human temperament from the Hippocratic school.

Writers who laid more stress on personal experience and habitual reactions held that facial expression furnished better clues than anatomical build and physical appearance. Of these the author most frequently quoted is J. K. Lavater (*Physiognomische Fragmente zur Beförderung der Menschenkenntnis*, 1778, to which Goethe contributed a chapter). His writings aroused the interest of the anatomist, Charles Bell (1806) and the biologist, Charles Darwin (1889). In its most plausible form this theory maintained that the various instincts common to man and animals express themselves in quasi-reflex changes in the expression of the face and in the posture and gestures of the body: if certain instincts and their accompanying emotions are repeatedly aroused or given free play, these muscular changes, as a result of sheer habit, would tend to become more or less fixed, and so alter the lines and wrinkles of the face; 'the bad-tempered man develops a permanent frown, and the merry man crow's-feet at the corners of the eyes'. Subtler differences were said to distinguish the 'observant man' and the 'thoughtful man'.

During the first half of the nineteenth century by far the most popular method of assessing mental characteristics was based on a theory elaborated by a Viennese anatomist named Gall. He called it 'cranioscopy'; but his most active disciple, Spurzheim, re-christened it 'phrenology'.

Everyone has seen in the phrenologist's shop-window those white plaster models of a bald head mapped out into about thirty-six little plots, duly numbered and named. Intellectual qualities—Perception, Memory, Reasoning, Language, Mathematics, and the like—are usually located behind the forehead; imaginative qualities—Creativeness, Fancy, Poetry, Art—at the side of the head; the cruder emotional qualities—Amativeness, Philoprogenitiveness, Appetite—at the back of the head; and the higher moral qualities at the top. The list varies from one writer to another; Gall's was derived largely from the classification popularised by the Scottish school of 'faculty psychology'. Each quality was supposed to have its own centre or organ within the brain. If any particular quality is strongly developed, the corresponding centre in the brain will be enlarged, and so produce a slight protuberance or 'bump' on the skull. These enlargements, it was alleged, could easily be felt by the expert. Herbert Spencer was for a while a keen believer in phrenology, and persuaded two of his young lady-friends, George Eliot and Beatrice Potter (who later became Mrs Sidney Webb) to have their heads inspected. We now know that, although in certain parts of the brain there is some degree of localisation, what are localised are relatively simple functions—chiefly sensory processes and muscular movements. The so-called 'centres' are merely relay-stations along the neural conduction-paths, leading from the sense-organs to the cortex of the brain and from the brain down to the muscles.

The majority of scientific writers remained highly sceptical of all these claims. Jevons (1874) summed up their attitude in a few terse words: 'there is in human character an unfathomable diversity; despite the boasted powers of science, we cannot apply scientific method to our own minds and characters, which after all are far more important to us than all the nebulae and stars'.

E

Need for Scientific Confirmation

Each of the foregoing pronouncements, however confidently asserted, was based on little more than armchair speculation, eked out by a few casual observations chosen to fit the theorist's pet notions. What Macaulay says of James Mill would hold of all of them, exponents and critics alike: 'A few vague principles are postulated, and from these ill-established premisses a whole science of human nature is synthetically deduced or summarily dismissed.' It is indeed astonishing that until quite late in the nineteenth century no one ever attempted to study at first hand the various problems raised or test the rival theories by direct scientific investigation.

The first to do so was Sir Francis Galton, 'the father' (as his biographer observes) 'of individual psychology and the half-cousin of Charles Darwin'. Galton's first important work on mental differences was entitled *Hereditary Genius* (1869); a better title, he remarks in a note to the last edition, would have been 'Hereditary Ability'. His studies, so he tells us, were begun shortly after Darwin published his *Origin of Species*, 'which first suggested both the problem and the general mode of approach. . . . At that time there was no lack of theories professing to explain the differences between individuals; indeed there were too many: what was plainly needed was a systematic attempt to confirm one or other of these more or less plausible guesses, and disprove those that were erroneous'. His twofold aim, he says, was to 'devise methods of assessing in precise quantitative terms first the particular characteristics to be studied, and then the relations between these characteristics and their presumable causes and symptoms'; and he ends his preface by claiming that he was 'the first to treat the subject in a statistical manner, and so arrive at numerical results'. 'I think,' wrote Darwin to Galton, after receiving a copy, 'I never in all my life read anything more interesting and original.'[4]

Galton's style is eminently readable. There are numerous tables supporting his conclusions; but his more elaborate mathematical proofs and formulae were relegated to the pages of scientific journals or the appendices to his later books. His psychological vocabulary is drawn from the language of everyday life; and he seeks to make his meaning clear by concrete examples rather than by a rigid or pedantic adherence to a technical terminology, with each key-word formally defined. One or two early reviewers com-

[4] A cheap paper-back edition is now available in the Fontana Library, with an introduction by Professor Darlington.

plained that his 'homely style and arithmetical calculations make rather dreary reading as compared with the picturesque illustrations and practical proposals of the phrenologists and physiognomists whom he so scornfully casts aside'. Galton's reply was sharp and to the point: 'Rather than humbug I prefer the humdrum.'

He starts by implicitly accepting the traditional tripartite classification of mental processes into knowing, feeling, and willing. As the academic textbooks put it, every mental activity has three main aspects—cognitive, affective, and conative. It follows (to keep to his own simple language) that, 'in order to achieve eminence, a man must possess great intellectual ability, a keen emotional interest in his chosen field, and a resolute will to work'. Time and again Galton and his followers are accused of an 'intellectualist bias': of 'supposing that everything depends on testable ability, and wholly overlooking the importance of personality-factors—of ambition, aims, and motivation'. Yet Galton went out of his way to forestall such criticisms. Although in his book he deals primarily with inherited ability, this does not, he insists, imply that he 'believes in capacity without zeal or industry', or that he overlooks the influence of education and social advantages: all are essential.

General Ability

Nevertheless, since a man's intellectual capacity inexorably sets an upper limit to what he can accomplish by a sustained interest or dogged perseverance, the most fruitful plan, so he argues, will be to start with the first of the three main qualities—the intellectual rather than the emotional or moral. The prevailing academic doctrine in his day was that 'all intellectual activities are the product of a small number of basic mental faculties, each highly specific'. In its usual oversimplified form, this doctrine, Galton maintained, was contradicted by the actual facts. 'Numerous instances recorded in this book', he writes in his chapter on 'The Classification of Men according to their Natural Gifts', 'show in how small a degree eminence can be considered due to purely special powers. . . . People lay too much stress on apparent specialities, thinking that, because a man is devoted to some particular pursuit, he cannot possibly succeed in anything else. They might just as well say that, because a youth has fallen in love with a brunette, he could not possibly have fallen in love with a blonde; it is as probable as not that the whole affair was mainly or wholly due to a *general* amorousness.' He does not deny the existence of what he calls 'special aptitudes', and those he mentions seem almost identical with some of the old-fashioned faculties. But he accords them no more than a subsidiary influence. 'Certainly', he says, 'without a special aptitude for mathematics, a man will not become a mathematician; but without a high degree of *general* ability, he will never make a great mathematician.'

The distinction was in fact by no means new. It had already been recognised by Aristotle: 'Some men', he says, 'appear to be intelligent all round, others only in part.'[5] Dr Johnson entertained a similar view. 'Had Newton applied himself to poetry, he could have produced a great epic.' Robertson, the Scottish historian, objected that one man might have the power of reasoning, another keen judgement, and yet another a finer imagination than anyone else: Caesar could not have written *Hamlet*, nor Shakespeare have commanded an army. 'No, sir,' retorted Johnson, 'it is only that one man has *more mind* than another. He may direct it differently: he may desire to excel in this study rather than that. Sir, the man who has vigour may walk to the East as well as to the West, to the North as well as to the South.' Carlyle held much the same opinion. 'I confess', he wrote, 'I have no notion of a truly great man that could not be any sort of great man—Poet, Prophet, Priest, King, or what you will. . . . True, there are natural aptitudes as well; Nature does not make all great men, any more than ordinary men, in the self-same mould. Varieties of talent doubtless, but infinitely more of circumstance.'[6]

Somewhat similar views were set forth, in a rather more systematic and erudite analysis, by Herbert Spencer in the second and much enlarged edition of his *Principles of Psychology* (1870). By then he had consigned phrenology to limbo. He describes in much detail how, during the evolution of the animal kingdom and the development of each growing child, the fundamental capacity of cognition 'progressively differentiates from a simple generalized form into a hierarchy of more specialized abilities, much as the trunk of an oak ramifies into boughs, branches, and twigs'. He distinguishes four main levels, emerging at fairly definite stages in animal evolution and fairly definite ages in the development of the individual: '(1) presentative, (2) presentative-representative, (3)

---

[5] *Nic. Eth.*, VI, vii, 2.

[6] Boswell, *Journal of a Tour to the Hebrides* (15 August); Carlyle, *On Heroes and Hero Worship*, Lecture III. Galton had been strongly impressed, so he tells us, by Carlyle's views 'on the influence of great and gifted men on the destiny of their own country and indeed on human history'.

representative, and (4) re-representative' or, in less portentous terms, sensation, perception, memory and imagination, judgement and reasoning. The fundamental capacity he termed 'intelligence'; and in Part IV of his *Principles* ('Special Synthesis') he devotes three chapters to describing its 'Nature', its 'Laws', and its 'Growth'. Later differentiations, he maintained, would be transmitted from parent to offspring; and, if they proved to be better adapted to current environmental conditions, they would become permanently fixed in the race, owing to the steady elimination of the less efficient stocks and 'the survival of the fittest'—a catchword first coined by Spencer. In Britain, however, as he observes in his Preface to the later edition, 'the notion of mental evolution was at that time frowned upon, even in the scientific world'. In view therefore of this prevailing scepticism Galton considered it necessary first and foremost, as he explains in his opening chapter, 'to show that man's natural abilities are derived by inheritance under exactly the same limitations as the form and physical features of the whole organic world'.

THE METHOD OF PEDIGREES

The method he adopted was, so to speak, an attempt to trace the evolution of some of the more efficient families and their most famous members by examining pedigrees; and the greater part of *Hereditary Genius* consists in a detailed tabulation of the family histories of nearly a thousand eminent men, supplemented by brief biographical studies to justify his assessments. He prefaces his analysis by carefully defining what he means by such words as 'eminent' or 'genius' .How many men are there, he asks, in the entire population whom common consent has recognised as having, directly or indirectly, made outstanding contributions to the survival and progress of the nation to which they belonged? To answer this question Havelock Ellis some thirty years later (*A Study of British Genius*, 1904) used the first twenty-six volumes of the Dictionary of National Biography; its records included over 30,000 persons; and, after eliminating minor personages and those who owed their inclusion to their birth, he assessed the number of 'genuine geniuses' at about 200 per century from the Renaissance onwards, with a sharp increase during the nineteenth century.

The *Dictionary*, however, did not start publication until near the end of that century. Galton therefore had to fall back on other sources. He began by examining such compilations as Routledge's

Dictionary of Men of Our Time, and checked the results by collating various biographical and obituary notices. All seemed to yield much the same result. Broadly speaking, men who were almost unanimously regarded as geniuses appeared to consist of the ablest 250 in every million—a proportion equivalent to one in every 4,000. This therefore was his definition of 'genius', or, as he preferred to say, of the 'truly eminent'.

He next collected detailed pedigrees for as many individuals as he could find who fell within this category and had made their mark in the history of their nation, and for whom reliable information was available in regard to their parents, grandparents, brothers, sons, and remoter relatives. His lists include poets, painters, musicians, statesmen, judges, men of science, men of letters, and military commanders. The crucial question he puts in the following terms: suppose a boy is the son of a genius, how far, if at all, does this increase his own chance of turning out a genius, and what would be his chances if a remoter relative—a grandfather, an uncle, or a cousin—has been a genius? After averaging all his figures, his answer was as follows. The probability that any boy picked just at random would be a genius is, by the very definition of the term, 1 in 4,000. If, however, his father was a genius, the probability is increased to 1 in 4—an amazing difference; if only his grandfather was a genius, it would be about 1 in 29; if only an uncle, the proportion is lower still, 1 in 40; and if only a cousin, 1 in 200, though here the figures are somewhat untrustworthy, owing to lack of information. Taken at their face value, the results are not entirely consistent. Supposing, he argues, that the number of surviving male children per parent averaged about four in each generation, which he believes to have been the case during the period with which he was dealing, then, could the figures be trusted, we should expect that the four sons of the grandfather would have included one genius, and that this one son in turn would have produced a genius, while his three brothers would have produced none. Thus among the grandsons we should expect one genius in 16, not 29. This suggests that the home and other aids which an eminent father can usually provide will raise the probability in the case of his son.

Environmental Influences

Galton's present-day critics constantly complain that he overlooked the environmental advantages that an able father is usually able to provide. 'The son,' says Dr Harrison, 'may owe everything to the favourable conditions in which he has been brought up. To be born into a family which already contains one or more geniuses must obviously stimulate the youth's ambition; he will doubtless enjoy far better educational opportunities both at home and at school, and receive a good start in his future career: thus all that Galton has done is to demonstrate the value of a cultured, well-to-do, privileged home.' Galton, however, states in the most explicit terms that he 'freely acknowledges the power of education and social influences in developing the active powers of the mind, just as [he] recognizes the effect of use in developing a blacksmith's muscles'; but the *power* must be there to begin with: and in both cases the power inherited at birth puts a limit on what can be achieved. Social conditions form only one factor making for intellectual success. After all, in spite of the advantages of a cultured home, most of the sons of a genius do *not* become geniuses; and, he adds, there are numerous cases in which a lad attained eminence in later life when the conditions under which he had been brought up were the very reverse of favourable.

As one among many instances he cites the story of young D'Alembert. During the winter of 1717, on the steps of the church of St Jean le Rond in Paris, the night watchman found an infant abandoned in the snow. The child was placed with an impoverished glazier, and christened after the church where he was found. The boy was eager to learn. But the glazier wanted him to follow in the same humble trade, and did all he could to thwart his attempts to study. Secretly the boy bought or borrowed books, reading them at night in his bedroom. He taught himself science and mathematics, and eventually, after submitting a highly original *mémoire* on the calculus, was elected a Member of the *Académie des Sciences*, at the unprecedented age of only twenty-three. Later he was appointed permanent secretary of the *Académie Française*, and became one of the founders of the famous *Encyclopedie*. His numerous articles and other publications, all highly original, range over philosophy, music, and the arts, as well as astronomy and dynamics. It was later discovered that he was the illegitimate son of the Marquise de Tencin, a celebrated novelist, sister of a Cardinal, and herself a nun, who, after renouncing her vows, had become the mistress of more than one French celebrity. Her cousin was a famous dramatist; another relative was a leading critic, the companion and literary executor of Voltaire.

'Abundant instances', says Galton, 'of this emergence from obscurity can be found in the pages of my book.' And it is easy to add to his list. Going through the family histories collected by

Havelock Ellis, Miss Cos, and several foreign biographers, I found that a large number of the intellectual geniuses in their lists were sons, not of well-to-do, cultured, or professional men, but of persons in the lowliest manual classes, many of them entirely self-taught. Kepler was the son of a drunken innkeeper; Gauss, acclaimed in Professor Bell's history as 'the greatest mathematician of all time', was the son of a German bricklayer; Laplace, almost as illustrious, the son of a French farm labourer; Wolsey and Defoe were sons of butchers; Watt, Whewell, and Abraham Lincoln of carpenters; Thomas Cromwell, David Cox, and Michael Faraday, of blacksmiths; Marlowe, Winkelmann, Hans Anderson, and James Mill, of cobblers; Luther, Zwingli, Cassendi, Knox and Burns, of peasants; Kant's father was a strapmaker, Franklin's a soap-boiler, Bunyan's a tinker, Carlyle's a mason, Sir Humphrey Davy's a shiftless wood-carver, Cardinal Richelieu's a soldier of the guard; and the catalogue could easily be extended. None of the published lists include eminent industrialists or eminent labour politicians. Many of the former, like Andrew Carnegie, worked their way up from the humblest jobs; many of the latter, like Ernest Bevin, were born in poverty-stricken homes and were largely self-educated and self-supporting.

Galton's study of the eminent and able, however, was merely the first exploratory step of a pioneer. As he remarked in the opening chapter of his book and repeated at the close, inquiries confined to just one end of the intellectual scale would be far from conclusive. Genius was exceptional; therefore its inheritance might be exceptional. It was equally important to study the dull and defective at the other end of the scale, and above all to investigate the average mass of the population. For these no pedigrees were available: unnamed and unknown in the pages of history, their ancestors have left no records of their lineage, or their progeny, or of their own success or failure in the several occupations. Some new method of investigation had therefore to be devised.

Instead of grading people by their reputation, it became necessary to judge them by their actual performance at some comparable task. This, however, proved difficult in dealing with adults who have little time or patience for examination by some inquisitive outsider. Galton therefore turned his attention to the study of school children. 'The school', he writes, 'is itself an anthropometric laboratory, ready and accessible for psychological research.' Quite apart from the theoretical value of such inquiries, the conclusions reached, he believed, would be of practical use to the teachers themselves. However, if the results obtained were to be reliable, such investigations would have to be quantitative. Hence the first requirement was to discover some way of measuring children's abilities in precise numerical terms ('Proposals for Anthropological Statistics from Schools', *J. Anthrop. Inst.*, III, 1874, pp. 308f.).

MENTAL TESTS

Individual Differences Among Children

Shortly after the publication of Galton's book, Forster's bill for a scheme of universal education was placed on the statute book. In 1880 Mundella's bill made school attendance compulsory. And all over the country there sprang up those gaunt three-storeyed edifices, which caught the eye of Holmes and Watson as they travelled across the London suburbs on the affair of *The Naval Treaty*. 'The new Board Schools', Dr Watson observed. 'Lighthouses, my boy,' cried Holmes with a gush of metaphors; 'beacons of the future! Capsules containing hundreds of bright little seeds in each, out of which will spring the wiser England of the next generation.'

But the seeds proved to be of widely varying quality. Most of the brightest and most docile youngsters from the more enlightened types of family had already been accommodated in the voluntary schools. In the poorer districts the huge school buildings quickly became packed with unruly and seemingly ineducable youngsters—'dullards who could not be taught, ruffians who could not be trained'. Soon the teachers were loud in their complaints. 'Every classroom in my school', said a headmaster from an East End slum, 'contains three or four pupils who are utterly unable to learn, and do their level best to hinder the others from learning what little they can.' The doctors suspected that 'all such children were probably pathological cases'; and in 1876, Dr Francis Warner, Professor of Anatomy and Physiology at the Royal College of Surgeons, was asked to examine pupils attending typical schools in six different areas, and report to a Special Committee of the Charity Organisation Society. His conclusion was that many of the more backward suffered from incurable mental defects, and that others needed transference to a 'special type of school where they could be treated and trained by the physiological methods already popularized in France by Edouard Séguin'. The result was a series of Acts of Parliament dealing with the subject of mental deficiency, starting with the Idiots Act of 1886.

The chief problem was the difficulty of diagnosis. How were the teachers or doctors to recognise those who required these special types of treatment or who were innately and incurably defective? According to the Acts dealing with school-children, the fact of deficiency had to be certified by a medical officer specially approved for the purpose by the Board of Education; and most medical officers treated the matter as a medical, not as an educational or a psychological problem. Influenced partly by their habitual preoccupation with the anatomical and physiological approach needful in dealing with the physically diseased, and partly, it would seem, by the phrenological theories which still found favour with many neurologists, Dr Warner and the other doctors looked for anatomical 'stigmata' and physiological 'nerve-signs'. Small, misshapen, or asymmetrical skulls, low, narrow, or bossed foreheads, narrow, high or V-shaped palates, lobeless ears, splayed or drooping hands—these and many other physical anomalies were held to signalise a reversion to some low, primitive, or degenerate type. Even when I joined the London staff as consultant psychologist in 1913, the school doctors still based their certification principally on the results of a physical examination—measuring the size of the child's head with a tape measure and looking for so-called stigmata.

Now it was Galton's firm belief that one should judge mental characteristics by mental symptoms, not by physical. In *Nature* (38, 1886, pp. 40f.) he published a brief note, showing that head measurements had but little correlation with assessments of mental efficiency: and this was later confirmed by Karl Pearson ('The Relationship of Intelligence to Size and Shape of the Head', *Biometrika*, V, 1906, pp. 105–46). Accordingly, at the 'Anthropometric Laboratory' which he established at the Science Museum in South Kensington and later moved to University College, he carried out a long series of experiments in the hope of standardising what he called 'mental tests'. The College still preserves several of his large orange posters announcing that 'A Laboratory has been set up for the measurement of human form and faculty, partly with a view to carrying out research, partly to familiarize the public with the need for a scientific approach, and partly for teachers and parents who wish to bring their children for examination to learn what are their bodily and mental powers or obtain timely warning of remediable faults in development: charge, threepence each to those already on the register, fourpence to those who are not.'

He began with simple tests of sensory discrimination, suggested by the experiments carried out by Fechner and Wundt in Germany, and then went on to devise tests for 'higher mental processes'. To illustrate the methods he had in view, he described in *Inquiries into Human Faculty* (1883) a typical sensory test and a 'test' or rather questionnaire on mental imagery. His most effective tests for general ability he naturally abstained from publishing, since many parents and teachers might start trying them out, and perhaps even coach their children before they brought them to the laboratory.

Galton's novel device was quickly taken up by teachers who visited the laboratory. As early as 1881 C. H. Lake, a London schoolmaster, was already applying tests of discrimination, memory, and intelligence in his school at Chelsea. A little later another of Galton's disciples, Miss Sophie Bryant, Headmistress of Camden High School, published results obtained with a set of mental tests which she had applied to her own pupils ('Experiments in Testing School Children', *J. Anthrop. Inst.*, XV, 1886, pp. 338–49: the earliest printed account of a systematic research on the subject). Sully (Professor of Mind and Logic at University College where he established the first psychological laboratory in the country) carried out, in collaboration with Galton, what he called 'psychometric experiments' on reaction time and attention: the individual differences thus measured, he wrote, 'vary pretty uniformly with age and with degree of intelligence, and might with advantage be taken as at least a rough criterion in estimating children's mental power as a whole' ('Experiments on Prehension', *Mind*, XII, 1887, pp. 75f.).

Mental Age

To measure you need a unit of measurements. In the case of children Galton had already hinted at the possibility of measuring intelligence in terms of mental age. During the elementary school period, that is from about five to thirteen, the average rate of both physical and mental growth is fairly uniform. With single individuals the rate often fluctuates from year to year, particularly as a result of ill health; but, if the figures for a large sample of individual children, obtained with tests that can be applied for several years running, are averaged, then the annual increments prove to be approximately equal up to the pre-pubertal stage; plotted to scale, the averages obtained fall very nearly on a straight line. It would therefore seem possible to take the annual change as the metric unit.

This principle had in effect been adopted by the officials of the old Board of Education. The Code which they drew up to govern the payment of grants specified in some detail the attainments to be expected of pupils during each year from the age of seven onward. To ascertain whether the majority of pupils in each age-group came up to requisite standards, the inspectors took round with them sets of test-cards to check the children's performances in reading, spelling, and arithmetic, and (at the later stages) in more general subjects. The normal performance of a child of seven was described as 'Standard I', that of a child of eight as 'Standard II', and so on, as far as 'Standard VII' for age thirteen. In my day a 'Standard Ex-VII' was added for the brightest thirteen-year-olds and any fourteen-year-olds who had stayed on. As a result it became the custom among the teachers to nominate for possible certification any pupil aged nine, who could not do the work of Standard I, and was thus at least three years retarded. The final decision lay with the school medical officer, who usually relied on the methods I have described above.

At the special schools established for such children classes were much smaller; teaching individual and practical; and particular attention was paid to the health, nutrition, and adequate clothing —all very necessary in the days when so many lived in conditions of the direst poverty. To these new types of school the doctors not unnaturally tended to transfer any backward child who could benefit by such salutary provision. As a result the finance committee complained of the expense; the parents complained of the slur entailed by the epithet 'defective'; and the teachers complained that the whole problem was educational rather than medical.

The Chief Education Officer had a new solution. Impressed by Galton's methods at his anthropometric laboratory, he advised the appointment of an educational psychologist who should rank as a member of the school inspectorate, not of the medical officer's department. It should be his task to examine 'all doubtful cases referred by teachers or inspectors [often at the request of parents] including, not only cases of alleged mental deficiency at the lower end of the scale, but also cases in which a child whom the teacher considered fit for entrance to a secondary technical or grammar school had failed at the regular examination'. The appointment was to be purely experimental, half-time, and for three years only. During the remaining half of the psychologist's working week he would be free to carry out research.

The Binet Scale

Very similar problems had already been encountered by the education authorities in France; and in 1904 the Minister of Public Instruction set up a commission 'to study and report on the diagnosis and training of subnormal children'. Its most active members were Alfred Binet, Director of the Psychological Laboratory at the Sorbonne, Th. Simon, physician at a mental institution at Saint-You, and M. Vaney, School Director of Paris. They recommended that 'three methods should be employed: (1) a medical method (dealing with hereditary antecedents, past development, and the results of a physical examination); (2) a pedagogical method (based partly on teachers' reports, and partly on tests of acquired school knowledge); and (3) a psychological method, consisting of direct examination and measurement of the child's ability': the 'measurements', they suggested, should be based on a series of tests specially devised and graded. And these Professor Binet in conjunction with his two colleagues proceeded to compile (*L'Année psychol.*, XII, 1905, pp. 191–244).

While studying at a biological laboratory some years earlier, Binet had become a convert to the novel theories of the British evolutionists—Spencer and Darwin. In the reviews he published of Galton's books and papers he found the ideas there put forward 'entirely convincing'. And when he turns to outline the procedures he himself has in view, he adopts much the same principles as Galton. Like Galton, he starts by distinguishing between cognitive and motivational characteristics. Of those pupils who cause persistent difficulties in school, he says, some are subnormal intellectually, others temperamentally or morally subnormal; 'their intellectual faculties may be perfectly intact, and their backwardness merely a secondary consequence of their emotional instability'. Like Galton, too, he goes on to distinguish between innate capacities and acquired knowledge and skill. And finally, he borrowed Galton's distinction between 'general ability' and 'special aptitudes'. In French the word *habilité* means something quite different from the English equivalent; so Binet fell back on Spencer's term 'intelligence'.

'How', he asks, 'are we to understand the term? There are many different kinds of intellectual processes, forming, as it were, a hierarchy; but there is one fundamental capacity of the utmost importance in all practical life—the faculty of *adapting* oneself to circumstances.' (Views plainly taken from Spencer.) Thus 'all the phenomena with which psychology is concerned are phenomena of intelligence—sensation, perception, memory, and so forth, quite as much as rational thought'. 'Are we', he asks, 'to examine all the child's psychological processes?' Clearly that would demand an impracticable amount of time. Except at the earlier ages the current laboratory tests of simple sensory processes are, he maintains, of little value. Accordingly, partly on the basis of general experience, partly after trying a variety of different tasks, he decides that tests of higher mental levels—tests of the logical processes of 'comprehension, judgement, and reasoning'—will be most effective.

Binet published several 'scales of intelligence tests', gradually enlarging his compilation of practical problems and questions. In its final form the various items were arranged in order of difficulty and grouped according to the ages at which they could normally be solved. The amount of intelligence possessed by any given child was then to be measured by 'taking the highest age at which he passes all the tests, with an allowance of one failure for that age' ('Le developpement de l'intelligence chez les enfants', *L'Année psychol.*, XIV, 1908, pp. 1–94; cf. 'Nouvelles recherches sur la mesure du niveau intellectuel chez les enfants de l'école', ibid., XVII, 1911, pp. 145–201).

The Mental Ratio

As a criterion for mental subnormality Binet suggested a backwardness of 3 years at about the middle of the child's school career: thus, a boy aged 10 by the calendar with a mental age of 7 or less would be regarded as subnormal. In the case of adults he suggested a mental age of about 8 or 9 as the borderline for the 'feebleminded', 6 or 7 for 'imbeciles', and 2 or 3 for 'idiots'. These limits were based on a preliminary application of his tests to inmates at the mental institution where Dr Simon worked. Now in the case of children the criterion proposed is far from satisfactory. A backwardness of 3 years means very different things at different stages in life: it would be far more serious at the age of 6 or 7, when most British defectives were certified than at the age of 16, when they were re-examined on leaving school; and a child of 2½ could not possibly be backward by 3 years. For adults Binet's own borderline implies a much greater degree of retardation than for children.

Galton, as it happens, had already indicated a possible method of circumventing the difficulty. In his book on *Heredity Genius* he observes that, judging by the published descriptions of adult defectives undergoing training in mental hospitals, it appeared that a feebleminded person was capable of working 'like two-thirds' of a normal man, while an imbecile worked with only half the efficiency of a normal man, and an idiot with only one-third. Later, in an address to teachers and doctors, he suggested that, when the defect was congenital, these rough proportions would probably remain constant throughout the years of growth, and therefore apply to school-children of almost any age. One or two doctors objected that the corresponding proportions did not remain constant in the case of physical measurements, and that Galton himself had argued that subnormal development in mental characteristics conformed to the same principles as subnormal development in physical characteristics. Accordingly Galton appears to have dropped the suggestion.

However, in my early work with mental and educational tests I tried to check Galton's argument by analysing actual data. I found that, alike in tests of educational attainments and in tests of general ability, the proportions did in fact remain approximately constant. The simplest way of verifying the principle was to calculate the average deviation (or some equivalent measure of variability) at every age. I chose Galton's own measure, the 'probable error'. I found that at the age of 5, it was half a 'mental year'; at 10, almost exactly one mental year; and at 15, about one and a half mental years; thus, when the age doubled or trebled, the deviation likewise doubled or trebled (cf. *Relations and Distribution of Educational Abilities*, 1917, p. 31, Figure 5). These results suggest that a child's intelligence should be measured, not by the *difference* between his chronological and mental ages, but by their *ratio* (Figure 2D, op. cit., p. 10 shows that the ratios are fairly constant from 7 to 15, though after 12 there is a slight tendency to decline); but, as was then noted, it holds good only of averages, and often fails in the case of single individuals.

In Germany, Wilhelm Stern, who had published the first systematic treatise on individual psychology (*Die Individuelle Psychologie*, 1911), and had made great use of Galton's work, independently proposed a similar procedure: a child's intelligence was to be measured by 'dividing his mental by his chronological age and expressing the result as a percentage'. This percentage he termed an 'Intelligence Quotient'; and the phrase was adopted by American writers, usually in the abridged form, 'IQ'.

The substitution of a ratio thus seemed to yield a measurement that was independent of chronological age. Could this conclusion be accepted, it would provide a rough and ready method of predicting at a fairly early age how a child's future development would turn out. Later studies in which individual children—defective, dull, average, and bright—were tested soon after entering school, and followed up during their entire school careers and often into adult life, showed that on the whole these predictions could usually be trusted to yield *probable* indications; but in nearly every child there are occasional fluctuations, and in some a marked decline or (more rarely) a slight improvement, particularly towards puberty. Hence, as I emphasised at the time, 'the claims for constancy are but imperfectly realized'; and specific examples were given of boys and girls whose mental ratios had shown appreciable changes when re-tested after an interval of anything up to 6 or 7 years (*Mental and Scholastic Tests*, 1921, pp. 151f.).

The criticisms of the IQ since advanced by writers like Professor Fleming in this country and Professor McV. Hunt in America seem to display an unfortunate ignorance of the researches they set out to criticise. Dr Fleming, for example, states that 'Burt and other writers in the first few decades of the nineteenth century . . . *did not hesitate to assume* that pupils who did well at an early age would maintain their relative superiority in later years', and similarly, *mutatis mutandis*, with those who received a low IQ (*Adolescence*, 1948: my italics). Dr Hunt is still more drastic in his attack on what he calls 'the dogma of the fixed IQ' (*Intelligence and Experience*, 1961). And their strictures are repeatedly quoted in current educational journals.

But the '*approximate* constancy' of the IQ was by no means based on mere 'assumption'. As will be seen from the passages I have quoted above, it was an empirical inference, carefully checked; and its limitations were explicitly noted. No reputable psychologist to my knowledge ever put forward the notion of a 'fixed IQ'. To the teacher the mental ratio or intelligence quotient seems a concept that can be easily understood; and for the practical purposes of classification and provisional prediction it is in my view of considerable use. Naturally the classifications and predictions tentatively arrived at after each child enters school would be reconsidered and rectified at a later stage; indeed I argued that these reviews should be carried out annually. On the other hand, 'for the theoretical purposes of scientific research', as I contended in my earliest reports, 'the IQ is quite unsuitable. . . . The employment of the standard deviation is indisputably the better device' (1917, p. 15; cf. 1931, pp. 33f. and Appendix on 'Curves of Growth'). The reason for this is obvious. The range and variability of IQs and mental ratios differ enormously from one type of tests to another: a child who has an IQ of seventy-five or more with the Binet scale may be given an IQ of only sixty-five or less with Cattell's.

Nevertheless, for most readers, even in these days, assessments exp_____ ___ ___itive or negative multiples of the standard deviatio_____ ___y own practice has bee_____ _ a conventional IQ wi_____ fifteen points. The ad_____ applied, not only to ch_____ o to adolescents and ad____.

L_____ __ _____ ____

F_____ _nce have come under h_____ the commonest ground f_____ pupils with a view to d_____ _een freely employed to _____ o are then relegated to _____ er end of the scale, they _____ _-plus examination for _____ _lder elementary schools _____ _ have been widely used _____ different streams. The _____ on various ideological _____ _ut the point on which _____ _sts.

_____ s that the children are _____ then quoted to show _____ or more years later, _____ _om perfect. A table _____ _al Society (1957) is _____ ng party responsible _____ _____ ___ most appropriate measure of good or bad selection is the proportion of pupils wrongly accepted or wrongly rejected' [as a result of tests such as those used for the eleven-plus]. Their calculations imply that 5 per cent were wrongly rejected and another 5 per cent wrongly accepted. 'Surely', say the critics, 'such a misclassification rate—5 per cent either way—is far too high. . . . Why should a child be condemned as subnormal or deprived of higher education merely because his test-score fails to reach some arbitrary norm?' (Campbell, 1956, Benn and Simon, 1970; cf. Mittler, 1971 and refs).

Evidently nothing but tests and predictions that are absolutely perfect would satisfy these critics. Yet in all practical matters infallible predictions are out of the question. 'Probability', said Bishop Butler long ago, 'is the guide of life'; and all that the psychologist can do is to increase probabilities. In other lines of business those who make their living by calculating probabilities—life-insurance actuaries, book-makers, dealers on the stock exchange—would be only too happy to achieve a margin of error that was no greater than '5 per cent either way'. And what has been said of them holds good of the psychologist: 'the best he can do is to *maximise the probability* that his expectations will be fulfilled and his decisions justified'.

What the critics omit to point out is that the intelligence test is but one item in the procedure employed; Dr Mittler indeed sharply rebukes psychologists for 'confining themselves to global tests, such as the Binet scale'. But, so far as I am aware, no educational psychologist ever adopted such a practice. In interviewing children referred on account of general backwardness or some other intellectual disability (as will be seen from the chapter on 'procedure' in *The Backward Child*), the psychologist also makes full use of tests for special capacities (sight, hearing, muscular coordination, memory, imagery, linguistic defects, etc.) and takes note of the child's temperamental characteristics. In the scholarship or eleven-plus examination tests of English and arithmetic were regularly included and reference made to the teachers' reports. The great value of standardised tests was that they served to equate the very different standards adopted by teachers in different schools. Nor was any child ever 'condemned as subnormal' or 'deprived of higher education' because of failure in an intelligence test. The function of such tests was precisely the reverse of what the critics imply—not to exclude children from a higher type of education, but to secure it for them. 'The object of introducing tests of general ability', I wrote, 'is to *prevent* children from being certified on inadequate grounds and to enable gifted children from illiterate homes to obtain a scholarship in virtue of their unrecognized potentialities. If a child *fails* in a test of intelligence, that does not necessarily prove he lacks intelligence' (he might fail for some quite irrelevant reason—emotional disturbance, temporary ill health, unsuitability of the type of test employed, or a dozen other reasons); 'if on the other hand he succeeds, that can almost always be accepted as proof that he does at least possess the degree of ability that his answers indicate.'

Alike in the primary and in the secondary school teachers who used such tests were always urged to repeat them at least once a

year, and correct any classification that seemed to be at fault. Nor
were they expected to 'confine themselves to a single global type
of test'. 'Tests', as I repeatedly stated, 'are but the beginning,
never the end of the study of the individual child'; and an
elaborate schedule was drawn up for the cumulative compilation
of a school record file for every pupil (Burt, *The Backward Child*,
pp. 627–33).

GENERAL ABILITY

The Definition of Intelligence

What then is it that intelligence tests, however inadequately, are
designed to measure? Perhaps the commonest complaint urged by
the critics of mental testing is that 'psychologists who talk about
intelligence seem utterly unable to agree on their definitions'
(Mittler, loc. cit., p. 6). Those who use this argument usually refer
to a symposium organised in the early days by an American editor
(*J. Educ. Psychol.*, XII, 1921, pp. 123f.): they generally fail to
mention that this was fifty years ago. A number of psychologists
were asked 'how should intelligence be defined so as to discover
how best to measure it?'. Some stressed analysis, saying, as
Spearman did, that the 'essential function' was 'sensory discrimination'. Others stressed synthesis, citing Ebbinghaus's well-known
'Kombinationsmethode' ('ability to organise facts into a comprehensible whole'). Terman suggested 'power of abstract thinking'.
The commonest suggestion was that already proposed (in slightly
varying terms) by Spencer, Binet, and Stern—'the ability to adjust
one's thinking to new requirements'. Some years later Boring put
forward 'an operational definition'—'intelligence is what intelligence tests measure', a proposal which plainly raises the further
problem—when is an intelligence test not an intelligence test?

However, these replies are not 'definitions' as the lawyer or the
logician understands that term; they are tentative descriptions,
explaining how the characteristic in question presumably functions, and indicating in what ways it can be most easily recognised
and measured. Such answers inevitably differed according to the
particular purpose the contributor had in mind: if he was interested chiefly in testing older children or adults, tests of abstraction
naturally seemed promising: if he was working with very young
children, he rightly preferred simple tests of discrimination.

But these are not matters of definition. What the logician
understands by a definition, as Mill taught us long ago, is a brief
statement specifying how some important word or some un-

familiar technical term is to be interpreted in the arguments that follow or in the branch of science to which it belongs. In the case of intelligence the formula I proposed was intended to express the way Galton and Binet had used the term. Both firmly believed they could detect the operation of a mental capacity which was (i) innate, (ii) cognitive, and (iii) general: (by 'general' they meant that, unlike special aptitudes or limited 'faculties', it influenced efficiency in everything we do or say or think). Instead of repeating a cumbersome phrase, twelve syllables long, it was obviously more convenient to adopt, quite arbitrarily, some single word to designate this novel and complex concept. Most of the contributors to the symposium took it for granted that 'intelligence' was being used in this sense. In those days the word had not yet passed into general circulation; and everyone working in that field automatically associated it with the ideas developed by Spencer and Binet. Hence, today when Professor Hunt tells us that 'a newer and better concept of intelligence consists of strategies for processing information which are acquired during the child's interaction with his environment', or when Dr Mittler says 'we now think of intelligence as a hierarchy of skills—habits of action learnt during the early years of life', they are not propounding a truer explanation of what Galton and Binet had in mind; they are simply proposing to use the old word in a new sense.

The crucial question of course is whether or not any trait, capacity, or tendency, corresponding to this triple specification, does in actual fact exist. So let us take each of the three assumptions in turn, and ask what evidence there may be in its support. First of all, therefore, let us inquire what facts can be adduced in defence of the notion of a *general* ability'.

The Neurological Evidence
The clinical work of Hughlings Jackson, the experimental researches of Sherrington and his collaborators, the microscopical studies of Campbell, Brodmann, and Sholl, and the more recent work of surgeons like Penfield and Delgado, have done much to confirm Spencer's theory of 'a hierarchy of neural functions', with a basic type of activity and a certain degree of specialisation in broadly distinguishable 'levels' within the central nervous system. In the spinal cord, medulla, and brain-stem, in the hind-brain, mid-brain, inter-brain, and fore-brain, there are numerous so-called 'centres' for a variety of processes, gradually increasing in complexity from the simplest physiological reflexes to extremely elaborate patterns of psychical activity. To the layman the

neurologist's old-fashioned term 'centre' is apt to be a little misleading; they are best regarded as relay-stations consisting of innumerable cell-junctions through which the nerve-impulses pass on their way from various sense-organs up to the surface (or 'cortex') of the brain and then down to certain muscle-groups. It became customary to distinguish four main levels, roughly classifiable according to the degree or range of 'integration' involved in each: (i) unconscious reflexes; (ii) sensori-motor processes (the basis of sense-perception, observation, and the like); (iii) processes of association (the basis of memory and habit); and (iv) relational processes (abstraction, generalisation, judgement, and reasoning). Although it is convenient to describe them in terms of the conscious experiences involved, each of the processes usually involves both a sensory and a motor aspect, though often one may predominate; and each of the higher and more complex levels incorporates and 'integrates' processes of the simpler and lower levels.

In surgical operations on patients suffering from epileptic fits it is now possible to use only a local anesthetic and lift a segment of the skull, so as to expose a large part of the brain. The brain is then explored by an electrical stimulus until the surgeon hits on the overexcitable part which seems responsible for the fit. The patient remains conscious; and his responses indicate that over a large part of the brain the stimulation apparently has little or no effect: nothing is felt. In other parts involuntary movements are excited; and in others flashes of light are seen, sounds heard, and memories vividly recalled. The points at which these results are obtained correspond pretty exactly with the 'centres' for these various functions as mapped out by earlier neurologists on the basis of their microscopical studies of incoming or outgoing nerve-fibres, and of experiments on various animals. Still more recently it has proved possible to insert very fine electrodes into the deeper parts of the human brain, and thus determine the functions of the inner centres. For example, in what is called the 'inter-brain' (diencephalon) there appear to be localised centres for certain emotional reactions—anger, fear, sex, pleasure, and so on. In the cortex of the brain the centres so far established are for relatively simple cognitive responses (vision, hearing, touch) or for specific movements of the limbs, with surrounding regions for different types of perception and imagery.

The post-mortem study of human brains under the microscope shows that there are wide differences in the minute structure of the brains of different individuals. The brains of mental defectives, for example, have fewer nerve-cells; the nerve-cells have fewer branches; and the arrangement of both cells and branches is far less regular and systematic than in brains of normal persons; and these characteristics are discernible in almost every part of the defective's brain.

Thus the observable differences in brain-structure clearly suggest two of the main distinctions, namely, the distinction between cognitive and emotional processes and between general and specialised abilities. Further, if differences in these respects are due largely to differences in the physical structure of the brain, then there is a strong presumption that, like other differences due to the structure of the individual organism, they will be partly influenced by heredity; and this presumption is reinforced by our knowledge of the way these structures have emerged and been transmitted during the evolution of the animal kingdom and the manner in which they develop and mature during the growth of the individual.

The Statistical Evidence

The foregoing inferences are admittedly little more than tentative conjectures. Hence they call urgently for more direct corroboration. And this, in my view, is most convincingly supplied by the results of statistical analyses of test-scores and similar data. The problem came sharply to the fore at the beginning of the century. In 1892 the Anthropological Section of the British Association had organised an anthropological survey of the British Isles, based on the measurement of height, weight, and various other physical characteristics; ten years later it was suggested that the survey should be repeated on a more elaborate scale, and should include mental measurements as well as physical. William McDougall, Reader in Mental Philosophy at Oxford, was appointed chairman of the psychological planning sub-committee. He accordingly set his research-students, William Brown, J. C. Flugel, and myself, to compile and try out suitable tests for this ambitious project. We were joined by C. S. Spearman, who had just returned from working under Wundt at Leipzig, and settled down in a village near Oxford.

The first question to be decided was what kinds of mental characteristics would it be possible to test? It had already been agreed that the psychological part of the programme could best be carried out in the schools; and McDougall, a keen supporter of Galton's views, proposed tests of two main types—general ability and special aptitudes—along the lines of a school examination. Brown, quoting a recent research by one of Cattell's students in America, doubted the whole conception of a 'general ability'.

Spearman, on the other hand, rejected the notion of special aptitudes as 'an obsolete survival of the discredited faculty psychology', and contended that we should confine ourselves solely to tests of 'general intelligence'; Flugel and I supported McDougall's suggestion.

It was generally agreed that the accuracy and suitability of the tests could best be measured by Pearson's method of calculating correlations. Each of us began by taking a sample of about twenty or thirty schoolchildren of the same age at some school where an experienced teacher could be relied on to rank the children in order of their general ability with reasonable accuracy. Each test (usually lasting about 15 to 30 minutes) was then applied to the children individually, and the order furnished by the tests was compared with the order furnished by the teacher. The amount of agreement was measured by a 'correlation coefficient', i.e. a fraction varying between 0 and 1, zero denoting total absence of agreement and unity denoting perfect agreement.

Now it seemed to me that the problems raised by our alternative hypotheses could best be settled by adapting a well-known mathematical technique used by Karl Pearson in classifying various bodily measurements. Suppose, for example, you have three tests presumably involving verbal ability—reading, spelling and composition, and three tests presumably involving numerical ability—addition, multiplication, and division; and you wish to check the validity of this hypothetical classification. You work out all the fifteen possible correlations between the tests taken in pairs, and examine the results. If Brown's hypothesis were true, you would expect moderately large correlations between the three verbal tests and moderately large correlations between the three arithmetical tests, but no appreciable cross-correlations between any of the verbal tests with any of the arithmetical tests. Such a result would confirm the simple twofold classification into verbal and numerical abilities. If Spearman's hypothesis were true, there would be positive correlations between *all* the tests (varying no doubt in size), since a general ability would be common to them all; and, what is more, if the correlations were arranged in a 6in. × 6in. square table, the figures in each row would be proportional to the figures in every other row, and similarly with the columns; this follows from a well-established theorem in matrix algebra. Owing to sampling errors and errors of measurement, the proportionality would not be exact. But a simple formula enables one to calculate the theoretical values one would expect on Spearman's hypothesis for the fifteen correlations. These can be subtracted from the coefficients actually obtained; and the discrepancies then tested for statistical significance. If none was significant, we should conclude that the twofold classification was fallacious: in other words, only one 'general ability' was operative, not two distinct 'special abilities'.

In our own investigations Flugel and I found no support for either of these simple hypotheses. Provided the number of children tested was fairly large, there were no near-zero correlations of the type required by Brown's hypothesis; but certain clusters of residuals were fully significant, so that Spearman's hypothesis was ruled out. In other words, we seemed compelled to assume that *both* general *and* specific abilities were operative. However, since the method was purely mathematical, we preferred to talk of components or 'factors' rather than 'abilities'. How far these abstract 'factors' could be plausibly identified with concrete abilities seemed a matter for a separate inquiry.

In our first investigation we applied tests for every cognitive level and for both sensory and motor aspects. Some of the tests were already in use in ordinary laboratory work; but many were invented by McDougall, who regarded this as his special task. To check the self-consistency or 'reliability' of each test, Flugel and I applied the same tests to the same children independently. The results in this, and indeed in most later experiments, were much the same. There was first a large 'general factor' entering into all the tests; second, one (or more often several) 'group factors', i.e. factors common only to certain groups of tests (e.g. tests involving predominantly verbal or predominantly numerical processes); third, certain 'specific factors', each peculiar to a single test, and presumably depending on some distinctive activity characteristic of each test; and fourth, a specific factor, loosely called 'error', indicated by the imperfect correlations between the two applications of the same test (cf. Burt, 1909, 1917, 1949; Vernon, 1950).

The identification of the various factors is now usually made by calculating the correlations between each factor and each of the tests: the types of test with the largest of 'factor loadings' (as such correlations are called) then suggest the nature of the factor. Flugel and I preferred to select individuals with the highest factor-measurements, and get them to describe the type of mental process which they used. Their introspections plainly indicated that, in most investigations of this type, the general factor is a cognitive not a motivational factor; and this is further confirmed, first by the high correlation between the factor measurements and the teachers' ranking for 'general intelligence', and, second, by

factorial studies in which assessments of emotional and moral qualities have been included as well as intellectual.

Analysis of Variance

However, to demonstrate the mere existence of a general cognitive factor is not enough: even if it exists, it may have no more than a slight or nugatory influence. What the practical teacher wants to know is the relative importance of all these various factors in the causation of the observable differences between one child and another. This again is a question which can be adequately answered only by quantitative analysis. The simplest way to measure the amount of individual differences in any particular characteristic is by calculating the extent to which each child differs from the average for his age-group; and the most convenient measure to adopt is what technically is termed the 'variance': (the non-mathematical reader may regard this as the *average* of all such differences). It then appears that, with schoolchildren under the age of about nine or ten, the general factor contributes well over 50 per cent to the total variance in assessments of mental efficiency, which with children usually means educational attainments: no other single factor accounts for more than about 15 per cent. With older pupils, as special abilities gradually mature, the relative importance of the general factor diminishes; and with adults it often plays a comparatively minor role. It is for this reason that students of child psychology have devoted most of their attention to 'general intelligence', and have tended to neglect the study of more specialised abilities and of motivational factors, such as industry and interest.

THE INHERITANCE OF GENERAL ABILITY

Popular Misconceptions

During recent years the notion that mental differences between individuals are largely the effect of differences in their innate endowment has become the subject of heated debate. Most of the controversy has arisen over the selection of pupils for different types of school, and especially the retention of the eleven-plus examination for entry to a grammar school. Professor Pedley states the case against selection in the following terms: 'Before 1955 public confidence in the fairness of the examination rested on the belief that intelligence tests could detect and measure inborn ability. The leading figure in the movement was Dr Cyril Burt. Burt and his followers, not only thought that heredity mattered far more than environment in determining mental ability, but believed they could distinguish inborn ability. . . . This led the Spens committee to recommend the establishment of three different types of school—academic, technical, and general. In the middle fifties the belief was strongly challenged by such university teachers as Philip Vernon, Brian Simon, and John Daniels, who demonstrated conclusively that this was not so' (*The Comprehensive School* (Penquin), 1969, pp. 15, 36).

These assertions are by no means accurate. Technical and academic types of secondary school, with special entrance examinations, were in existence long before I joined the staff of the London County Council; my own recommendation was merely to add an intelligence test to the existing examination for the academic ('grammar') type of school; my reason was that, when confined to English and arithmetic, such examinations tended to handicap children from the poorer and illiterate families. The only publication by Vernon which Professor Pedley cites is the inquiry carried out under the auspices of the British Psychological Society, and which Vernon edited (*Secondary School Selection*, 1957). It is true that this report denied any suggestion that intelligence tests measure '*purely* innate ability'; but no psychologist ever suggested any such thing. In the final chapter, consisting of a 'Summary and Conclusions', it is expressly stated that 'the intelligence test is so consistently successful that it should not be dispensed with'. In the section on inheritance reference is made to the view of 'a number of left-wing writers, who have claimed that intelligence-test results largely or mainly reflect social class differences'. But this view is firmly repudiated; and evidence is quoted to show that class differences are as much the effect as the cause of differences in intelligence.

The weakness in the arguments adduced by Pedley and other critics whom he mentions arises partly from the fact that they adopt an entirely out-of-date conception of heredity, and partly from their reliance on armchair arguments. Heredity, they assume, means merely 'the tendency of like to beget like' (the oft-quoted definition of the *Oxford Dictionary*); and the evidence for heredity, it is therefore assumed, must consist chiefly in calculating co-efficients of correlation to measure the degree of likeness between parents and their offspring or between siblings. For the rest their arguments are almost wholly verbal, and based solely on *a priori* assumptions. This is as though one persisted in proving from an *a priori* assumption that the orbits of the planets were circular, and ignored the mathematical calculations which indicated they were elliptical. No modern breeder of animals or plants sits down and just argues verbally whether or not this or that characteristic is inherited.

With one or two notable exceptions few critics nowadays go so far as to affirm that heredity has no influence whatever on mental characteristics: their contention is rather that, even if heredity exercises some effect on mental differences, that effect is too small to be of any practical consequence when compared with the overwhelming influence of environmental conditions—social class, poverty or wealth, and the training provided at home and at school. But to assess the relative importance of such factors it is essential to undertake a quantitative analysis. This they never attempt; nor do they discuss or examine the detailed analyses already published.

Genetic and Environmental Factors

As may be seen from the papers cited in the Psychological Society's report, the procedure used by my co-workers and myself in our earlier researches consisted in extending the technique of factor analysis to correlations between members of the same set of families, related by varying degrees of kinship. As in so many factorial inquiries (cf. above, p. 87f.), we found four main types of factor: first, a 'general factor' common to all members of the same family, no matter what their degree of kinship, or whether they had been brought up in the same homes or not; second, a 'group factor' common only to those who had been brought up together in the same homes and at the same schools; third, a 'specific factor' peculiar to pairs of identical twins, whether brought up together or apart; and finally, specific factors peculiar to those who had been brought up in an environment away from all other relatives, or (so it seemed in certain cases) who had been treated differently at home because of age, or individual disposition.

In all factorial studies the most interesting result is the relative size of the factor variances. We found that the first and third had the largest proportional variances, the third (surprisingly enough) being almost as large as the first. The second was smaller in the case of intelligence-tests and certain body-measurements (height, for example), but much larger in the case of educational attainments.

The Mechanism of Inheritance

How were these results to be explained? At the beginning of the present century—that is, soon after Galton and Binet had published their more important conclusions—a number of biologists, interested in the breeding of livestock and grain, started a series of experimental researches on the problems of inheritance and the peculiarities of the cells involved in reproduction. The results threw an entirely new light on the way in which inheritable tendencies are transmitted from one generation to the next. The methods and hypotheses adopted were due largely to the investigations of an Augustinian monk named Mendel, who had made a special study of hybridisation. Mendel had published his results in 1865; but his work remained buried in a local scientific journal, and was re-discovered only in 1901. His experiments were confined to plants, chiefly peas and beans, which he grew in the monastery garden at Brünn. His conclusions will be easier to follow if we consider the analogous results obtained by later British investigators with animals and birds.

Let us begin with pure-bred specimens of black and white Andalusian fowls. If a white bird is crossed with a black, all the offspring will be grey (poultry fanciers call them 'blue'). If we mate the grey with one another, the next generation will consist of birds of three different colours—white and black (which now reappear as so-called 'throw-backs') and grey or 'blue'. On an average the proportions will be 1 white, 2 grey, and 1 black. The white if mated together, and the black if mated together, will always breed true; but the grey will produce three types as before in similar proportions. Evidently, although the colours we observe appear at times to blend, the inheritable constituents which are responsible for these colours do not: they segregate, and then temporarily recombine. The proportions, be it noted, are what we should get if we tossed a penny for the male parent, and another for the female parent; and then, in a lengthy series of trials, counted the number of heads and tails: in the long run we should get two heads, two tails, a head and a tail, and a tail and a head an equal number of times. The laws of heredity are thus essentially laws of chance: in a rather novel sense, 'marriage is a lottery'.

The inheritable constituents are now termed genes. The genes are carried on minute thread-like structures known as 'chromosomes', visible under the microscope in cells just before they divide to produce daughter cells. Except in the reproductive cells (sperm and egg), they are present in pairs, the number varying according to species. Every human being has forty-six pairs, each no doubt carrying hundreds of genes. In the older Andalusian breed, we may imagine, there was originally a gene responsible for producing a chemical pigment which made the feathers look black. Then in certain cases some accident or other (possibly some sudden change in temperature or electric radiation) caused the gene in certain birds to change its chemical composition, with the result that their offspring developed no pigment, and so became albinos. If this novel type was carefully raised and preserved by breeders, its progeny would survive; there would thus be a gene existing in two alternative forms; let us call them *B* (for black) and *b* for the mutant form. If we start with a black cock (or a black hen, the sex does not matter), we may assume it carries on both the two corresponding chromosomes in each cell the black-producing form of the gene, so that its 'genotype' can be represented by *BB*. Let us mate it with a white fowl, represented by *bb*. The union of the sperm and egg must consequently produce either *Bb* or *bB* (the first letter denotes the gene from the male). When these are mated we shall evidently get *BB*, *Bb* = *bB*, and *bb*; and here the *Bb* and *bB* genotypes presumably develop only half the usual amount of black pigment, so that these fowls appear grey.

Often, however, no such intermediate colour results. If we mate a pure-bred rabbit having the brown fur of the normal or wild type with an albino rabbit having white fur and pink eyes, all the offspring will be brown. When these are mated together, their offspring will be either brown or white; and in the long run the proportion will be 3 brown to 1 white. In this case the hybrid *Bb* or *bB* have the same dark colour as the pure-bred *BB*. Accordingly the brown colour is said to be 'dominant', and the albino 'recessive'.

The same types of inheritance are found in human beings. Some thirty years ago a Norwegian biochemist, working at an institution for mental defectives, noticed that several of the inmates exuded a peculiar smell; and on looking up their case-histories found that these children were often related: several were first cousins. Further investigation revealed that the children in question were lacking in an enzyme in the liver which disposes of an aromatic amino-acid called phenylalanine. The presence of this substance in the blood interferes with the growth and functioning of the brain. Normal persons carry a gene on both chromosomes responsible for manufacturing the enzyme that gets rid of it. But the gene has a mutant form which fails to produce the necessary enzyme; and, if *both* genes are of the mutant form (as may occur when relatives carrying a single mutant marry), the child becomes mentally defective. But one normal gene suffices. The abnormal condition is therefore recessive. There are now known to be a number of different types of mental deficiency due to the action of single genes: sometimes the condition is recessive, more rarely it is dominant. This mode of inheritance is called unifactorial, and the genes responsible are called major genes. Unifactorial inheritance plays an important part in certain characteristics which lead to a classification of individuals into two distinctive types, one usually normal, the other often abnormal; e.g. colour-blindness, eye-colour, left-handedness, and several bodily diseases. Sometimes the gene exists in more than two forms, as in the case of blood-groups.

In human beings, however, most normal characteristics exhibit not just a simple two-fold qualitative difference, but graded quantitative differences: instead of a clear-cut classification into types, there is a continuous variation from one extreme to the other. The height of British males, for example, varies by almost imperceptible amounts from 57 in. to 77 in. Such differences, so far as they are due to innate influences, must be caused, not by one or two genes taking only two different forms, but by a large number of such genes, each capable at most of adding only a minute fraction of an inch to the individual's stature. These genes are called polygenes; and this mode of inheritance is known as multifactorial inheritance. The same laws of inheritance are assumed to govern their transmission, although the effects of each separate gene can no longer be traced in the pedigree tables.

The implications of such a mechanism can easily be calculated. Thus, for characteristics like height or intelligence, well over a hundred genes at the very least must be operative, each capable, in one of its alternative forms, of adding a small unit to the child's intelligence. Suppose, for the sake of simplicity, that there are exactly 200. Imagine that in the father of two boys 140 of his genes are favourable. If he mates at random, his wife will probably have about 100 favourable genes. Now each child receives half his genes from his father and half from his mother; thus we should expect each to have about $70+50 = 120$ favourable genes. Evidently in a large group this would produce a correlation between either child and either parent of approximately one half or 0·50. But, unless the two brothers (Tom and George, say) are identical twins, the individual genes inherited by Tom and George will not be the same. If we think of the analogy with coin tossing, we should expect only half the genes received by Tom from his father to be the same as those received by George; and the same with the genes received by each from their mother. Hence the correlation between the two brothers will also work out at about 0·50. The genes that are common to both brothers (and in a lesser degree to all blood-relatives) are responsible for the large common factor in our factorial analysis and form a common genetic factor; the genes which are peculiar to each brother are responsible for the difference between the two, and thus act as specific genetic factors. If, however, Tom and George are identical twins, developed from the splitting of the same fertilised egg, all their genes will be identical: hence in their case what in ordinary sibs we regard as specific factors will now operate as an additional common factor. If there are differences between such twins, those differences can be due only to environmental causes.

In regard to intelligence, however, mating is by no means random. Restrained by the barriers imposed by our class system, impelled by a variety of personal prejudices and predilections, human marriages have always been in some degree preferential: like chooses like. The consequent similarity between fathers and mothers appreciably increases the correlations actually found. If, on the other hand, (as seems probable) certain genes are dominant in their developmental action, this must tend to lower the correlation between ordinary sibs by magnifying the specific genetic factor; but it will not affect the correlations between parent and child.

Every observable characteristic is the joint result of both genetic and environmental factors; and there are often complicating interactions and correlations between them. When two members of the same family—father and son, or a pair of brothers—are brought up or live together under the same roof and in the same cultural environment, that will usually increase the resemblance between them. Nevertheless, even though they have spent their whole lives in the same home, and the same neighbourhood, the environmental influences affecting them will never be *exactly* the same: the first born, for instance, so long as he remains an only child, will receive all his parents' attention; but by the time a younger sib appears, the circumstances of the parents may have been materially altered. In these and other ways therefore environmental factors may help to diminish the correlations as well as to enhance them. All these complicating influences must be borne in mind.

Analysis of Variance

Our main purpose, it will be remembered, is to analyse the variance which we actually observe on testing the abilities of a representative batch of individuals, into its component causes. Since variance is additive, we may, if we accept the foregoing specification of the causal factors chiefly concerned, express the total variance as the sum of four main contributory factors: this procedure admittedly involves some slight simplification, and may need further amplification later on; but let us begin with it as a practicable starting point. This fourfold analysis yields the following fundamental equation:

$$V_T = V_{GC} + V_{GS} + V_{EC} + V_{ES}, \tag{1}$$

where V_T denotes the total observable variance, and the subscripts G, E, C and S indicate 'genetic', 'environmental', 'common', and 'specific' factors, respectively. We thus have four unknowns whose values are to be determined from our observational data. However, since all we are interested in are the *relative* amounts contributed by the several components, we can put $V_T = 1$ (or 100, if we prefer to think in percentages rather than fractions); we then need only three observed quantities to determine the various proportions.

The easiest figures to collect are the correlations (i) between sibs reared together, r_{st}; (ii) between sibs reared apart (e.g. one in a foster-home or residential institution, and the other with his own parents), r_{sa}; and (iii) between monozygotic (i.e. 'identical') twins reared together, r_{mzt}. A correlation may be regarded as stating the ratio of two variances, viz., (a) the variance of the factors common to the two correlated sets of individuals to (b) the total variance. Recalling the arguments set out above, we can thus put

$$r_{sa} = \frac{V_{GC}}{V_T}, \tag{2}$$

$$r_{st} = \frac{V_{GC} + V_{EC}}{V_T}, \tag{3}$$

$$r_{mzt} = \frac{V_{GC} + V_{EC} + V_{GS}}{V_T}. \tag{4}$$

Evidently therefore, if we have obtained empirical values for these three correlations, we can calculate the component variances by a process of successive subtraction. In columns 2, 3, and 5 of Table 1, I give the correlations obtained for 200 sibs reared together, 100 sibs reared apart, and 68 monozygotic twins reared together. In this early investigation the test-scores for intelligence and attainments were obtained during surveys of ten-year-olds carried out in 1919–22. However, to secure an adequate number of twins and of sibs reared apart a few cases outside these age-ranges were included; in every case an age-correction (never very large) was applied where necessary. We included correlations for height, since one of our main objects was to check the theory that the inheritance of mental ability was similar to that of physical characteristics (cf. Burt, 1923; the tests used are described in Burt, 1921).

In the present table I have added two further sets of correlations. Column 4 gives the median correlations published by a number of other investigators, not only in the United Kingdom, but also abroad (chiefly Canada and the USA). The number of pairs tested in these reports amounts to nearly 8,000 sibs reared together, about 300 reared apart, and over 1,000 monozygotic twins reared together (the exact totals are uncertain, because several investigators failed to state the numbers on which their correlations were based). I have also added figures for counts of finger-print ridges (Holt, 1961): in this case the correlations cannot possibly be increased by environmental conditions or assortative mating, though environmental or developmental conditions may help to reduce the resemblances.

Table 1. Observed correlations

	Fingerprints	Height	Intelligence Burt	Attainments Other Investigators	
Monozygotic twins reared together	0·950	0·926	0·897	0·874	0·908
Sibs reared together	0·500	0·523	0·516	0·551	0·656
Sibs reared apart	0·487	0·471	0·433	0·472	0·385

As the reader can ascertain for himself in Table 2 on page 98, the figures in Table 1 yield estimates for the contributory variances. I have converted decimal fractions to percentages.

It would therefore seem that genetic endowment contributes about 90 per cent to physical characteristics, and about 80 per cent to scores obtained with intelligence tests. The common environmental factor contributes less than 10 per cent to the scores for intelligence, but nearly 40 per cent to those for attainments. In face of these figures—and they include (be it remembered) the results of numerous other investigators besides myself—it is

Table 2. Variances for genetic and environmental factors: percentages of total

Factor	Fingerprints	Height	Intelligence Burt	Attainments Other Investigators	
V_{GC}	48·7	47·1	43·3	47·2	38·5
V_{GS}	45·0	40·3	38·1	32·3	25·2
V_{G}	93·7	87·4	81·4	79·5	63·7
V_{EC}	1·3	5·2	8·3	7·9	27·1
V_{ES}	5·0	7·4	10·3	12·6	9·2
V_{E}	6·3	12·6	18·6	20·5	36·3
V_{T}	100·0	100·0	100·0	100·0	100·0

impossible to suppose, as so many contemporary writers have contended, that intelligence tests are simply 'yet another test of attainment'.

Identical Twins Reared Apart
It is, however, not altogether satisfactory to rely on assessments for sibs, particularly sibs reared apart. One can never be quite sure how far difference in age affects comparability; and in choosing foster homes it is easier with ordinary sibs to find parents corresponding in social level to that of the child's own parents (as those responsible for placement usually strive to do): with twins this is seldom possible, since the need to place one of the children in a separate home is not realised until it is discovered that the mother is about to produce twins instead of just another sib. Thus with monozygotic twins reared apart one avoids the complications of selective placement, and with dizygotic twins reared together the effects of difference in age. Unfortunately, twins, whether identical or not, are much rarer than ordinary sibs; and consequently it is only possible to obtain reasonable numbers of identical twins reared apart, if one continues to collect such cases over a long period of time; and even then the sampling errors are far greater than they would be with the larger samples available for ordinary sibs. However, in a huge area like London two or three such cases can be discovered almost every year; and with the co-operation of the care committee workers it has been possible over the years to accumulate a moderately large number. In Table 3 I give data both for cases collected in London (Burt, 1966) and for those investigated by Newman and his co-workers in America (1937).

Table 3. Correlations for twins

	Burt				Newman et al.			
	Number	Group tests	Individual tests	Attainments	Number	Group tests	Individual tests	Attainments
Monozygotic twins:								
reared together	95	0·944	0·918	0·983	50	0·923	0·881	0·892
reared apart	53	0·771	0·863	0·623	19	0·727	0·767	0·583
Dizygotic twins:								
reared together	127	0·552	0·527	0·831	51	0·621	0·631	0·696

Table 4. Distribution of individual differences in mental ability

IQ	Under 50	50–60	60–70	70–80	80–90	90–100	100–10	110–20	120–30	130–40	140–50	Over 150	Total
Number	1	3	19	68	161	248	248	161	68	19	3	1	1,000

To obtain values for the contributory variances the same type of calculation can be used as before, substituting for the equation used with r_{sa} the equation appropriate to r_{mza}, $(V_{GE} + V_{GS})/V_P$. I leave the calculations to the reader. The important point to notice is that, in both Newman's figures and my own, the correlations obtained with intelligence tests are distinctly higher for monozygotic twins reared apart than they are for dizygotic twins reared together: dizygotic twins of course are merely ordinary siblings who happen to be born at the same time; hence they are no more alike in their genetic endowment than ordinary siblings. To explain this higher correlation by the effects of selective placement is, in our own inquiry, out of the question. As a glance at the supplementary table printed in my paper indicates, there was no correlation whatsoever between the social conditions of the twins brought up with their own parents and those of the brothers or sisters who had been sent soon after birth to a foster-home or residential institution (Burt, 1966, Table 1). The high correlations for the separated twins therefore cannot possibly be attributed to a similarity in environment. The fact that before birth they developed within the same womb is more likely to have produced differences than similarities, since one twin is usually more favourably placed than the other, as indeed differences in their birth-weight, health, and general condition so often show. With attainments the situation is completely different: in both Newman's data and my own there is a difference of over 0·300 between the correlations for identical twins brought up together and those brought up apart.

There has been a good deal of misconception about what we were trying to discover. Writers who quote our figures generally treat them as 'estimates of the extent to which heredity influences intelligence', and then observe that they seem 'incredibly large'. But by 'intelligence', as the context shows, these writers evidently understand *actual* mental efficiency. That, however, is not what we had in mind. Our aim was not to estimate how far the innate element in mental capacity determines *actual* efficiency, but to ascertain how accurately different tests and methods of assessment appear to measure that hypothetical *innate* element. Actual efficiency varies widely with the particular activities in which the writer or investigator happens to be interested. With children it presumably means progress at school and the educational attainments which they eventually acquire; in that sense genetic endowment contributes an amount usually varying between 40 and 70 per cent, averaging about 60 per cent, as in the table set out above. With adults the interpretation will vary largely with their trade or profession; and here the percentages are lower still.

Most of our critics have neglected to refer to the original research reports, and have apparently taken the figures at second-hand from some text book or other where they are quoted (e.g. Fuller and Thompson, 1960, p. 323). Reference to the original papers (e.g. Burt and Howard, 1956, or Burt, 1958) will show that we gave results for three different methods of estimation—(1) a typical group test; (2) a typical individual test (with children the London revision of the Terman–Binet tests); and (3) what we called the 'final adjusted assessments': these were obtained after first submitting the raw test-scores to the children's teachers, and then re-examining (usually with performance tests) every child about whom there were appreciable discrepancies. The tabulations indicated that there was a considerable variation in the accuracy of the assessments thus provided: on average it amounted to about 75 per cent for the group test, 80 per cent for the individual test, and 85 per cent for the final adjusted assessments.

The Agreement between Theoretical and Empirical Estimates
The attempt to determine the accuracy of these various methods of assessing innate capacity obviously assumes that such a capacity exists; and the high degree of accuracy implied by the results goes far to confirm its existence. However, the main argument for a genetic factor proceeds rather differently. It takes the two-fold form of every complete inductive proof.

(A) If environment rather than heredity is the main cause of the differences we observe, then certain observable consequences would follow: e.g. (i) we should expect the assessments obtained for children's abilities to resemble the assessments of the material and cultural conditions of their homes. Often they do not. We not only find extremely dull children in families of well-to-do professional parents, but also extremely bright children in families where the home conditions, one might have thought, would condemn every child to hopeless failure. (ii) Second, we should expect the assessments for unrelated children reared together from birth in the same institution or foster-home to agree far more closely than the assessments for ordinary siblings reared apart. They do not. The correlations for the latter are nearly twice as high as those for the former. (iii) Third, we should expect the assessments for dizygotic twins reared together in their own homes to agree far more closely than those for monozygotic twins reared apart. As we have seen, they do not. In the case of educational attainments the environmentalist's expectations *are* to a large extent confirmed, though not so completely as to rule out *all* genetic influence.

(B) If on the other hand heredity (as understood by the modern neo-Mendelian geneticist) is the main cause of the differences in the test scores and other assessments, then very different consequences would follow. On the basis of the multifactorial hypothesis formulated above, it is easy to deduce the correlations to be expected between relatives of varying degrees of kinship, ranging from identical twins, half-sibs, parents and children, grandparents and children, to first and second cousins. In the literature of the subject one can find correlations reported for nine different types of kinship; in our surveys we covered twelve types. In almost all these cases there was a remarkable concordance between the values predicted by the genetic hypothesis and those actually observed (Burt, 1966, Table 4). It would be quite impossible to account for these remarkable coincidences on a purely or predominantly environmental hypothesis.

I have no space to discuss the inheritance of other types of mental difference. For these anything like conclusive evidence must await the findings of further research. A study of pedigrees strongly suggests that certain special abilities and disabilities are inherited, for example, memory, mathematical, musical, and verbal ability; and some, e.g. verbal ability and visual imagery, appear to be partly sex-linked.

The causation of motivational tendencies is far more elusive. On applying the same factorial techniques that we used for intellectual characteristics, my co-workers and I found much the same types of factor as before—general, group, and specific. The general factor making for emotional stability or instability, the group factors responsible for the so-called extraverted and intraverted types, and certain specific factors, analogous to what biologists term 'instincts' (e.g. sex, aggressiveness, anxiety, wandering)—all seem in part dependent on innate disposition; but they are far more amenable to social and other environmental influences, particularly in early life. Unfortunately tests of personality and character have a deplorably low reliability; so that at present any precise quantitative treatment remains out of the question.

THE RANGE OF INDIVIDUAL DIFFERENCES

The Normal Distribution
Even the most hardened critics of mental inheritance do not deny

that many defectives at one end of the scale, and many geniuses at the other end, owe their unusual intellectual characteristics to their inborn constitution. These cases, however, are either passed over in silence, or dismissed as exceptional, if not pathological. This makes the task of the teacher, school doctor, and educational psychologist partially embarrassing. Since all 'normal' children are presumed to be innately equal, any signs of backwardness or 'subnormality', and even of early precocity or 'supernormality' the anxious parent infers must be due to some morbid disturbance.

But where are we to draw the lines? The 'subnormal' or dull merge into the mediocre, the mediocre into the moderately bright, and so on, until we reach the 'supernormal' genius. As the particulate theory of Mendel and Galton suggests, an unbroken continuum stretches from helpless idiots with IQs of 10 or less to the philosophers, scientists, and great statesmen of the past with estimated IQs of 200 or more. These variations, so far from being pathological, are as normal as differences in face or eye colour.

If the reader will think once again of the analogy with coin-tossing, it is easy to see what kind of frequencies we should get. Toss 11 pennies 2,000 times, and count the number of heads: there would be 12 grades in all (0 to 11). The most probable number of heads would be 5 or 6; and the relative proportions would be not unlike those shown in Table 4 below. However, the number of genes affecting such characteristics as bodily height and general intelligence is not 11, but well over 200. In that case the frequency-distribution would approach what is known as the 'normal probability' curve (the limiting values of the binomial distribution as the number of coins is assumed to increase indefinitely). This is the kind of distribution actually found in anthropometric surveys for physical characteristics such as bodily height: and it yields a very good fit to the frequency-distributions obtained with intelligence-tests (Burt, 1917, 1921; Terman and Merrill, 1937).

Surveys carried out in London schools yield figures closely approximating to the theoretical frequencies obtained for a normal distribution with a mean of 100 IQ and a standard deviation of 15 IQ; (the standard deviation may be regarded as the average deviation of the individuals from the general mean of the whole population, calculated by taking the square root of the variance). Table 4 shows the numbers of children that we might expect to have the IQs indicated out of a school population of a thousand. Those who are not accustomed to thinking in terms of IQs may imagine a decimal point inserted before the noughts; the figures will then indicate mental ages at the chronological age of 10·0.

Thus among every 1,000 ten-year-olds we should expect at least one to possess the mental capacity of an average child of only five, and at least one to possess the mental capacity of an average child of fifteen. Half of them would have mental ages between 9·0 and 11·0, i.e. would differ but little from the general mean. In actual practice the proportion of children with IQs over 140 is as a rule slightly higher than indicated in the table, and the proportions of those in the lower categories (below 80, IQ) are still larger.

These figures have an obvious bearing on the organisation of classes within the school and of schools within the country generally. Some of the more ardent advocates of 'comprehensive education' contend that 'a genuinely comprehensive school should cover the entire range of ability'. It may be doubted whether such critics realise how wide 'the entire range' actually is. Most comprehensive schools draw their pupils from their own immediate neighbourhood; and within a given educational area the occupational composition of one neighbourhood often varies widely from that of another; the residents in one district may consist mainly of manual workers; those in other districts may belong chiefly to the upper or lower middle classes. Thus in London districts like Hampstead and Lewisham produce ten times as many children with IQs over 130 as poorer boroughs like Limehouse and Bethnal Green; and the latter have well over ten times the number of children with IQs under 80 than are found in the former. Even in neighbourhoods where the population is more heterogeneous, the comprehensive schools, however large, are unlikely to cover 'the *entire* range of ability'.

What principally excites the protests of the critics is 'the traditional practice of selecting certain pupils, and assigning them to schools of different types'. Few expressly deprecate the segregation of the subnormal, in spite of the additional cost of providing such schools with smaller classrooms, special equipment, and specially trained teachers. Their sharpest strictures are reserved for those who advocate a similar policy in the case of the supernormal—selecting the ablest pupils by means of some special examination and then transferring them to a grammar school where once again the classes are small and the masters specially trained. The reason most frequently advanced for abolishing this procedure is that 'it unduly favours children from the middle classes'. 'The proportion of working-class children', we are told, 'who go to grammar schools, public schools, and eventually to the university is far smaller'; and this, it is contended, 'is flagrantly unjust and socially divisive'.

The disparity in numbers is undeniable. But for this the main cause is obvious: the percentage of children possessing the innate level of ability needed for a grammar school course is far smaller in the manual than in the non-manual classes. Nor is the reason for the disparity far to seek. It is the cumulative result of the constant interchange between social classes which started centuries ago, as soon as the rigid feudal structure imposed by the early Normans gave way to freer mobility. Ever since the days of the legendary Dick Whittington, and indeed long before his time, bright and energetic youngsters from the poorest homes have steadily worked their way up to the merchant or professional classes, while the duller and lazier children of the middle or upper classes have tended to drift downwards. And this dispersal must have been still further accelerated by the prevailing rule of primogeniture. The eldest son of a franklin or yeoman would inherit his father's strip of land and the tools with which to cultivate it or prepare its produce, while the younger sons set out to seek their fortune. And much the same occurred with younger sons of higher rank.

From the time of the Plantagenets onwards both the earlier Catholic and the later Protestant monarchs, or rather their political advisers, deliberately attempted to seek out the ablest children in any and every social class, and train them to meet the need for an ever-increasing number of administrative or theological posts. As early as the fourteenth century William Wykeham, Edward III's chancellor, founded a 'New College' at Oxford, and a subsidiary school at Winchester, endowing both with generous grants to assist 'poor and needy scholars proficient in the grammaticals' who were to be 'prepared as clerks'. This system of scholarships to grammar schools and universities became one of the distinctive and most envied features of British education.

Few of the critics I have quoted appear to realise the extent of social movement that has continued in this country for over six centuries and its inevitable results. If exceptional ability is not merely innate but also inheritable, then in each successive generation such families would probably produce two or three able youngsters who with luck might manage to climb one step higher in the social ladder. Sir Anthony Wagner (*English Ancestry*, 1961) gives numerous genealogies which illustrate how certain well-known families have risen from the lowest to the highest social rank, 'thanks to the industry and high ability of its members'. One striking instance must suffice. In the fifteenth century, a Norfolk villein named Geoffrey Boleyn escaped to London. His son started a prosperous business as a hatter, eventually becoming Mayor of London; his grandson was created Earl of Wiltshire; and the earl's daughter was Anne Boleyn, mother of Queen Elizabeth I. Let me add two examples of the opposite trend. Early in the present century a genealogist named Ruvigny set out to trace all the descendants of King Edward III; he got as far as the 54,000 descendants of Richard Duke of York (who contested the crown with Henry VI and was slain at Wakefield), and found that the vast majority belonged to the trading or labouring classes. Some years later a claim to the barony of Dudley made it necessary to trace possible heirs who would thus be descendants of King Henry VII: these included a butcher, a gamekeeper, a toll-gate keeper, and several others of even humbler status. With the free social mobility which has obtained in England, the emergence of distinct social classes, based largely on differences of innate capacity, was a natural consequence: (for first-hand studies of these upward and downward movements during recent years may I refer to my paper on 'Intelligence and Social Mobility', *Brit. J. Statist. Psychol.*, XIV, 1961, pp. 3–24).

THE GIFTED CHILD

The Achievements of the Gifted

Usually an observant and experienced teacher quickly discovers who are the most gifted individuals in his class; but he rarely seems to recognise *how* gifted some of them are, or how much they could achieve with adequate help and facilities. Take just a single illustrative case—one (strange to say) that appears neither in Galton's list nor in those of Havelock Ellis and Catherine Cox— William Hamilton, not the Scottish philosopher, but the scientist and mathematician. By the age of five he could read Latin, Greek, and Hebrew, and recite long passages from Homer and Milton; a few years later he added French, Italian, and Sanskrit. At thirteen he boasted that he had mastered one foreign language for every year of his life. A few months later we hear of him presenting a flowery address in Persian to the new Persian ambassador. About this time, however, he had become interested in the feats of Zerah Colburn, the famous calculating prodigy; and this turned his attention to mathematics. Here, so he claimed, he owed his great originality to the fact that he was entirely self-taught. After reading one of his early memoirs the Astronomer Royal declared: 'This youth—I do not say *will be*, but already *is*, the greatest mathematician of his time.' At the early age of twenty-two he was elected professor of astronomy, but retained his interests in languages and philosophy. There is no need to enumerate his highly ingenious work in both mathematics and science; I will only note that a century later his fruitful analogy between optics and dynamics, and particularly the equation expressing what is now known as 'Hamilton's principle', proved of the utmost value in elucidating and formulating the basic issues of quantum mechanics.

The detailed records we possess about the early life of such geniuses as Mill, Macaulay, Galton, and Norbert Wiener (to name only a few) show that their early achievements were just as precocious; and the autobiographies of the last two (as of many other brilliant geniuses) repeatedly deplore the inadequate and inappropriate teaching they received at school. I calculate that in the whole of the country there must be at least 3,000 children with IQs of 150 or more, and that 300 of these have IQs ranging from 180 to 200 or more. As things are, in the majority of cases their exceptional gifts pass unrecognised.

In London from 1913 onwards we endeavoured to follow up the subsequent careers of those boys and girls who gained junior county scholarships. The main results have been published from time to time in official reports, and are tabulated and summarised in a long article on 'The Gifted Child' in the *Yearbook of Education* (Burt, 1962). By far the most thorough inquiry is that begun in the schools of California by Professor Terman and his colleagues in 1921 and resumed at intervals until quite recently (Terman *et al.*, 1925, 1947, 1959). These and other longitudinal studies clearly demonstrate both the possibility and the importance of discovering at a very early age those children who are innately endowed with exceptionally high abilities, no matter from what social class they come. From the table set out above it will be seen that each of the larger comprehensive schools may be expected to contain anything between one and eight or nine pupils with IQs of 140 or more, many with highly specialised abilities and interests. It would manifestly be impossible to staff each of these schools with teachers of the same high ability as these children need. Surely it would be at once more efficient and more economical to gather such pupils into big batches and transfer them to selective schools which will provide them with the advanced education they deserve.

The richest of the nation's assets consists of those whom I have called 'the exceptionally gifted'. Think of what this country owes to the 900 geniuses whom Havelock Ellis sorted out from the

Dictionary of National Biography as being 'those who have built up British civilisation from its early beginnings nearly two thousand years ago'. Think too of what the world owes to the forty-seven Britons who in recent years have been awarded a Nobel prize for their spectacular achievements in physics, chemistry, physiology, medicine, philosophy, and literature. And by way of warning let us also recall how, time and again in the course of human history, nations and empires have declined, sometimes temporarily, sometimes for ever, in power, in prestige, and in the general well-being of their citizens and their subjects, simply because at the crucial moment leaders of high ability and character were lacking in the political, economic, or military sphere; and Plato's prophetic oracle was irreparably fulfilled.

REFERENCES

Bell, C., *Anatomy and Philosophy of Expression* (London: Longmans), 1844.

Benn, C., and Simon, B., *Half Way There* (London: Macmillan), 1970.

British Psychological Society, *Secondary School Selection* (London: Methuen), 1957.

Burt, C. (1909), 'Experimental tests of general intelligence', *Brit. J. Psychol.*, III, pp. 94–177; *The Distribution and Relations of Educational Abilities* (London: King & Son), 1917; *Mental and Scholastic Tests* (London: King & Son), 1921; *Annual Report of the Psychologist* (London County Council), 1923; 'The Structure of the Mind', *Brit. J. Educ. Psychol.*, XIX, pp. 100–11, 176–99, 1949; 'The Inheritance of Mental Ability', *Amer. Psychol.*, XIII, pp. 1–15, 1958; 'The Genetic Determination of Differences in Intelligence', *Brit. J. Psychol.*, LVII, pp. 137–52, 1966.

Burt, C., and Howard, M., 'The Multifactorial Theory of Inheritance and its Application to Intelligence', *Brit. J. Statist. Psychol.*, IX, pp. 95–131, 1956.

Campbell, F., *Eleven Plus and All That* (London: Watts), 1956.

Darwin, C., *The Expression of the Emotions in Man and Animals* (London: Murray), 1889.

Fuller, J. L., and Thompson, W. R., *Behavior Genetics* (New York: Wiley), 1960.

Holt, S. B., 'Quantitative Genetics of Fingerprint Patterns', *Brit. Med. Bull.*, XVII, pp. 247–50, 1961.

Jevons, W. S., *The Principles of Science* (London: Macmillan), 1900.

Mittler, P., 'The Influence of Social Class on Psycholinguistic Abilities', *Forward Trends*, XV, pp. 6–11, 1971.

Newman, H. H., Freeman, F. N., and Holzinger, K. J., *Twins: A Study of Heredity and Environment* (Chicago: Chicago University Press), 1937.

Terman, L. M. *et al., Mental and Physical Traits of a Thousand Gifted Children* (Stanford: Stanford University Press), 1925.

Terman, L. M., and Merrill, M. A., *Measuring Intelligence* (London: Harrap), 1937.

Terman, L. M., and Oden, M. H., *The Gifted Child Grows Up* (Stanford: Stanford University Press), 1947; *The Gifted Group at Mid-Life* (Stanford: Stanford University Press), 1959.

Vernon, P. E., *The Structure of Human Abilities* (London: Methuen), 1950.

4

Equality and Education

G. H. BANTOCK

I

The concept of 'equality' inevitably arouses notions of 'sameness' or 'similarity'; the dictionary defines 'equal' as being 'of the same in quality, degree, merit, etc.'. The movement towards equality in social terms can be charted as manifest in the growth of specific 'samenesses' or similarities institutionalised in the social structure of the community. What starts as a bare awareness of a common humanity recognised as operative in little else except the grave:

> Sceptre and crown
> Shall tumble down
> And in the grave be equal laid
> With the poor crooked scythe and spade

gradually takes on increasing customary and legalistic substance. In education, for instance, we start when all must go to school; we move on to the time when all must be provided with secondary school, then that all should go to the same sort of secondary school. Further refinements of equality are introduced when it is suggested that all should undertake a common curriculum, even a common syllabus, for at least a length of time. Then it is urged that the school shall be organised in such a way that each form should contain a roughly similar range of ability. Here the aim is a common experience to produce the similarity of understanding thought relevant to a democratic community. Even the way in which the curriculum is transmitted may be affected. Where the order and continuity of subject-matter is concerned John Dewey considered,

'The basic control resides in the nature of the situations in which the young take part. In social situations the young have to refer their way of acting to what others are doing and make it fit in. This directs their action to a common result, and gives an understanding common to the participants. For all *mean* the same thing, even when performing different acts.[1]

Yet here surely we are pulled up short. Notions of consciousness and the meanings which accompany consciousness are central to the whole task of Western formal education. Education, in this sense, is concerned with the handing on of such part of the cultural heritage as is responsive to formal transmission—as a matter, that is, of conscious transaction between teacher and taught. These parts of the cultural heritage are manifest as collections of significances, modes of understanding, skilled activities and the like—'meanings' in a broad sense—which require for their successful assimilation particularised orientations on the part of the pupil. To have introjected in any significant sense one of these 'meanings' is to have achieved an inwardness with specific concepts and their interrelationships, styles of argument, data, etc., to a degree which is usually in some measure publicly testable in ways which are likely to reveal defined gradations of understanding. Externally, in terms of school provision and organisation, it may be possible to produce at least superficial impressions of sameness or at least similarity. But when we get to the very core of the educational process, we need to ask to what extent it is possible to agree that all in fact do *mean* the same thing in either their actions or their understanding. Put it another way, as cultural meaning extends in depth, range and subtlety, to what extent can it be argued that all can share equally in the full range of meanings implicit in the formal curriculum of the schools? For this is the central issue which faces those who through organisational manipulation would seem to seek to produce at least an appearance of a common submission to an equivalent experience; and it is with this issue that we are ultimately concerned in any discussion of educational equality.

[1] *School and Society.*

II

One important effect of the eighteenth-century enlightenment was to substitute an abstract vision of the earthly perfectibility of humanity for the old historical Christian view of fallen man and the effort necessary for the attainment of grace. Basically, the new view was anti-historical, though in fact it often drew on a series of carefully selected historical examples to support its apocalyptic vision, especially those drawn from the supposed nature of a primitive society. It was anti-historical, however, in the sense that it laid the blame for human shortcomings on the historical situation in current society, and postulated human regeneration through a manipulation of the human environment which would permit a fresh start—perhaps through preserving an original innocence, as in *Emile*. Naturally the easiest way of manipulating this environment would seem to be through education. As Helvétius expressed it: 'l'éducation nous faisait ce que nous sommes'; manifest differences of attainment were to be blamed on the circumstances in which men were placed and especially on the particular form of the political system and government under which they existed. Genius was common, but it needed extraordinary conditions to bring it out—'il est beaucoup d'appelés et peu d'élus'. A characteristic twentieth-century theme was already in process of formulation and promulgation. Locke and indeed Quintilian before him had already advanced the proposition that inequality in minds resulted from differences in education; though at that time much the more usual view was that a 'natural' hierarchy existed which was reflected in the diversity of social rank and roles, arising out of disparities of birth and that virtuous conduct which was supposed to be the justification of aristocracy. A combination of circumstances which, on other grounds, focused on the importance of education helped to make Locke's proposition more widely acceptable than it had previously been, though even then its full force was not appreciated until nearly our own times in the world of practical educational politics.

Yet, at the same time that the role of education was receiving increasing theoretical emphasis, the beginnings of great social and structural changes in Western society consequent upon scientific, technological and industrial development produced the specific social conditions which enabled theoretical speculation to feed into practical policies. The educational revolution of the Renaissance period had instigated the important notion that men of government (the 'Courtier', the 'Governor') needed also to be men of education; and so the comparatively mindless chivalric ideal of the middle ages was fused, during the early Tudor period, with the Italian humanistic model derived from classical antiquity to form a new conception of ruling aristocracy. 'Understanding' becomes an important factor in the justification of the hierarchic orders of 'degree'; it was no longer bound up with the habit of contemplation which during the middle ages had associated it more with the clergy and the monastic orders than the activity of government: as Sir Thomas Elyot put it: 'In vain were your long travail in study and learning, if actual experience did not shew forth their fruits.'

But the learning remained broadly classical, despite periodical attempts to widen the curriculum and make it more relevant to developing mercantile and commercial interests. Even with the accelerating technological and scientific needs of the later eighteenth and nineteenth centuries, the classical curriculum retained much of its prestige down almost to our own times. Nevertheless, in reality, great changes had already taken place by the beginning of the twentieth century, as the ideal of the classically educated, 'amateur' gentlemen began to seem increasingly irrelevant to the rapidly developing demands of industry and of the industrial and governmental bureaucracies which accompanied industrialisation. The net effect of these changes was to create a new socially inspired image of the acceptable educated man, that of the Expert. Growing technical demands of differing sorts necessitated the production of an increasingly functional elite, one capable of supplying the specific demands implicit in the new fragmented technological order. The older conception of the essentially amateur if knowledgeable man of affairs was increasingly challenged by the newer professionalism, a challenge which ultimately resounded in the central corridors of power itself. The recent injunctions to 'Get Britain Moving' have included a presumption that the amateur no longer has a place in government.

The implications of all this for education I will spell out shortly. It is relevant to point out, however, that the technological and scientific developments which have been alluded to above have been accompanied, inevitably, by social and political changes which are of the greatest importance for my theme. The great watershed here is the French Revolution and the destruction of the *ancien régime* which resulted. The net result of this essentially political move was the breakdown of a whole network of traditional allegiances: 'In our days', as de Tocqueville wrote, 'men see that the constituted powers are crumbling down on every side; they see all ancient authority dying out, all ancient barriers tottering to their fall, and the judgement of the wisest is troubled at the sight.' The net result at the lower levels, for instance, was to prise the labourer out of his traditional framework and redeploy him at the mercy of the market as a 'hand'. The consequence was both liberation (of a sort) and atomisation; but the ground was being prepared for a degree of upward and downward mobility unknown to former times. Furthermore, the concept of social class entered into our social and political thinking, and the old conception of traditional hierarchy based on the notion of a 'chain of being' was replaced by the idea of stratification on class lines. Part of the significance of the difference lies in the opportunity afforded to think of the new status differentiation of class as the product of the play of social forces rather than as an unquestionable characteristic of the social order. Another of the profound legacies of the eighteenth century and of the Revolution which concluded it was the belief that the social order, like the natural order, was subject to human manipulation.

If these two legacies of the Enlightenment and of the cataclysm in which it culminated are brought into relationship with the movement towards the perfectibility of man noted in my opening remarks, the scene is set for some sort of questioning of the inequalities of the new class differentiation which was replacing the old traditional hierarchic organisation. As Professor Robert Nisbet has pointed out in *The Sociological Tradition*, there were, broadly speaking, two attitudes which developed towards the new stratified system:

'Was the new society that was being ushered in, a society founded upon citizen, entrepreneur, and technologist, a society based upon the imperious, if uncertain and often misled will of the masses, dominated by new structures of administrative power and flooded by new forms of wealth, driven by novel and incessant pressures for educational religious and social equality; was this society to be, as had all previous forms of society, organised primarily in terms of class layers, each holding the same union of economic, intellectual, educational, and political properties that had characterised social ranks in the old order? Or, in sharp contrast, could the acids of modernity be seen working in as destructive a fashion upon the bases of social class —in any viable sense of that word—as they were upon village community, extended family, and the whole network of moral-cultural relations that had also been born in the pre-capitalist, pre-democratic, pre-rationalist age?'[2]

One of these attitudes, then, saw the new stratification in terms of a reproduction, in the new industrial order, of the old rigidities; the other posited a much more fluid system, 'a scrambling of social categories to an individualisation of stratification which would result in the ascendancy not of class but of social status— which is at once more mobile, individually autonomous, and diversified than class'. As Professor Nisbet warns, the contrast must not be over-emphasised; neither group of thinkers was oblivious of class in some form or other. But the one saw it as a rigid solidified series of strata, the other as something more flexible, shifting and subject to the play of the market.

Now these two views of the nature of the developing industrial order are likely to assign somewhat differing roles to education. It is true that they will not have been as explicitly formulated at the time as they appear in Professor Nisbet's analysis; rather they constitute summations of attitudes drawn up with the advantages of hindsight. Nevertheless, one can see that even without full conscious realisation of the logic of their positions, holders of each view are likely to differ in their attitudes to equality and in their views of how one of the tools which might help to bring it about, education, should be employed. Their differing approaches may be revealed in their diversified handling of the notion of equality of opportunity. Those who stress the fluidity of society are likely to advocate equality of opportunity as contributing to this fluidity. Approaching the problems of the developing industrial-bureaucratic state pragmatically, they are likely to be impressed with the need to develop many of the new skills which society is going to require through education, and to advocate an increasingly open society, affording opportunities for status differentiation to individuals as both a means of satisfying the new restless aspirations of various sections of the developing social order and as a means of feeding the new demands of industrialisation. So great are these latter that it becomes necessary to call upon sections of the community hitherto depressed to provide some of the new recruits, on the assumption that there may be concealed among them a small reservoir of talent which, given an opportunity, may provide the necessary expertise for the new order.

Hence there develops the idea of the 'ladder of opportunity'. A more equal exposure to the life chances provided by education

[2] Op. cit., p. 148.

would enable children of talent from the lower classes to take their places in the higher levels of power in the new social order which was evolving; indeed, without these new recruitments it would hardly be possible to sustain the new society. Thus the equality implied was one at the starting post—a more equal opportunity to become unequal, as it were. Mobility was possible, desirable and should be assisted. As the society developed there was seen to be an ever growing need for talent, and so 'opportunity' was slowly increased. At the same time, there has been increasing pressure in the twentieth century to provide the rest of the population with an education suitable to their capacities and needs; so that the further implication of the equalising process becomes one of providing education which is *equally appropriate but different*. This solution to the problems of equality which had been inherited from the eighteenth century I will term the 'meritocratic' one. We were to take advantage of the fluidity which had been diagnosed as the characteristic feature of the new industrialisation by reinforcing it by education. Indeed, educational attainment became a chief criterion by which the new mobility could be implemented.

Educationally speaking, the chief consequence of this approach was, initially, the setting up of a new universal system of schooling, the chief curriculum requirement of which was cognitive in orientation. The latter point is important because it provided a curriculum which, in many of its manifestations, could be assimilated, given the necessary cognitive ability, by the culturally unsophisticated. An inwardness with the old humanistic culture with its many faceted artistic and literary implications depended as much on a process of slow assimilation as on conscious instruction. Those who achieved most were those who participated in the way of life to which this culture was native; the historical inadequacy, bordering in many cases on gross incompetence, of the instruction in many of the schools and universities was therefore not a matter of such vital importance, though it was not a matter of total indifference either. But there were other informal ways through which the necessary knowledge and more importantly, taste, could be acquired. Ideally, the introduction was not simply into the ways of knowing characteristic of the classical culture, but into its ways of feeling also; and the latter was not something which could necessarily be best transmitted through schooling.

But the new curriculum with its concentration on positive knowledge, its emphasis on science and on the semi-scientific subjects, like geography and history, and its comparative neglect of the arts and literature (literature, when it appeared, often occurred as subject-matter for grammatical exercise) could be much more easily assimilated through the processes of formal instruction. In view of criticisms which I will raise later of the whole meritocratic implication, it is important to bear this in mind.

For the moment, however, I wish to return to consider the implications, for the implementation of the notion of equality, of the other view of social stratification, that which saw it as mere translation, into nineteenth-century terms, of the old rigidities of the pre-industrial agricultural society. The tendency now is to use education as a device, a tool by which these rigidities can be overthrown and a more equal and therefore desirable society produced. It is therefore no longer a question of equality at the starting line, but rather at the finishing post; the means to this is *sameness* of provision. This I will refer to as the 'egalitarian' solution. Clearly the stubborn irreducible facts of human differentiation, however explained, make it difficult to maintain this view in practice for long; but as an ideal it has exercised a certain influence on the specific educational provisions of certain nations in recent years. Thus for quite a long time the Soviet system retained a mass element as its defining characteristic. The aim here was not to use education as a selective sieve for catching the ablest and discarding the rest; the stress, in the earlier years of the Soviet system, was on 'providing a basic general education, covering the same ground and on the same terms for all, regardless of background or future occupation'.[3] Hence equality comes to imply sameness in experiential terms. In this of course it is only in line with Marxist-Leninist ideology, where the paramount emphasis is on the building of a communist society and on the use of education as a tool to that end. 'Without teaching there is no knowledge,' Lenin once remarked, 'and without knowledge there is no communism.' Initial differences in aptitude were regarded as the result of unequal environmental pressures, not as due to hereditary equipment: 'The Marxist believes that human nature is not basically pre-ordained, but rests in the hands of man himself,'[4] and the whole notion of intelligence as innate ability became highly suspect. The influence of the Enlightenment is patent here, too. If Marx and Lenin were not, basically, egalitarian, it has to be

[3] Nigel Grant, *Soviet Education* (Penguin), 1970, p. 30.
[4] Ibid., p. 46.

admitted that there were initially strong egalitarian implications in the ideology of the system which they helped to evolve.

III

There is a further issue arising out of the intellectual and political events of the late eighteenth and early nineteenth centuries which is also of importance to our theme—the problem of cultural authority. As political authority was gradually extended to the masses the question of the maintenance of cultural standards implicit in the old aristocratic culture became increasingly pressing. Mill and Arnold, among others, both attempted to face this problem—and clearly, for education, it becomes one of central importance, though institutional inertia common to the development of societies has not made it a pressing one at school level until our own day. Nevertheless, the ideological issues implicit in the problem were argued throughout the nineteenth century. They were raised by the utilitarian programme of reform and its appeal to the numerical majority as the true arbiters of moral and cultural purposes. Bentham's ethical theories rejected in any form the notion of an absolute hierarchy of values. A combination of utility and association psychology made man 'totally the product of circumstances and motivated solely by egoism'. Here was no principle of authority which could be appealed to to maintain a cultural tradition against temporary ebullitions of interest or desire.

Various attempts to face the dilemma implicit in the felt need for social reform and the equally pressing need to preserve a cultural heritage and the authority implicit in it were noted and have been excellently expounded by Dr Sheldon Rothblatt in his book *The Revolution of the Dons*. There Dr Rothblatt applies his analysis to the crisis over university education (expressly with reference to Cambridge) in the mid-nineteenth century. Mill sought a solution through the dissemination of educated men throughout the main institutions of Victorian society so that the principle of cultural authority would be diffused through the community at large. Arnold appealed to the State as the repository of cultural authority—culture being 'The best that has been thought and said'. Neither solution, of course, was satisfactory. It is necessary, however, to refer here briefly to the dilemma which Mill and Arnold—among many others—faced and which has been charted in detail by Mr Raymond Williams in *Culture and Society*

(1780–1950) because the argument implies a third line of cultural and social concern relevant to my theme, in addition to the meritocratic and egalitarian strands indicated in the previous section—and one, moreover, in some degree of conflict with the other two. The implications of this third element I will reveal when I come to deal with the contribution of T. S. Eliot to the current debate over equality. For the moment, however, I wish to pursue further the implications of the other two.

IV

As we have already glimpsed, there are strong pressures towards equality *of outcome* in the work of John Dewey, the American educationist whose work is more immediately relevant than that of the Marxists to a study of equality—in the egalitarian sense— and the British scene. Furthermore, as we have seen, Dewey raises questions of meaning and communication which take us to the central curricular issues of equality (conceived of as sameness) where education is concerned. To Dewey education was explicitly an instrument in the promotion of a more democratic society; and the egalitarian implications of 'democracy' for him can be guessed at in his formulation of the characteristic features which he wishes to promote in his democratic society:

'A democracy is more than a form of government; it is primarily a mode of associated living, of conjoint communicated experience. The extension in space of the number of individuals who participate in an interest so that each has to refer his own action to that of others, and to consider the action of others to give point and direction to his own, is equivalent to the breaking down of those barriers of class, race and national territory which kept men from perceiving the full import of their activity.'[5]

The emphasis is on the nature of the community experience. Democracy is more than a political device; the essence of the democratic way of life would seem to lie in the extension and proliferation of shared meanings ('interests') in contradistinction to those barriers of class, race, or nationality which at present tend to prevent people from sharing a common experience. Dewey is too aware of the diversity of human make-up to count as a rigid egalitarian; nevertheless, there are strong equalising tendencies in the direction of sameness implicit in his views of men's develop-

[5] *Democracy and Education* (New York: Macmillan), 1966, p. 101.

mental potential and in his asserted need for an increased community of experience open to all. He is a relentless enemy of the Platonic hierarchy; '. . . progress in knowledge has made us aware of the superficiality of Plato's lumping of individuals and their original powers into a few sharply marked-off classes; it has taught us that original capacities are indefinitely numerous and variable'.[6] At the same time he argues that a man would not be 'an individual if there was not something incommensurable about him'. Yet in the context the stress on 'incommensurability' is a strategy directed against the suggestion that men differ in levels of ability rather than a device for indicating an ultimate incommensurability between human beings. The argument is that men's talents are more varied than the hierarchy of class, with its implications of the sharp demarcation of human talents, would suggest. But the possible deduction that greater variety might make communication even more difficult is avoided. In any case, the idea that some division into classes may be a rudimentary recognition of the variability of human endowment and provide an elementary way of coping with it in socially organisational terms does not, of course, strike Dewey.

Dewey's view of social efficiency, indeed, involves what he calls the 'socialization of mind': this necessitates 'breaking down the barriers of social stratification which make individuals impervious to the interests of others'. He desires a 'cultivated imagination for what men have in common and a rebellion at whatever unnecessarily divides them'. And, however much he may protest in the name of 'diversity' and 'incommensurability' it is difficult not to detect a strongly collectivist-egalitarian implication in his explicit repudiation of the cultivation of an 'inner' life as a desirable educational aim:

'. . . the idea of perfecting an "inner" personality is a sure sign of social divisions. What is called inner is simply that which does not connect with others—which is not capable of free and full communication. What is termed spiritual culture has usually been futile, with something rotten about it, just because it has been conceived as a thing which a man might have internally—and therefore exclusively. What one is as a person is what one is as associated with others, in a free give and take of intercourse.'[7]

6 Ibid., p. 105.
7 Ibid., p. 143.

In the last sentence individuation seems to become co-extensive with socialisation; the person is dissolved into his social relationships.

I am sure that Dewey himself would have been shocked at the implications I am drawing from his remarks; but the 'other-directed' emphasis of his analysis is unmistakable. The precise nature of the claims which the social should make on the individual must always be a matter of fine and delicate discrimination—usually a matter of refined argument in particular cases. But Dewey *could* be interpreted through some of his remarks as denying any area of autonomy to the individual apart from the claims which social intercourse should make upon him. On the one hand he seems to be stressing the uniqueness of personality. ('For how can there be a society really worth serving unless it is constituted of individuals of significant personal qualities.') On the other hand, he seems to think that these 'significant personal qualities' are such that they can be developed by all, in such a way that more, not less, communication will take place. It is as if greater heterogeneity of talent will lead to greater homogeneity of shared experience, a curiously perverse proposition.

The position, then, seems to be: everyone is unique and should have an opportunity of developing his 'distinctive' capacities; but what is developed should be equally capable of being communicated in its fullness to all, otherwise that social efficiency which results from the socialisation of mind will not be gained. It is interesting that in his view of desirable culture Dewey finds that all worth-while accomplishments, manifestations of experience inherently praiseworthy, should be accompanied by results of value to others. The ideals of self-sacrifice and of self-perfection, both of which imply a self which exists apart from others, are not to be recommended, for they are both manifestations of a dualism which is inherently undesirable; 'for that reason, it is the particular task of education at the present time to struggle on behalf of an aim in which social efficiency and personal culture are synonyms instead of antagonists'.[8] Social efficiency, as we have seen, he equates with a widening of social sympathy, the socialisation of mind which leads to the breaking down of the barriers of social stratification; hence the desired culture is manifest in 'the capacity for constantly expanding the range and accuracy of one's perception of meanings' in order to achieve the goal of complete cultural homogenisation: 'to have the same ideas about things

---

[8] Ibid., p. 144.

which others have, to be like-minded with them, and thus to be really members of a social group, is to attach the same meanings to things and to acts which others attach'.

Now in so far as a major function of education is that of cultural transmission the precise view which the educator holds of the nature of culture is clearly of the greatest importance in assessing the viability of his educational aims. One of Dewey's major purposes lies in this promotion of a barrierless social efficiency, and his instrument a culture which is capable of free and open communication. But all this emphasis on social communication is, as we have noted, at odds with Dewey's slightly less emphatic but none the less very real emphasis on the uniqueness of the individual, attention to which is also part of his view of social efficiency. The explicit use of the word 'incommensurable', which implies the *lack* of a common measure, is at odds with his insistence on the possibilities of total communication and the reciprocity of social experience. One is left asking how this unique, incommensurable quality manifests itself; and, in so far as a culture can be interpreted as the total pattern of meanings in which a society's significant life manifests itself one is left, if one wishes to apply Dewey's views, with the irksome anomaly, which can be demonstrated empirically as a common and identifiable problem, of the differentiated interpretations of meaning which occur between different individuals at the one time, as well as the changed emphases which historical perspective often imposes on that which has up till then been accepted as an agreed meaning. It is precisely the uniqueness and incommensurability of human beings which makes certain ranges of meaning capable of ambiguity or diversity of interpretation and which also makes the socialisation of mind in Dewey's sense an impossibility except in a wholly totalitarian environment where the inhabitants are willing to accept, at the will of the party, total standardisation of meaning (as in Orwell's *1984*), that, for instance 'War is Peace', 'Freedom is Slavery' and 'Ignorance is Strength', i.e. that all meaning is *one* meaning. One cannot both have uniqueness and total communication—for total communication implies the total receptiveness of the listener and the consequent erosion of any uniqueness.

This problem of meaning, as I have been hinting all along, is a crucial one for the egalitarian. One feature of Dewey's work may have helped to conceal this from him, another may indicate that indirectly he may have realised it. Dewey's major interest was in science, and his general philosophy amounted to an attempt to apply rather primitive scientific principles to life itself. Basically his instrumentalism involved the application of the technician's approach to everyday problems: to quote his own words, the 'hypothesis that works is the true one'. Now science provides meanings that are unequivocal; whether stated in words or formulae they should be capable of only one interpretation; nuance or ambiguity are rigorously excluded as of intent. Clearly, in the logical progression which makes up a science as a body of knowledge an individual student may reach a ceiling of understanding, but at least he is not faced with the complexities of ambiguity as an essential element in the very nature of the discourse he is studying. The early stages of a science are simple and wholly apparent; the poems of William Blake are simple but incredibly opaque. Difficulties over meaning may arise as a science advances because of increasing difficulty and the gradual realisation that concepts *intended* to be unequivocal in meaning are, as a matter of fact, more ambiguous than suspected; but they are not built in to the very substance of the discourse. Behind the attempt at cultural homogenisation lies a shift in cultural attention, as science, rather than the arts, has constituted the paradigm of cultural meaning.[9] For when science is the paradigm of knowledge, there is likely to be a built-in prejudice in favour of finding meaning clear and communicable, especially if the science believed in is of a pretty elementary sort; and Dewey was still Baconian in his scientific outlook. When such a person comes to look at the arts (implying the traditional, 'aristocratic' arts springing out of the renaissance tradition) he is likely to interpret them also as being equally open and clear to the gaze; and this is precisely what we find in Dewey: 'Since art is the most universal form of language, since it is constituted, even apart from literature,

---

[9] The implications of the movement have been very well analysed in their effects on English prose by Professor L. C. Knights in an essay on 'Bacon and the Seventeenth-Century Dissociation of Sensibility', reprinted in *Explorations* (Chatto & Windus, 1946). There Professor Knights points to the diminution of meaning implicit in Bacon's 'subordinating the emotional and expressive to the descriptive and analytic' and the Royal Society's prescription 'reducing all things as near the mathematical plainness as they can'. Under this régime metaphor comes to be illustrative ornament rather than explorative of the phenomenon under consideration: 'the function of the images (in Bacon's writing) is not to intensify the meaning to make it deeper or richer, but simply to make more effective a meaning that was already fully formed before the application of the illustrative device'. Elizabethan metaphor at its finest (e.g. in Shakespeare) implies overtones, ambiguities which far transcend in meaning the new plainness.

by the common qualities of the public world, it is the most universal and freest form of communication.'[10] Though he does see art as imaginative and innovative, he sees the experience of art as essentially shaped by traditional social experience and its expression as 'public and communicating' and as striking 'below the barriers that separate human beings from one another'. Mind, to Dewey, is a mode of activity, not an isolated entity within which things happen; it is therefore essentially in contact with its surroundings, 'objects and events, past, present and future'. It is little wonder, then, that he attended to the process of communication rather than to the nature of what was being communicated by a mind necessarily separate from its fellows. Once you focus on the meaning of what is being communicated as a separate entity, you raise questions about its communicability and intelligibility as a received entity in another mind; and it is a short step from there to ask questions about the capacity of the receiving mind to receive. The notion of mind as an essentially public communicating organ focuses on the process rather than on the nature of what is communicated—hence the belief that 'barriers' to communication are removable by external social policies rather than built in to the very uniqueness of individual mind.

For to every message there must be a receptor; and meaning is the product of two separate acts of attention and will, not of a single process of interaction. Once seen in this way, the possibility of non-comprehension is apparent. What goes on *in* the mind of the communicator and what goes on *in* the mind of the recipient may be two different things. The communication of meanings is the basic function of education; and the crucial task which faces the educator is that of making his meaning clear and apparent; but failure to transmit is a universal experience of educationists and one of the fundamental reasons for this failure must, on occasions at least, be accorded to the sheer inability of the recipient to grasp what is offered—either because it is too 'difficult' or because by nature it is opaque and ambiguous in transmission. One is faced by a sheer dissimilarity of mental functioning, for whatever reason, a dissimilarity which, in part, can be defined in terms of various levels beyond which certain minds demonstrably do not grasp. I am not for the moment concerned with whether this inability stems from inherently inferior mental powers—the product of heredity—or whether it stems from unhappy experiences, for instance of an emotional nature, which produce

[10] Dewey, *Art and Experience.*

emotional disturbances inimical to response. What I am concerned with is the gap which exists and can be shown by tests to exist, between the higher and subtler forms of meaning and what demonstrably certain pupils grasp. The life of the educator is constantly brought to recognise the empirical validity of William Blake's famous aphorism that 'a fool sees not the same tree that a wise man sees'.

V

Now Dewey, in other parts of his work, seems implicitly to accept differentiations of level of response; for in his handling of the whole complex of meanings relevant to the life of an educational institution which we call a curriculum he seems to accept a priority of meanings in terms of those which have significance for the majority. The curriculum, he urges, must be organised in order to lay fundamental emphasis on the widest range of available meanings; everything else is to be regarded as frills: '. . . the curriculum must be planned with reference to placing essentials first and refinements second. The things which are socially most fundamental, that is, which have to do with the experiences in which the widest groups share, are the essentials.'[11] Here there is suggested an order of value priority which seems to imply that certain disciplines are beyond the range of certain people, indeed, of the majority itself—these constitute the 'refinements'. At the same time, such attribution of priority to some disciplines rather than to others is at odds with another statement where he repudiates any idea of a hierarchy of studies:

'We cannot establish a hierarchy of values among studies. It is futile to attempt to arrange them in an order, beginning with one having least worth and going on to that of maximum value. In so far as any study has a unique or irreplaceable function in experience, in so far as it marks a characteristic enrichment of life, its worth is intrinsic or irreplaceable.'[12]

Dewey does not deny that in certain circumstances it may be more desirable to follow one activity rather than another; but 'In the abstract or at large, apart from the needs of a particular situation in which choice has to be made, there is no such thing as degrees

[11] Dewey, *Democracy and Education* (New York: Macmillan), 1966. p. 225.
[12] Ibid., p. 281.

or order of value'. One is, then, presented with a democracy of curricular objectives, each having its own intrinsic merit, and subject in choice apparently only to the momentary desire of the protagonist. Here there would seem to be an extended liberality. No criteria of relevant value other than the vague appeals to 'enrichment of life' and 'uniqueness' are allowed; and who could deny that in certain limited circumstances and in certain limited ways, even pushpin might be said to enrich life. A slackness of individual aspiration is encouraged—why bother when almost anything can gain approval! At the same time, in another context, a principle of choice is introduced in the idea of the prior importance of those curricular elements which have the widest appeal. The effect is to weaken resolve to tackle the difficult and the unpopular and to substitute the appeal of the universally acceptable if inevitably undemanding.

This shift of emphasis has a number of counterparts in the modern world. For instance, we are at present witnessing in our society an attack on traditional moral valuations—in the spheres of sex, authority and the like—which paradoxically seems to enhance the choice of the individual by making him/her the arbiter of how to behave, about whom to sleep with, whether to take drugs and so on. In other words there seems to be no principle of moral or cultural authority to which the individual can appeal other than individual whim and 'doing one's own thing'. At precisely the same time, certain other sorts of choices are being imposed—as to the sort of school to which one can send one's child for instance—in the name of social and public good. What we are seeing indeed is not so much a loosening of moral imperatives, but a shift of their nature and in the basis on which they are considered acceptable. What may be said to contribute to certain private moral aspirations and restraints is being broken down because these may perhaps reveal different qualities as between people, between those capable of self-discipline, for instance, and the self-indulgent. In the field of private morals, then, people are being encouraged to consider their whims and desires as ultimate criteria. In the public realm, however, a specific set of moral imperatives operate which are again directed against possible differentiations of life quality arising out of attendance at different educational institutions offering different curricular and therefore different life experiences. In both cases the net result is to foster a uniformity of life style at a lower level of aspiration, in the one case by encouraging restriction of choice in a democracy of moral alternatives, there being no suggested principle of discrimination other than that of desire or want, and in the other by explicitly introducing, for example, 'commonness' ('the common school') as the sole offering. In the same way Dewey proclaims that each school subject has an intrinsic worth and deprives the seeker of principles in terms of which he may judge the relative value of what he is offered; and at the same time offers as the exclusive principle of choice the social criterion of majority capacity.

The aim, then, would seem to be to destroy 'aristocratic' differentiation and substitute, as the principle of cultural authority, majority cultural experience: Dewey here is symptomatic of what later was to appear in this country. Hence the attacks on the public schools, the grammar schools and even the universities in the name of comprehensivisation; hence the insistence on the common curriculum in the comprehensive schools for the first two or three years and the imputed need for all to gain a common social experience under the same roof. Of course, it will not work, because it encounters an essential and irreducible hierarchy implicit in the structures of meaning which make up the school curriculum. It is possible to slough off certain traditional elements redolent of an inegalitarian past, such as Latin and Greek; but it is not possible to democratise the curriculum beyond a certain point simply because some at least of the traditional meaning structures—in the sciences and technology, for instance, which are only superficially democratic even if 'open' and in theory inspectable by all—are essential as ways of implementing the running of the modern world. Put it another way, one is faced, at least, with the ineluctable necessity of selecting certain sorts of expertise, people who have grasped advanced technical or scientific principles necessary for keeping the machines running. Paradoxically, what started as democratic and within limits, egalitarian (i.e. science), has achieved a logical complexity which demands high expertise and high intelligence, of a sort, for its full understanding. The arts can be, are to some extent being, democratised and proletarianised, as indeed they have become in the post-Dada period, especially our own period of the counter- or anti-culture. For Dada represented a demotic snook-cocking at the whole essentially aristocratic renaissance tradition; and the reverberations of Dada have spread far into the modern art movement, in the conscious break with tradition, the emphasis on momentary impulse or skeletal abstraction, in the very abdication of the artist himself and the appeal of chance. The hierarchical principle —in the form of meritocracy—has passed, for the time, paradoxically, to the sciences. And *modern* science does not support

Dewey's essentially primitive view of its universal communicability.[13]

Dewey, then, represents in the American environment a foretaste of the attack on that value differentiation in meaning which sustained the aristocratic principle throughout the centuries. He points forward to a developing situation which we face in the seventies. Egalitarianism has passed beyond the phase of seeking to establish certain equalities of a specific nature—before the law, for instance, or in the right to vote; it is attempting to invade the very spheres of cultural 'experience' itself. This is one of the reasons why Dewey is so symptomatic a figure; because in him we find a view of experience, of meaning, which increasingly is invading the central areas of our culture—though in ways which it is reasonable to suppose Dewey himself would never have guessed; he would indeed have been repelled by much of what today he would see.

VI

Of course, there have been reassertions of the renaissance principle in the sphere of the humanities. In his opposition to both the egalitarian and the meritocratic we see the significance of the contribution of T. S. Eliot both to our thinking about our culture and to education as a manifestation of that culture. Eliot, in an oblique way, takes up the theme of cultural authority mooted in Section III—'oblique' because he did not attempt to face the philosophical problems which exercised Mill and others as to how we were to justify the value differentiation implicit in the old aristocratic culture, but rather set about the sociological task of defining the conditions under which the traditional culture could flourish given the assumption that we wished to preserve it. In the process of doing so he introduces a factor of equality absent from many nineteenth-century discussions of the problem, which were

[13] This may seem to be at odds with what I have said earlier (p. 123) where I have suggested that it is art and literature (the humanist tradition) which is complex and ambiguous and therefore opaque, and science which is 'clear'. In fact this is not the case. Art can, of course, be democratised—and in fact is being so, cf. Roy Lichtenstein and Andy Warhol at the Tate Gallery—a painting of a Campbell's soup tin is quite unequivocal and demotic. The high culture tradition of complex literature and painting is gradually being destroyed. On the other hand, science which is basically 'clear' at an elementary level has far surpassed in complexity Dewey's primitive view of it and has come to seem the paradigm of 'knowledge' and 'understanding' in the scientific-technological era.

broadly concerned with locating the principles on which a high minority culture could be preserved and justified. Eliot's innovation is to see the problem of high culture as only *part* of the problem of preserving a healthy state of culture. To achieve such preservation it is certainly necessary to preserve the quality of the culture of the minority by keeping it a minority culture; but in addition, *every* level in the community needs to contribute its appropriate cultural offering, at the level of consciousness it can achieve, in order that the well-being of the whole shall be preserved. After all, 'Fine art is the refinement, not the antithesis of popular art'; the minority, Eliot thinks, cannot sustain itself in isolation, cut off from society at large and the nourishment a healthy popular art can provide. In Eliot's view, then, each level of the community must make a contribution which is *equally* appropriate but necessarily different.

In his attempt to define the sociological conditions in terms of which each section of the population can make this appropriate contribution, Eliot departs from the atomisation of individual offering implicit in both the egalitarian and the meritocratic view of educational opportunity. The assumption throughout his work is that people are not capable of achieving similar levels of consciousness, and attempts to equalise even opportunity may produce unfortunate results. He once said: 'You can have equality; you can have culture; but you cannot have both.'[14] The 'headlong rush to educate everyone' (i.e. to afford everyone opportunities) was, he considered, leading to a lowering of standards. Why should this be so?

Eliot's answer to this crucial question can be inferred from his cultural diagnosis, where indeed it is all but explicitly stated. As we have seen, he clearly accepted as empirical fact the manifestation of different levels of consciousness among the individuals of the community: but he saw that such different levels of consciousness arose from more than simply individual differences in measured capacity. He noted that the primary agency for the transmission of our culture was not, as the modern world sees it, the individual as an atomic entity but the family as manifest in the lives of different generations of that family. Environmentalists challenge the view that such differences in achievement as undoubtedly exist are inevitable; they tend to put them down to the force of unpropitious external circumstances, bad housing or schooling, but they confine the argument within the limits of the

---

[14] Personally to the present author.

I

negative effects of these factors on the releasing of talent. To some extent Eliot accepts the environmentalist case but urges that the intimacies of family cultural continuity afford a positive case for differentiating those capable of high levels of consciousness from the rest. In other words, he advises that we should be more aware of the *positive* advantages to the health of our culture in having certain persisting families at the highest levels who can supplement the work of the formal system by the nature of their informal interests and commitments. Here both heredity and propitious environment can work positively to maintain the appropriate level of consciousness.

Let me expand this further. The communication problem lies at the heart of Eliot's social and specifically educational thinking. He sees education as one means of transmitting the culture from generation to generation; but he also sees that the formal education system can only transmit part of that culture: 'There is . . . a danger of interpreting "education" to cover both too much and too little; too little, when it implies that education is limited to what can be taught; too much, when it implies that everything worth preserving can be transmitted by teaching.'[15] Hence, for instance, the need for a continuity of families charged with the transmission of the most conscious part of the culture. This, he states, does not constitute a 'defence of aristocracy', but a 'plea for a form of society in which an aristocracy should have a peculiar and essential function, as peculiar and essential as the function of any other part of society'. Put another way, he implied that in the consciousness of certain family environments there is an accumulation of cultural and social wisdom which, if neglected, can only lead to a general social deprivation. Meritocracy is not enough because meritocrats meet only in terms of a specific expertise, of a professional interest; thus 'they will meet like committees', and will communicate only at this level, at which much of the nuance and subtlety of cultural meaning will be lost. 'Men who meet only for definite serious purposes, and on official occasions, do not wholly meet.'[16] A society based on meritocracy implies a too great mobility and this in turn a lack of a continuity of meanings.

The great service which this analysis by Eliot performs is to draw attention to the respective roles of both formal and informal education. A system of education is essentially a formal structure,

[15] T. S. Eliot, *Notes towards the Definition of Culture* (Faber), 1948, p. 47.
[16] Ibid., p. 85.

and teachers and pupils meet in terms of explicit and conscious learning structures only. These structures, as a matter of fact, are primarily cognitive, in the very nature of the modern school curriculum. But one of the major themes of Eliot's poetry is that of the complexity of meaning and communication. In it he speaks of the 'intolerable wrestle with words and meanings'; but more, he is haunted by the power of memory and the indestructible quality of time:

> Time present and time past
> Are both perhaps present in time future,
> And time future contained in time past.[17]

So consciousness is inevitably and unavoidably an historical consciousness, not simply an individual one:

> The world becomes stranger, as we grow older the pattern
>   more complicated
> Of dead and living. Not the intense moment
> Isolated, with no before and after,
> But a lifetime burning in every moment
> And not the lifetime of one man only.
> But of old stones that cannot be deciphered.[18]

This sense of the historical dimension makes him aware that communication is of many different kinds, some of them much more subtle than can be made explicit in a classroom lesson; furthermore, that the subtler sorts of communication take place through the informal agencies of our society: 'For the schools can transmit only a part, and they can only transmit this part effectively, if the outside influences, not only of family and environment, but of work and play, of newsprint and spectacles and entertainment and sport, are in harmony with them.'[19]

That informal agencies play a vital role in the whole business of cultural transmission is irrefutable. As Dr Rupert Wilkinson has pointed out in his book, *The Prefects*, the informal elements in a public boarding school have tended to play the major socialising role in the upbringing of its inhabitants, rather than what is explicitly taught. The pressures (to use Wilkinson's terminology) are aesthetic and manifest in etiquette and 'good form'; the classical curriculum, the explicit subject-matter of

[17] T. S. Eliot, 'Burnt Norton', *Four Quartets* (Faber), 1944.
[18] T. S. Eliot, 'East Coker', *Four Quartets* (Faber), 1944.
[19] T. S. Eliot, op. cit., *Notes*, p. 106.

'teaching', though not entirely unproductive, has proved a narrower and less broadening affair than it has been made out to be because of the way it has been taught.[20] The long hours of translation have left little time, as Wilkinson points out, for the broader considerations of literary content and meaning. It was the profoundly influential *style* of the school life which produced the much more lasting effect—its emphasis on loyalty and co-operation, its acceptance of minute differentiations of rank, its dissolution of youthful egotism, the assumed association of social status with moral superiority, its reference back to a certain class of family life. In the same way, in other spheres we have become aware of the profound influence of the home environment, so that the efforts of schools are often brought to nought unless their work is backed up by parental support. This indeed has been so well documented as hardly to require elaboration; it remains a constant barrier to the self-realisation of certain working-class children who sometimes fall behind their middle-class peers not necessarily because of lack of ability but because of lack of parental support and because of cultural deprivation in the home. Dr J. W. B. Douglas's evidence in *The Home and the School* has been widely accepted in its view of the profound influence the home has on educational success. But if families have this negative effect they may also be allowed to have a positive effect, though this is not the inference which has so commonly been drawn from the findings. If subtle matters of attitudes among parents produce this considerable effect on the learning characteristics of their offsprings, is not the whole question of indirect informal educative influence of the profoundest importance, and is it not likely also to affect those subtleties of meaning and communication with which Eliot is concerned?

Now as a matter of undeniable empirical fact we are faced, in the schools, for whatever reason, heredity or environmental, with a vast differentiation in terms of levels of measured achievement. This is the primary datum of the educational situation. Some interpretations of the notion of social justice would seem to indicate an attempt at equalisation of achievement by a vast

[20] Dr R. R. Bolgar makes the point in a study of Renaissance education that the quality of Renaissance culture relied much more on the interest of adults than it did on the school system which, where the transmission of classical culture was concerned, was often woefully inadequate. Cf. R. R. Bolgar, 'Humanist Education and its Contribution to the Renaissance', in *The Changing Curriculum* issued by The History of Education Society (Methuen), 1971.

programme of compensatory education, on the grounds that present deficiencies spring largely from environmental short-comings. What, however, no one could possibly contemplate is an attempt to equalise parents in terms of cultural commitment; and yet some such enterprise would seem essential if compensatory education is to have any real chance of producing lasting results. In other words, it is necessary, assuming the accepted importance of informal education, to compensate not only within the formal system, but within the informal system also. Once stated in this way, the difficulty of the notion of compensatory education and the reason for its comparative lack of success in America become more apparent.

There are, indeed, two possible interpretations of the idea of social justice. Normally it is interpreted in terms of an equalisation of provision for the individual members of society, who are regarded as having prior claim to attention. In this sense, the notion has become either a device of the meritocracy to ensure the identification of talent or a means of which the egalitarian society seeks to induce a sameness of cultural experience. A more profound interpretation of the notion, however, might have regard to the benefit accruing to all from a revival of cultural vitality—i.e. 'justice' to the conditions necessary for cultural health rather than justice to atomic individuals in society. The difference lies in whether the individual or the state of society is accorded priority.

If we admit the claims of society in terms of its cultural health then we need to note carefully the historical pressures implicit in the society as a going cultural concern. Granted that historically the hierarchic order of society has never matched precisely the diffusion of cultural levels of consciousness throughout the community—which is why a degree of mobility has always been important—we may note nevertheless that some social continuity of such levels is implicit in the primary unit of all known historical societies, the family. Hence, paradoxically, even to do justice to individuals it becomes necessary not to impose a common curriculum on all irrespective of observed ability to benefit (to treat education as an 'abstraction', as Eliot puts it, according to which 'it has come to be assumed that there must be one measure of education according to which everyone is educated simply more or less')[21] but to seek curricular differentiation in ways which allow all an equal opportunity to achieve their appropriate level of consciousness and hence to make their own proper contribution

21 T. S. Eliot, *Notes*, p. 105.

to the cultural health of the society. In other words, we should look to the viability of the offering rather than seek to impose a uniformity, a sameness, where the living complexity of individuals within the social order makes this unacceptable. I shall revert to this point again later when talking of comprehensive education.

Those concerned with a greater equalisation of opportunity for individuals have had their way for some time because, appalled by the spectacle of historical poverty, the desirability of some equalisation of shares (of what beyond economic resources has usually gone undefined with any distinctness) as a means to ameliorating the lot of the deprived has seemed of paramount importance. Though complete equality of income has not been achieved nor seriously contemplated, a greater equality of income and of access to remunerative positions, and the banishment of the problems of extreme poverty to the margins of our lives have been achieved. Some such equalisation in the economic sphere can be regarded as desirable; but the notion of more equal shares cannot so easily be transferred to other spheres. Differentiation of job remuneration can be compensated for by artificial devices of the economy; differentiation of minds imposes irreducible limits to attempts to induce a sameness of cultural experience, more especially when 'mind' is seen to be a matter of interaction between hereditary endowment and early cultural opportunity.

The position where education is concerned is complicated because the educational system fulfils two separate functions. One is that of cultural transmission where it is sensible to seek to transmit that level of culture which the pupil can encompass; the other provides the means by which the occupational system is fed. The desire therefore to afford people, economically, equal chances interferes with the more basic need to induct people into that level of culture from which they may gain most satisfaction. If the aim is simply to recruit to the meritocracy, then similarity of provision becomes excusable on the grounds that all should as long as possible be in a position to achieve the desired occupational goals; the prices to be paid are unsuitability of provision for many who demonstrably fail to benefit—and to some extent the distortion of what is provided by the need to prepare candidates to leap the necessary hurdles. The seeking of cultural satisfaction—the aim of the liberal educationist throughout the ages—is in some degree of tension with the need to provide life chances. This has been recognised from the time of Aristotle onwards—it has always been emphasised that a liberal education is intended for leisure; and today, a liberal education exists in a particular state of tension with that demand for expertise which is so much the aim of modern specialised education.

In an age which has learnt to accept (almost) the priority of the economy above all things, it makes sense to ask if the culture matters. When the answer is that it is the culture which structures the highest and most complex human consciousness of the age and that the economy constitutes simply one aspect of that culture, it is perhaps not too much to claim that it does. Culture, of course, is a word that can be used in both a neutral (in the sense of the total pattern of a society's thought and doings), and an evaluative sense, as (to quote Matthew Arnold) the 'best that has been thought and said'. Education is a concept that carries with it inevitably evaluative overtones, and it is culture in its evaluative sense which is relevant to its functioning; in other words, the culture the school is concerned to transmit constitutes, basically, the truth-meanings of its generation. It is therefore surely fundamental to the quality of the life of its times, and individuals will be the richer for submitting themselves to the requirements of a vital cultural order rather than claiming consideration solely as atomic economic units.

VII

Before I proceed to apply the insights gained from the foregoing discussion to a study of those aspects of our educational system where the notion of equality has become most manifest—the move towards comprehensive education and the arguments over school organisation—it is desirable briefly to recapitulate the characteristics of the three main positions which have emerged from my analysis of the historical movement towards equality which has culminated in our own day. I will distinguish these as the egalitarian, the meritocratic and the cultural, and I will attempt to spell out some of their implications in purely educational terms.

The egalitarian seeks to achieve the maximum sameness possible, a sameness which, at secondary level, should not only become manifest in the provision of a common school which all should attend, but in a subjection to similarity of curricular requirement, even, indeed, to quote the LCC's pamphlet *London Comprehensive Schools*, 'to have, as far as possible, a common syllabus'. The egalitarian's fundamental aim is a common social experience, as many and as varied points of common social contact, to quote Dewey. His aim is the common cultural meaning, his instruments compensatory education, the common school, the common curriculum and the internal organisation of non-streaming among others.

The meritocrat will be concerned with sameness at the beginning of secondary schooling because of the difficulties of selection and the social need to identify talent. He will want a common curriculum not in order to provide a common social experience but in order to hold open the options of selection as long as possible; without some common element in what is learnt, transfer between streams, for instance, becomes difficult. In general, however, he will approve of internal setting and/or streaming, and the teaching of the ablest children by the most highly qualified teachers. The tendency here will be for hierarchic tripartitism to reproduce itself inside the school. His fundamental purposes, however, will be examination success and the close relevance of school provision to occupational requirement. In both these positions the aim is ultimately social-functional. The egalitarian desires social harmony through the abolition of barriers dividing man from man, seeking in the last resort the equalisation of meaning as between mind and mind, so that all come to *mean* the same thing in a heavenly bliss of classlessness and harmony of interests and purposes. The meritocrat is not so naïve; he sees that the actual functioning of the society for which he is seeking to educate makes certain irreducible demands—for instance, in terms of specific expertise of a scientific and technological nature. As the functioning of society is essentially hierarchical and not all can occupy the top governmental or expert positions—nor are all capable of doing so—his educational aims are closely tied to the occupational structure, so that society is fed with the varieties of expertise it needs for its efficient functioning: functional efficiency, the production of 'educated manpower', sums up his aspirations.

The cultural position is different. Here there will be a tendency to accept the diversity of talent with which we are faced as giving some indication of the different levels of cultural consciousness for which he should provide. Anyone who holds the cultural position will, indeed, be hostile to any attempts at equalisation of meaning except in the fundamental sense that each pupil should be provided with an education which, although showing great diversity and difference in content, nevertheless attempts to be equally appropriate to his or her level of potential. His scepticism over any equalising in the content of provision will spring partly from his acceptance of the importance of the hereditary and early environmental element in assessing the possible ceilings of human attainment—though he will concede that wise educational provision may exploit successfully an inevitable imbalance in the generations which allows a certain measure of flexibility for the possible development of talent. He will, however, consider that this can be more easily achieved by special and varied provision exploiting what is known about the various ability levels than through an attempt to impose a common though unsuitable provision and thus evoking repugnance among sections of the school population. For he is impressed by the fact that human beings are more difficult to engineer than the physical environment and that the individual pupil is subject to pressures which lie deep in the historical consciousness of the race; such a pupil should not, therefore, be treated as an atomic unit apart from family culture and the psychic expectations implicit in family culture. These indeed will work both ways, both assisting the school experience of certain sections and tending to make the school an alien institution to those whose life and family experience foster different priorities; though there will, of course, be exceptions to these. He therefore will seek to encourage that level of cultural commitment which is feasible in the light of a careful socio-cultural analysis which includes a historical as well as purely individual dimension—though he will bear in mind T. S. Eliot's warning, when speaking of a 'continuous gradation of cultural levels'; '. . . it is important to remember that we should not consider the upper levels as possessing *more* culture than the lower, but as representing a more conscious culture and a greater specialisation of culture.'[22] His aim, indeed, will be liberal rather than functional, his concern with quality and inherent satisfaction rather than the rat race. What, indeed, is claimed for him is that, his analysis of the human predicament being the more profound, what he has to offer shames the thinner rationalism implicit in the diagnoses of the other two. Cultural diversity and the satisfaction appropriate cultural offerings can foster provide a richer quality of living than either harmonisation of interests based on a reduction of all human wants and achievements to the same level, or the limitation of differentiation to functional provision.

VIII

It will be appreciated that it is rare to find any of the three positions outlined above in their purest forms; and perhaps it should be added that it is rare to find the last of the three at all.

[22] *Ibid.*, p. 48.

What indeed we tend to find in the argument about comprehensive schooling are various admixtures of the first two.

It was early apparent that there was a fundamental confusion about the arguments in favour of the changeover to comprehensive education in this country. On the one hand there was the argument from wrongful selection. Although the 1944 Act had tried to ensure parity of esteem as between three kinds of secondary education, such was the prestige of the grammar schools that what was intended as a test for allocation of pupils to the sort of education for which they were most suited became in effect a competitive examination for those desirous of entering the grammar school. Inevitably many were disappointed, and hence controversy about the nature of the eleven-plus test (in effect, a ten-plus test) arose.

At least three major criticisms were directed against the examination. It was considered unfair that so much should depend on a test taken on a single day, especially when sickness or nerves might interfere with the performance of candidates; the psychological effects of the strain of taking the tests were harmful to the young candidates; it was difficult to predict with the necessary accuracy the future performance of the candidates by an examination taken at so early an age—hence selection could never be 100 per cent accurate.

Whatever truth there may have been in the first contention became less accurate as the years went by when, as a result of intense public interest in the outcome of the examination, greater and greater care was taken over actual selective processes. Research was initiated in the attempt to discover which of the various techniques of allocation (e.g. teachers' ratings, intelligence tests, achievement tests, interviews, etc.) were likely to produce the best predictions of future attainment; in fact, teachers' ratings were found to be among the best of the available techniques; but in any case, the proliferation of methods of assessment gave the lie to those who still criticised the system of allocation as dependent on a single day's test. Where the second criticism was concerned, investigation carried out by the British Psychological Society and published in 1957 led the Working Party responsible for the report to conclude that

'there is little evidence to support the notion of widespread and severe mental health effects. The psychologists who were consulted considered that most of the breakdown cases who came to the clinics were caused by other factors, such as gross inadequacies in the family relationships, active in the early years of childhood, and that at most the selection system was likely to contribute to situations already in existence, e.g. that it might constitute a further source of anxiety to a child already rendered prone to anxiety by its earlier constitution and environment.'[23]

At the same time the Working Party referred to the impossibility of a completely accurate prediction on the basis of eleven-plus tests:

'. . . predictions can never approach perfection. Of pupils scoring in the top 5 per cent, one in twenty are likely to prove failures in the average grammar school; and among pupils who score below the national average at 11, one in a hundred might turn out well if given the chance. Thus, the border zone, which received special consideration before allocation is decided, should be considerably wider than is usual at present.'[24]

In thus drawing attention to the inability to achieve perfection in allocation, and to the importance of the border zone, the Working Party was undoubtedly correct. In further research the National Foundation for Educational Research, which described the eleven-plus examination as one of the most carefully conducted examinations in the world, nevertheless expressed the opinion that there was likely to remain 'a margin of error which in the most favourable circumstances cannot be expected to be less than 5 per cent either side of the border line'. Hence the need for later opportunities for transfer was stressed, and some 'blurring of the edges' between types of schools by the provision of GCE courses in secondary modern and technical schools advised. Further testing refinement at the time when the pamphlet on 'Procedures for the Allocation of Pupils in Secondary Education' was published seemed unlikely to make much improvement in testing procedures. It is, however, relevant to point out that this pamphlet was published in September 1963; since then there have been attempts to improve intelligence tests, and creativity tests of, at present, rather dubious value have been developed. Nevertheless it has to be accepted that selection is unlikely to be made perfect and a minimum of 10 per cent error must be accepted as inevitable if selection is to be retained.

The focusing of attention on this argument emphasises the

[23] P. E. Vernon (Ed.), *Secondary School Selection* (Methuen), 1957, p. 61.
[24] Ibid., p. 172.

importance of selection both because of the children themselves and because of the national need to develop talent to the utmost. At the same time it points to an assumed meritocratic requirement, the need to afford a greater opportunity to more children to become unequal. The other major argument in favour of comprehensive education is the social one, 'The desirability', in the words of Miss H. R. Chetwynd, former headmistress of Woodberry Down School, 'of educating adolescent boys and girls in an environment planned to encourage social unity through mutual understanding, respect and shared experience'; '. . . it would be invaluable for (the liberal scholar)', Professor Pedley considers, 'to understand the minds and outlook of scientists and technicians— and indeed of craftsmen and shop assistants and unskilled workers —through meeting them in the same environment of college clubs and societies; on the games field and in the students' council.'[25] In deploying this argument, attempts were made, as has been hinted above, to attribute gross differences in achievement to environmental effects rather than to innate qualities. The implication was that in a school where they did not feel 'rejected'—which was the implication of being allocated to the secondary modern— children of lower achievement would be encouraged to give of their best, and would indeed benefit from constant contact with the academically brighter so that they would attain a greater equality of achievement. Here, then, the attempt was to induce, in the name of democratic living, a more equal experience in terms of a common environment for all, in some cases undifferentiated class teaching groups and in many cases a common curriculum for all for one, two, or three years of the secondary school age range. Indeed, in 1968, in 606 comprehensive schools containing the 11–14 age range, 80·5 per cent had a common course for all pupils in the first year, of these 48 per cent maintained the common course for three years, 30 per cent for two years and only 18 per cent for the one year only.[26]

Now here, or so it seems to me, we find the same basic conflict that we noted in Dewey's equivocations between the autonomies of the individual and the implied needs of the community, between the liberalising and the collectivist implications of the process of democratisation. It is indeed a conflict that de Tocqueville had noted in the earlier years of American democracy:

[25] R. Pedley, *Comprehensive School* (Penguin), 1969.
[26] Figures taken from B. Simon and C. Benn, *Half Way There* (McGraw-Hill), 1970, p. 144.

'In the principle of equality I very clearly discern two tendencies; the one leading the mind of every man to untried thoughts, the other inclined to prohibit him from thinking at all. And I perceive how, under the dominion of certain laws, democracy would extinguish that liberty of the mind to which a democratic social condition is favourable; so that, after having broken all the bondage one imposed on it by ranks or by men, the human mind would be closely fettered to the general will of the greatest number.'[27]

If it is not immediately apparent how de Tocqueville's analysis is relevant within the confines of a school, it is only necessary to consider concretely the possible plight, say, of children from a middle-class background in a predominantly working-class school, when the virtues of social mixing may be less apparent in actuality than they can be made to seem in the abstract. We live at a time, indeed, when among certain sections of the intelligentsia middle-class values are derided and romantic notions of working-class virtues are promulgated. Whatever the rights and wrongs of this argument—and one would have thought that grace was not necessarily exclusively on either side—it can hardly excuse the cruelty that can easily arise when children nurtured predominantly in the ethos of one way of life encounter a majority brought up in another. If middle-class superiority over questions of accent and behaviour can be wounding to children brought up without this sort of nurturing, the crudity of working-class manners and habits can be terrifying to children bred in a different and on the whole gentler atmosphere. It is as well to remember that children, like adults, differ not only in terms of measured achievement but over a whole range of other qualities, of morals and manners, in personal relationships and capacities for restraint. Regardless of the debatable point as to which constitutes the 'correct' form of behaviour, these differences form a definable part of the world we inhabit, though in the overriding concern for life chances or the equalising of experience as the criteria of social justice in terms of which the debate over comprehensiveness has been conducted they have often been lost sight of.

An article by Dr Derek Miller in *New Education*, however, draws our attention back to them and to our almost total negligence in applying our imaginations to what is likely to happen in a school where the different social classes are brought into close

[27] de Tocqueville, *Democracy in America* (Oxford: World's Classics), 1946, p. 299.

proximity. Dr Miller's testimony is the more impressive in that he openly confesses to being a confirmed supporter of comprehensive education. But his clinical experience at the Tavostock Clinic in London has brought him up starkly against the deep psychological upsets that can occur when groups with quite different backgrounds are brought together, especially when they are children who have not yet achieved some of the inner restraints which comes to most adults of whatever social origin. Dr Miller warns:

'. . . the mixing of social class groups, especially among adolescents, if not pre-adolescent, children, is infinitely complex. If it is desirable to mix social classes in a comprehensive school with the aim of producing healthy social change in society, this should imply a planned experiment with an understanding of what is being attempted. Teachers and departments of education will need to know a great deal more about the effects of social systems on human behaviour, the psychological effects of social mobility and the way different groups of our society live.'

As Dr Miller points out, there is little known about the different ways of life (for example in respect of human relationships, the handling of sexual and aggressive feelings, the significance of language as a communication medium) which characterise different social groups in this country; and he proceeds to give examples of the effects of working-class sexual aggressiveness on middle-class children and the anti-academic feelings engendered in a school where non-academic children have the ascendancy of numbers. One bright boy of fourteen had been referred for clinical treatment because he feared to lose his place in an accelerated academic stream and be required to mix with aggressively anti-academic children: 'He felt rather like a Jew expected to leave the safety of the ghetto in the Middle Ages.'

This is the sort of evidence which is ignored in glib talk about the need for social mixing and the desirability of the classless society. One can see its relevance, at the childish immature level appropriate to a school, to de Tocqueville's diagnosis; on the one hand there is the school as an instrument of liberal education, ostensibly leading its pupils on to the attempting of as yet untried thoughts; on the other hand there are the pressures implicit in the school as a social system. These may be of two sorts; there may be anti-academic pressures from certain sections of the staff or even, on occasions, the headmaster (I know of at least one comprehensive school headmaster who has overtly indicated that he is not interested in the bright children but only in the average and less able). No one who has been concerned with the training of pre-service and in-service teachers needs to be told that both groups contain their fair share of academically indifferent teachers whose interest in their subjects is minimal and whose cultural outlook in other respects is of the most philistine; this combined with a certain jealousy of the very bright child—a noticeable characteristic of some teachers—means that broadly anti-academic attitudes can characterise staff rooms as well as many of the children. Where the latter are concerned, there is a good deal of evidence from American comprehensives to demonstrate the pervasively anti-academic atmosphere of many high schools. There are reports of the same sort of thing in this country. The other pressures will be those from the peer-group—those I have already sufficiently indicated.

Basically, however, my point—which I now wish to take further—is that there exists a degree of tension as between these two fundamental impulses behind comprehensivisation. There are, of course, many other arguments for and against comprehensive schools; but these are the ones which have most relevance to issues of equality. The co-existence of arguments, one of which looks to a greater equality implicit in the organisation and curriculum of the school, and the other of which places no obstacles in the way of differentiation other than an initial concern that there should be sufficient similarity in the earliest years in order that late developers shall be in a position to move upward in the hierarchy of streams without finding themselves too far behind what is being done in the more academically able forms, means that in effect schools and their heads may take up a whole spectrum of emphases in their concern for the analogous wide spectrum of talent by which they are faced. Hence comprehensive schools may at one extreme prove highly meritocratic in ethos, and at the other highly egalitarian, where the 'expressive', pastoral role of the teacher is thought much more important than the instrumental pedagogic role.[28]

[28] Mr G. Bernbaum's recently published account of Countesthorpe College (in *Case Studies of Educational Innovation, Vol. III, At The School Level* (Paris: OECD), 1973) provides an admirable study of a school which stresses the instrumental over the pedagogic. I would draw attention to the first headmaster's (Mr Tim McMullen's) views on 'grass roots participatory democracy'; and a comment by Mr Bernbaum: 'That there might be a shift from the overtly educational goals . . . to goals more immediately concerned with social control can be seen from one teacher's comment about . . . difficult pupils that "though they're great big boys they'll sit and play with Lego for hours; I'm quite prepared to let them play with Lego—but I don't know about

In actual practice, however, certain inescapable elements in the educational situation, especially the way in which it is ineluctably tied to the occupational structure, have led to the predominance of the meritocratic comprehensive school—to an extent, indeed, which has led to a split within the ranks of the comprehensive supporters themselves. Thus a headline in the *Times Educational Supplement* proclaimed that 'Comprehensive Reorganisation is no longer enough'; the feature it announced was concerned to summarise an article by Mr Dennis Marsden which had been published in the autumn issue (1969) of *Comprehensive Education.* Here indeed, we are told that the present comprehensive school has tended to remain distressingly meritocratic in orientation and advised that we ought to seek the 'egalitarian school'. Such schools, apparently, 'measure their success by good class mixing, out-of-school activities and high quality art, music and drama'. Even my own enthusiasm for these disciplines would not suggest to me that they should become the sole focus of qualitative consideration in a school curriculum intended to provide for the whole ability range, though in view of Mr Marsden's egalitarian enthusiasms it is pleasing to note even so much concern for quality.

In effect, the 'good class mixing' which Mr Marsden sets as one of his major criteria of school success, as might have been anticipated by those who remember their own school days and are not bemused by the pipe dreams of the classless society, tends to occur in only limited ways. In one of its more recent publications, *Comprehensive Schools in Action*, edited by T. G. Monks, the National Foundation for Education Research has produced evidence to show that

'There is a strong tendency for pupils to choose their best friends from among pupils in the same ability, social, behavioural or ethnic groups.'

'This in-group preference appears more strongly in ability and behavioural groups than in social groups.'

In other words, sympathy of intellectual capacity is one of the best means by which an inter-mixture of social classes is likely to be

their parents".' The recent rows over Countesthorpe College and Wreake Valley (also a Leicestershire experimental comprehensive school) which have been widely publicised, indicate the dissatisfaction of many middle-class parents with schools in which achievement seems to play a secondary role (and in which it would seem that social and behavioural attitudes may be fostered which are at odds with views of middle-class upbringing).

achieved. Otherwise, apart from children who belong to similar behavioural or ethnic groups, social class differences are likely to be reflected positively in friendship patterns.

Another smaller piece of evidence that the comprehensive school is not likely to prove the solvent of social class differences that its more idealistic supporters had hoped it might be is to be found in Dr Julienne Ford's *Social Class and the Comprehensive School* where she tested two hypotheses relating to social class mixing in a single comprehensive school and compared her results with what she found in a grammar and secondary modern school. She discovered in this admittedly very small sample, among other things, that 'if any type of schooling diminishes the likelihood of class bias in informal relations within the classroom this is not the comprehensive but the grammar school'—an interesting confirmation of a point which has been made by upholders of the grammar school for long enough. According to the *TES*, indeed, Dr Ford considers that, 'The divisions manifest in the tripartite system are just as evident in the comprehensive schools; but then they are just between streams, not between schools.'

But there is a further interesting feature of Dr Ford's analysis; for she also tested three hypotheses which related to the academic success of the particular school she was investigating. Again, she found that there were no grounds for thinking that comprehensive schools fostered a 'greater development of talent than tripartite schools', or that they necessarily provided 'greater equality of talent for those with equal talent'. Attempts have, of course, been made to produce figures which would demonstrate the superiority of long-established comprehensive schools vis-à-vis the tripartite system. The most notorious of these derive from Professor Pedley, who attempted to show on the basis of a 73 per cent return from sixty-seven fully established schools that their 'A' and 'O' level results were in certain respects superior to the overall results throughout the rest of the country of the tripartite system. Professor Pedley's attempt has been roundly attacked by Mr John Todd in Black Paper 3, partly on the grounds that it is at least possible that those not replying to Professor Pedley's questionnaire may have neglected to do so because their results bestowed little credit on the school—in other words, that the sample is a distorted one and that therefore it is unreasonable to derive from such figures as he has collected the implications that he has. There is undoubted force in these and the other arguments which Mr Todd employs.

The NFER indeed, has made it quite clear that in the present

K

confused position in this country neither side in the debate is in any position to appeal firmly to definitive figures indicating clearly superiority on one side rather than the other. One then needs to fall back on such evidence as one can glean to indicate that there is still need for caution and that initial feelings that educational changes carried out at such a crude level as that of organisation are unlikely to produce the educational millennium which some of its more ardent supporters have looked for; that, indeed, at best reorganisation is likely to do little more than the sceptics have hinted at from the beginning, which is to replace one set of problems by another. For, as I have already indicated, whether we like it or not, the schools are inelectably tied to the occupational structure in some degree. It is inevitably through the educational system that selection and differential training for major adult roles are effected. While society remains unavoidably hierarchical in terms of skill requirements, equally unavoidably the schools will be used to feed this hierarchy of skill. It is for this reason that no one should be surprised that so many comprehensive schools have tended to reproduce inside the school the tripartitism which previously existed in different institutions. At the same time confusion over the notion of equality is likely to inhibit in certain schools and in varying degrees a full-blooded concern for the able.

It is this risk to the able which probably explains why a number of advanced industrial societies which have preceded this country in the setting up of a comprehensive system of education are now returning to various forms of selection. In the United States of America, for instance, concern for the low standards implicit in the comprehensive high school preceded even our own move towards comprehensivisation and the fact of the matter is that now in metropolitan areas the comprehensive high school is the exception rather than the rule. Dr James B. Conant has said in his book on the comprehensive high school 'I admire the comprehensive high school in the towns with one high school and see it as an instrument of democracy', but he adds, 'the metropolitan areas of the country are almost without high schools that in regard to the curriculum are widely comprehensive in nature'. In an article in the *Times Educational Supplement* entitled 'The Myth of the Comprehensive High School' Mr Lloyd P. Jorgenson spells out in detail the actual position in a number of highly urban American centres, pointing to the large number of special purpose secondary schools which exist.[29] In Czechoslovakia, it was clear

[29] Issue of 21 February 1969.

by June 1968 that the comprehensivisation of schools had led to what was described to me by a member of the Pedagogical Faculty in the Charles University in Prague, as a catastrophic fall in the standards of University entrants; conferences, I was informed, were about to take place to discuss changes in the system which could re-establish standards.[30] In the first place, fifty highly selective schools were to be set up in various parts of the country in order to provide opportunities for the most able academic children. Since then, and following on the Russian invasion, selection has been diverted to selection in particular fields after the Russian model. For instance, children in Prague and other main centres are at present being selected at the age of eight years in order to attend highly specialised language schools. These, it should be noted, are separate schools and not simply specialised streams within a school. Children are also being selected at the age of eleven who show special talent for mathematics and gymnastics. This tends to follow very much the Russian plan. It has been known for long enough that in Russia selection at the age of fifteen/sixteen has been made for special mathematical schools; but now selection for these schools is taking place at the age of eleven, and experiments are being made in an attempt to discover whether it is possible to select budding mathematicians as early as at the end of the first year of school which, in Russia, is seven. There are also indications that there are special language schools for talented linguists in the USSR and there are special schools also for talented musicians. Similar selection is said to take place in Hungary. Furthermore, it was openly admitted to me by a high official of the Swedish Ministry of Education in 1968 that comprehensivisation in Sweden had led undoubtedly to deterioration in the achievement of the most able children. He, however, was convinced that the gain in democracy was worth the sacrifice. It is particularly interesting that this admission should be made about Sweden when it is appreciated that Sweden is almost exclusively a rural country with very few large urban centres and it is in rural centres faced with the need to run small, uneconomic schools with a very restricted curriculum that comprehensive education would seem to have most to offer. Hence its comparative success in such areas as Anglesey and the Isle of Man in this country.

It is not, however, only the highly able children who may be at

[30] I was in Czechoslovakia for ten days in June 1968 attached to the Charles University. Czech educationists were very informative about the failure of their own comprehensive system—and the development of selection in Russia.

risk in the comprehensive school. It is also the least able. As I have already pointed out, an important feature of the comprehensive curriculum is the need in the name of equalisation of opportunity for all children to follow a common curriculum in the first one, two or three years. We are thus faced with such monstrosities as children, hardly able to read or write their own language, having to learn a foreign one as well. One of the most important and pressing needs in education in this country today is to develop a theory of popular education which will provide genuine opportunities for those who figure in the Schools Council Enquiry *Young School Leavers* as the bored, frustrated and rebellious—the less intelligent from the culturally restricted home.

IX

It is here indeed that the relevance of the cultural model I have developed earlier is perhaps most easily apparent in the circumstances of today. Two fundamental and highly intractable problems have arisen out of the scientific and technological revolution of the last three and a half centuries, and the industrialisation which has accompanied it. In the education of the ablest we need to find a substitute for the old classical curriculum as the central humanistic and civilising discipline, one which penetrated into so many aspects of our social and cultural life and which provided a moral image and a style deeply nutritive to the developing West. For this profoundly energising force science with its skeletal models of material behaviour and its concern for efficient means is no substitute; what is needed is what the ancient world provided —something with the affective force of myth. The only serious attempt at substitution has been Dr Leavis's suggestion of our national literature as the energising and sensitising agency; but heroic though the attempt at definition has been, one does not anticipate its universal acceptance; how could it be when even the problem, in the current concern for meritocracy rather than cultural authority, is not even appreciated?

At the bottom end, however, our desperation is greater and therefore the more apparent. The attempt at cultural homogenisation explicit in the meanings of the watered down high-cultural curriculum which is their traditional school fodder has lamentably and palpably failed. Yet we lack a theory of popular education which would provide the children I refer to with *cultural* satisfactions designed to afford them the opportunity to live rewarding lives. They are drop-outs of the meritocratic system; they are the victims of an inability to grasp the meanings implicit in the well-intentioned egalitarian attempt to provide a common experience.

The aim must be to provide them with an education which, while admitting their incapacity for certain types of advanced cognitive education, nevertheless genuinely liberalises. Work has, for such children, become too narrow and restricted in scope in the modern factory to provide, as traditionally it did, a focal point for the extension of their awareness of significant meaning; nor must they be dismissed with a simple life adjustment programme which seeks to exploit everyday practicability at the most mundane levels—counting the change and mending the motor bike.

The gateway to the cognitive curriculum is the act of reading—the assimilation by the inner consciousness of inert material in solitary contemplation. The principle of entry into minds unfitted for such primarily cognitive orientations is to be found in the kinetic with its opportunities for emotional control and expression and communal participation.

The justification for seeking an alternative principle to the cognitive curriculum in the education of the emotions lies deep in the socio-cultural history of the folk as well as in the findings of modern psychologists and sociologists. Briefly it is implied in the affective basis of the oral tradition and of the arts and crafts which in pre-industrial times constituted the higher levels of their work experience. Their orientation is practical—but with opportunities for imagination within the area of the practical and concrete. Hence the releasing potential implicit in Laban-inspired movement education, with its applications with dance, dance-drama, mime and imaginative play. In this way the world of language can be entered—as imaginative expression rather than as cognitive discourse. They will not in general cope with such a syllabus as well as would able children; but its orientation lies along the grain of their traditional consciousness, working with rather than against.

I have written at greater length elsewhere about this revised syllabus and its rationale in terms of their level of consciousness;[31] the attempt too is to exploit appropriate contemporary media of communication as well as the print culture. My purpose in this brief reference is simply to bring out the relevance and applicability of the cultural model in preference to either the meritocratic or the egalitarian views I have analysed. For at bottom both these imply a false notion of equality, though more so in the latter than in the former case. The fault of the meritocratic model lies in its

[31] In two articles published in the *Times Educational Supplement*, 12 and 19 March 1971.

too frequent indifference to the living potential by which we are faced in order to serve the purely functional efficiency of the industrial-bureaucratic society; that some concessions in this direction are necessary, indeed inevitable, is no justification for not considering the price we pay for not working out an adequate theory of education for the less able. Yet in the meritocratic school at least certain sections of the potential are reasonably catered for. The able are not neglected or despised. The fault of the egalitarian model lies even deeper—a perverse attempt to homogenise both ends of the spectrum in a mediocre common experience satisfying to neither. The attempt to induce a common meaning constitutes a most serious threat to the future of our civilisation—it degrades the able without satisfying the intellectually backward. The cultural model at least looks to satisfactions beyond the functional —and to an attempt to provide an equally appropriate but essentially differentiated school experience—differentiated in terms of cultural expectation and potential. Educationally this is the only sort of equality which is viable, for the abstract 'sameness' which produces the political solution of 'one man, one vote' is simply not possible within the complex requirements of a curriculum. Here, the very nature of the meanings concerned, their specifically involved and complex structures, palpably and unmistakably fail to coalesce with minds too restricted in capacity for cognitive development to benefit; the hope that such restrictions are the result of environmental pressures (and thus, it is thought, subject to manipulation) rather than hereditary endowment has recently taken so many knocks (notably from Professors Burt, Eysenck, Jensen and Butcher, among others) that it can be dismissed.[32] Ineluctably we are faced with a broad spectrum of

---

[32] Of course, environment plays an important part, but almost certainly not even the major role. But, of course, even if it were conceded that human beings were *totally* formed by their environments, there is no reason to assume that this would make much difference to the range of achievement by which we are faced. For one thing, as a matter of historical fact, environments are, educationally speaking, both good (culturally rich, emotionally supportive) and bad (deprived emotionally, culturally impoverished). This must be conceded. Now the hope is, of course, that these inadequate environments can be rapidly improved. In fact, in many cases, this will prove impossible. Families are going to continue to split up, parents are going to continue to neglect their children, husbands and wives to separate and divorce, thus causing those emotional troubles in their offspring which we know to represent a major factor in lack of achievement. Furthermore, other families, even when emotionally supportive, will fail to offer the cultural nourishment necessary for achievement. In the wider environment, impoverished cultural offerings via the mass media will continue to retard mental and emotional development

talent, and its need for diversified cultural satisfactions appropriate to its varied levels of consciousness. In this way, we could aspire to a revitalised cultural order and the *individual* satisfactions this could afford—a forlorn hope perhaps in the degradation of our times, but worth the consideration of good men.

This much of the essay was completed in April 1971; the long sad illness and untimely death of Dr Tibor Szamuely has held up publication, and made a coda on the most recent theoretical developments desirable. On re-reading, the essay seems as cogent as when it was first written; nothing at the level of practical politics has occurred to outdate what it has to say other than a sense of growing public disenchantment with comprehensive schooling and a stout unwillingness to be pressured into destroying good schools on the part of the former Secretary of State.

Nevertheless an interesting recent development in educational thinking has focused attention (albeit in ways unacceptable to the present writer) on the cultural problem as disillusionment with specific organisational devices to produce equality of achievement has grown. As it has become clear that, even in comprehensive conditions, working-class children continue to do worse than middle class, and compensatory programmes fail to produce any very startling results, the attack, briefly noted earlier, on what is termed 'middle-class culture' has developed in the name of the putative equal value of working-class culture. In this way, the inferior achievement of the working classes is disguised and the myth of cultures different but equal is fostered.

The line of argument receives a further boost from recent developments in the field of the sociology of education. Interest in the sociology of knowledge, dormant since Mannheim's day, has been revived, particularly with reference to the determining

---

—indeed, it is not unreasonable to assume that the situation will deteriorate rather than improve as even high cultural standards are sacrificed in a general cultural mediocritisation. In fact the human situation cannot be manipulated with anything like the ease with which, in the technological era, we have learnt to control the natural environment; and even if it could, there is no reason to assume that the cultural standards of the manipulators would prove, in any profound sense, to be educative. Why should one assume that control of manipulation would be seized by the educated (the 'philosopher kings') rather than by commercial interests or dictators on the twentieth-century model? All the evidence goes to show that in the current situation, *these* are likely to exploit such human manipulation as is possible. But, of course, environmentalists always naïvely assume that the environment will be adjusted to serve *good* purposes.

power of the curriculum. The traditional curriculum, indeed, is no longer to be seen as having an autonomy implicit in its meaning-structures, but is to be viewed as 'socially constructed as sets of shared meanings' representative of the dominant power structure of society; subject disciplines are 'socio-historical constructs of a particular time' without absolutist validity. The line is that such 'socio-historical constructs', being only regarded as factors in a social power game, are means to domination and not valuable in themselves: thus 'Formal education is based on the assumption that thought systems organised in curricula are in some sense "superior" to the thought systems of those who are to be (or have not been) educated' and such implicit 'superiority' should be questioned. The link with the less technical working class/middle class argument set out above is explicitly made by Mr M. F. D. Young when he criticises Douglas and Plowden for their views of what constitutes failure:

'By using a model of explanation of working-class school failure which justified reformist social policies, they were unable to examine the socially constructed character of the education that the working-class children failed at—for instance, the peculiar content of the grammar school curriculum for the sixteen-year-old in which pupils are obliged to do up to ten different subjects which bear little relation either to each other or to anything else.'[33]

The veiled hostility to the grammar school curriculum implicit in the terms in which this is set out is to be noted.

The net effect of all this is to throw into doubt the nature of the meaning-structures the school seeks to transmit not (as I have argued) because some cannot encompass it, but because such meaning-structures draw much of their validity as weapons in the political power struggle as means through which the dominant classes keep the lower orders in subjection.

Now clearly a culture is a 'social' phenomenon if 'social' is interpreted as the sum-total of all the meanings comprehensible to the total population of a society; but in fact the meaning of 'social' implied is a much more restricted one, indicating some measure of domination—a 'social' device for preserving hegemony. Yet surely the meaning-structures implicit in the school curriculum have a logic and autonomy which makes them

---

[33] Michael F. D. Young (Ed.), *Knowledge and Control*, (Collier-Macmillan), 1971, p. 24.

independent of any such particular attempt at social domination—
as the history of Nazi Germany and Soviet Russia constantly
demonstrate. If such disciplines were reducible simply to political
devices for domination, then no independent assessment of, for
instance, Lysenko would be possible; but much of Lysenko can be
shown to be false because his theories are not true to biological
behaviour not because they were simply reflections of the current
power structure; the criticism comes from within the area of
biological studies, not simply from socially deviant groups.

It is indeed idle to argue the equal validity of working-class
culture with that which is implied by the reference to middle-class
culture (presumably the traditional 'high culture'); for the skills
and insights, scientific and humanistic, which sustain our civilisation have been developed by those who either are middle class or
have become so in the process of acquiring such skills. Working-
class culture in this sense is a myth; and indeed the argument can
only be given the slightest appearance of plausibility by juggling
with two senses of the word 'culture'. In the anthropological
sense, the working classes may be said to have a culture, for their
patterns of living show definable differences from those which
characterise the middle classes. (In passing it might be pointed
out that the working classes themselves show considerable
diversity of culture pattern in this sense of the word.) But in the
qualitative sense (the sense of Arnold, of what one implies in
referring to a 'cultured man') the working classes no longer have
such a culture. Once, in pre-industrial England they did; and our
lives have been permanently enriched by the craftsmen, the songs
and legends of the oral folk tradition. Now, even as prejudiced a
witness as Mr Brian Jackson can summon up little more than
'brass bands' and 'pigeon fancying' as representative of the
indigenous cultural activities of the working classes; industrialisation has reduced the range and scope of their work, sometimes
catastrophically, and their culture has suffered accordingly.

Yet the concept of 'cultural deprivation' is now being subtly
undermined on the grounds that working-class children have their
own culture, different but equally rich; and the offering of 'opportunities' to such children in terms of an introduction to 'middle-
class culture' is deprecated partly on the grounds that they have
available their own alternative amplitude, and partly, as indicated
above, on political grounds. The idealisation of working-class
life implied is explicable as a current version of pastoral—a
nostalgia for a simpler life which reappears in numerous guises in
European history; in the eighteenth century there was a fashion

for (classically inspired) shepherds and shepherdesses; today they appear in dungarees. It is a sillier and more restrictive version of the myth, but it has the potential power to destroy a culture, as Russia and China illustrate.[34]

[34] Another strategy is to recommend the introduction of 'pop' culture into schools, on the grounds that this has become the new 'folk' culture and is therefore 'relevant'. This strategy is accompanied and sustained by all sorts of pretentious claims for 'pop', especially in the field of music. (The mingling of 'high' and 'pop' elements by the *avant-garde* is a matter of great social interest and cause for some concern.) Pop is largely about profits—as *Vox Pop* by Michael Wale, a book in no way hostile to pop, makes clear; at its best it provides distraction, as did the popular music of the twenties and thirties, to which it is no whit superior; indeed it is appreciably worse mannered. Its introduction into schools should be strongly resisted.

5

The School,
Equality and Society

DR RHODES BOYSON

Equality is a concept like goodness, liberty, freedom and fraternity with which good men are supposed to agree. Yet it is no ultimate good to which all other goods bow; indeed, certain of the concepts are contradictory—if you give men freedom they will certainly not end up equal. The seeker for utilitarianism might also argue that stability and security in a status society were preferred by most people to equality.

To maintain the view that all children are born with equal brain potential when in every other way they are different in height, weight, the colour of their eyes, stamina and sporting ability, is to make people with flat earth beliefs positively rational.

Given genetic differences, and most geneticists consider the heredity element determines 70 to 80 per cent of a person's intellectual abilities, then there can be no equality of achievement. The environment of the family itself, which history has shown is the most basic and continuing of all units, means that genetic differences at birth will have been further increased by environmental factors before children commence school. The only environmental alternative to the family is the removal of the child at birth to some collective institution, yet the efficiency of the nurses and ancillaries employed there will itself differ. Even if robots were programmed to replace human nurses in this early training the relative efficiency of their supporting mechanics would be a further limiting factor.

Most people would, however, subscribe to the need to give

equality of opportunity to all children to develop their hereditary intelligence and abilities. This is very different from supporting equality of rewards or accepting equality of abilities. Some people, however, do support these latter views. Equality of rewards is possible by political action but it will be achieved only in a completely oppressive state-controlled society, whether labelled fascist, communist or socialist, all of them extreme left-wing concepts, which look for the solution of men's difficulties in his collective nature because they have no belief in his individual nature. Men who hold such views are the ultimate Jeremiahs of mankind.

In society there must be a balance between equality of opportunity to develop to the full the facilities with which one is born and the need for security and stability as creators of happiness in human life. Many people do not want to move out of their class structure: they are happy and secure there and would be miserable in a society where they were compelled to move irrespective of their wishes. Indeed one of the attacks that the egalitarians made on the grammar school was that it imposed middle-class values on the working-class. If these values mean industry, thrift, reliability, honesty, and ambition then it showed how little the egalitarians, most of them middle-class in upbringing, knew of the life of the artisan working-class in the 1930s with its protestant and predominantly nonconformist beliefs in personal responsibility. But the middle-class egalitarians would reply that this nonconformist ethic was itself an opium maintained by the middle-classes to subdue and control the working-classes.

The good society must firstly provide the maximum freedom for the individual to choose for himself whether he wants to partake in social mobility and must second make the educational facilities available so that he can move if he has the intellectual qualities required and the desire to develop them. It is as well to recognise that there has never been a completely structured society where no movement occurred because so stagnant a society would quickly die. In Tudor England, Archbishops and Lord Chancellors could come from the labouring classes. There was considerable social mobility at the time of the Industrial Revolution and very many employers had begun as ordinary workers.[1]

Modern society changes so rapidly—note the rapid increase in world population, the rise of new powers, the quick collapse of the British against the slow decline of the Roman Empire, the

[1] See Rhodes Boyson, *The Ashworth Cotton Enterprise* (O.U.P.), 1970, p. 87.

development of new products—that one can argue that there is a conflict between the need for social mobility as required by the state and status and security as desired by the individual. A powerful state requires rapid social mobility and change to allow its continuance as a first-class power while the individual for his happiness often desires less mobility and more security. The growing militancy of trade unions in Britain aims more at preserving the status of craft or employment than increased wages and this is a symbol of Britain's economic decline. Opposition to coloured immigration was and is largely a desire for a settled unchanging environment, although it might be cogently argued that such immigration was economically disastrous in that it dangerously delayed British mechanisation of industry by keeping wage rates low so that the man was cheaper than the cost of any machinery substitute.

The widening of opportunities for equality of opportunity in the primary and secondary schools has now focused attention on the upbringing of the under-fives. Many educational psychologists argue that the earliest years are the most formative in the life of any person and without special programmes for the under-fives there will never be real equality of opportunity. This view is supported by many advocates of the common or comprehensive school who note that it is doing little for social equality and look elsewhere for some means of achieving their desired ends.

There is no doubt that by the age of five the attitude of a child to schooling and in many cases the beginnings of numeracy and of verbal and of reasoning capacity have been developed. The best person to encourage this development is the mother by talking to her child and fostering his interests. An intelligent and concerned mother will discuss topics with her children and will answer their questions, and reasoning ability and a knowledge of words and their meaning will develop. As Professor Bernstein has pointed out, a harassed or ineffective mother will simply use words as commands and her child will only be praised when he is not interrupting her. Even if children from two such homes started with the same innate intelligence they would be of different intellectual calibre by the time they arrived at school.

Pre-school play groups meet only about two to three hours a day whilst their mothers shop or have coffee. Their advantages are that children meet other children and parents usually play a full part since they generally organise the groups themselves. Some good play groups do attempt to develop ideas through play. Real development of children up to the age of five comes, however, more from intelligent converse with adults. This is where the mother fulfils a vital role in giving her undivided attention for at least part of the day to her child. It is also arguable that when such a mother is busy her child will play alone developing his imaginative facility, which will be of more value than the chasing games of the pre-school play group.

An extension of nursery classes and nursery schools for the three–five year olds is now part of the Conservative and Labour Party programmes. Such schools gain support both from social workers concerned with the deprivation of young children in depressed city areas and from professional middle-class mothers in suburban areas. The latter can well afford their own provision since nursery classes normally free a mother to rejoin a profession and earn considerable income, but the former might need special help.

The Minority Report of the Plowden Committee recommended fees in state nursery schools and since these schools are very expensive this suggestion must be seriously considered.[2] Further expansion of state provision of education financed from rates and taxes would mean more squalor all round. The cost limits on new school buildings were in 1973 so low that it is arguable whether the new school buildings were preferable to the buildings they replaced. The level of taxation in Britain is also too high yet hospitals, certain social services and old people need more money spent on them. If governments wish to establish more state nursery schools then economic fees should be charged with provision for reduced fees on a means test for the parents who cannot afford to meet them. Such a plan could help deprived children, like those from the one-parent family, who need help while ensuring the professional mother covered the cost of her child's place instead of it being a charge on the rest of the community. This development would also mean that private provision of nursery facilities could compete on equal terms with state provision to the benefit of efficiency and the variety of our way of life. State-subsidised or totally-provided monopoly here, as elsewhere, would be dangerous to the continuance of the free society.

These nursery schools will have to be generously staffed or they will be counter-productive. If the ratio of teachers to pupils is low then the children will listen to one another instead of to the teacher

---

[2] The average annual cost of each nursery school pupil in England and Wales in the year 1970–1 was estimated at £202·2. The cost of the average primary pupil was then estimated at £97·0 and the secondary school pupil cost £186·3.

and they would be better at home with mother. Dr Sula Wolff, a child psychiatrist, told a conference of the Nursery School Association in 1971 that nurseries could not provide the one-to-one relationship of adult and child which was vital in the early years for basic social and intellectual skills.[3]

The results of the Headstart Programme in America have not been very encouraging. Pupils learned quickly but fell back again when normal schooling was commenced. The experience of some infant teachers in Britain also throws doubt on the usefulness of pre-school play groups and nursery schools, since children come to associate school with play and join the infant school expecting play to continue, so that they are slow to concentrate on learning. In the United States it has been found by the Office of Economic Opportunity that a weekly session at which mothers listen to experts talking on children's health and intellectual development is more useful than child attendance at nursery schools and mothers are encouraged to attend by being paid £2 a session.

In the infant school (5–7 years) and the junior school (8–11 years) we enter the area of four controversies with regard to equality of educational opportunity: the neighbourhood school, the whole question as to whether compensatory education can serve any useful purpose in deprived city-centre areas, the teaching of the apparently bright in separate groups from the apparently dull and the use of experimental so-called 'progressive' methods of teaching as against the traditionally successful methods of teaching.

The catchment area of a school is governed by the length of a pupil's stride. An infant school must draw from a smaller area than a junior school and a junior school from a smaller area than a secondary school. How far this general rule will be modified by the increased use of the private car for bringing infants to school at an early age and for sixth-formers to drive themselves at the older secondary age is a matter of conjecture. Small drawing areas mean that schools for younger children will tend to be drawn from a single social class unless care is taken in zoning areas or in siting schools.

There are arguments for and against the neighbourhood school. A one-social-class school can be attacked as providing little or no social mixing and 'bussing' or movement between areas to produce artificial mixing has proved a failure both in America and Britain.

[3] *Times Educational Supplement*, 14 May 1971.

It is unsettling to a child to remove him from his safe environment in which he is secure to another environment to which he does not desire or possibly can never belong. A sop to social engineers, it is a move to the atomisation of social groupings into what Trotsky called 'human dust' so that they might be manipulated by the state without the disruptive influences of family, locality and such loyalties.

Dr Eric Midwinter, director of the Liverpool educational priority area project, said in 1971 that even the attempt to wean children away from the values of their homes and community was inducing a form of schizophrenia. He continued:

'Different social groups require different types of school and the idea of handing out dollops of compensation is false. . . . The successful middle class school identified closely with the local community and working class schools should do likewise, although teachers might find that a very difficult thing to do.'[4]

One great advantage of the single-social-class school in a deprived area is that the deprivation of the pupils will be so obvious that remedial action is likely to be taken. The attempt to give compensatory benefits to deprived areas goes back in history to the foundation of charity schools in the worst districts of our cities. The state through its organs moved to compensatory education in Britain soon after the passing of Forster's 1870 Act. In 1884 the London School Board introduced a special allowance for teachers in 'schools of special difficulty': head teachers received an extra £20 per annum and assistants an extra £10. The first fifteen schools were chosen from the worst of the central slum areas but their number was later increased. The same principle was recommended by the Plowden Committee on Primary Education in 1967, and teachers in schools in difficult areas can be nominated by their local education authority for the special 'educational priority area' allowance but in this egalitarian age the assistants are to receive the same £75 a year as their head teachers. The Inner London Education Authority has also allocated extra non-teaching staff to some fifty schools and an extra capitation allowance to some hundred schools.

Yet one wonders if such compensatory education can ever be really effective. The £75 per annum is a negligible sum, swallowed up in the high fares of London travel. The requirement that all

[4] *TES*, 8 January 1971. Also note his speech to the conference organised by the Comprehensive School Committee and the progressive magazine *Forum* on 8 May 1971. See *Education*, 14 May 1971.

teachers should teach for five years in difficult areas before they received promotion could in theory be more effective but with low teacher salaries it would only mean that many well-qualified candidates never entered the teaching profession. Some difficult schools are well staffed because of inspired headship and high school morale but other such schools are staffed by late applicants or weak teachers who did not obtain places in the lusher areas in which they hoped to teach under a particular authority. Few teachers can find reasonable accommodation in 'deprived' areas and many teachers who apply for appointments in difficult schools may do so for the wrong reasons—the wish to study sociological conditions and turn the children into guinea pigs, or the wish to assuage some guilt complex about a secure, probably middle-class home background against which they are in revolt.

Extra money for neighbourhood schools catering for deprived children which can be spent on books, games, pens, felt pens, spirographs, tangrams, plasticine and paints is very useful. A careful siting of new schools by building them in the best-regarded part of their drawing area can pay rich dividends. I notice more and more, particularly in secondary schools, that the determinant of the compensatory value of a school is less related to the intake area than to the neighbourhood's assessment of the social standing of the road in which the school is actually sited. Parents like their children to attend a school in the most highly regarded part of their neighbourhood.

One of the best ways of bringing people together in schools other than on a neighbourhood basis is on a religious basis, where other values are held in common irrespective of social class. This can help teachers in raising the hopes and ambitions of both pupils and parents. It is also possible that, if parents were given a choice of school according to the type of discipline, method of teaching and curriculum offered, families would come together because they shared certain views of life not restricted to a social class. It is a pity that education officials continue their fiction that all their schools are equal. If the differences between schools were recognised and publicised and parents were encouraged to choose schools according to their ideas and beliefs, then parents would more easily identify with the schools. This is probably the biggest factor in promoting the progress of their children's education.

The streaming of children—their division into teaching groups within the year according to their academic ability—is normally defended by the same teachers who defend traditional methods of teaching. It has been asserted that streaming in the primary school was itself a product of the eleven-plus selection examination, in so far as those likely to pass the examination were taught separately from those who were considered of too low an academic standard to contemplate entry. But streaming can be defended as the most efficient way of teaching all pupils, particularly by the traditional methods. If pupils in a year are split into two or three teaching classes each of approximately equal ability the teacher can adjust his lessons to the average ability in each class and all pupils will proceed at a more satisfactory speed. The teacher can teach each class as a whole and they can all have 40 minutes instruction and work, without being in despair because they are left behind the brighter pupils or bored because they are waiting for the laggards to catch up.

The opponents of selection assert that this streaming often reflects social divisions (which themselves largely reflect intellectual divisions?) and that pupils will reflect their teachers' judgements on their abilities in that the bright will become brighter and the dull duller. In argument the opponents of streaming assert that it is either self-confirmatory or that it is inefficient. If pupils taught in different streams then show on external tests that they are of widely different attainments it is said that this is because their achieved standard reflects the expectations of the teachers. If on the other hand the pupils in different streams do not show these wide differences in achievement at the end of their course then streaming is attacked as inefficient. It is almost like being asked whether you have ceased to beat your wife.

C. C. D. Kemp after studying 50 London primary schools in the 1950s decided that streaming was at least as effective a method of organising teaching as were mixed ability groups.[5] Further useful evidence on primary school streaming is that of Mrs Joan Barker Lunn for the National Foundation for Educational Research.[6] Her first report indicated that pupils in streamed junior schools scored some 6 per cent higher marks in mechanical arithmetic, problem arithmetic, English and reading than did the pupils in unstreamed junior schools. Her second study was surprisingly inconclusive. The interesting point in the first study was that the higher marks in the streamed junior schools apparently arose from the more able children obtaining higher marks than did the same ability children in unstreamed junior

[5] C. C. D. Kemp, 'Environmental and Other Characteristics Determining Attainments in Primary Schools', *Brit. J. of Psychology*, 1955, 2, pp. 67–77.
[6] J. C. Barker Lunn, *Streaming in Primary Schools* (NFER), 1970.

schools. This bears out a common belief that streaming does encourage the brighter pupils to proceed more quickly.

The decision to stream or not to stream in the junior school, as in the secondary school, depends upon the size of school, the attitude of the teachers and the type of intake. In a small school in a homogeneous area there is probably little or no requirement to stream but in a large junior school with a wide spread of ability then there generally comes a point when teachers will favour streaming from a particular age. A four-year-old pupil with an intelligence quotient of 125 is only one year ahead of the pupil of average ability of the same age with an intelligence quotient of 100, but at the age of eight he will be two years ahead and as he approaches the age of twelve he will be three years ahead. The argument for streaming can be seen with greatest clarity when it is realised that in every 100 pupils the range of mental age at the chronological age of 6 will be from 3 to 8, at age 10 they will range from mental age 6–14 and at age 14 they will range from mental age 8–19. This clearly shows the difficulty, if not the impossibility, of teaching unstreamed groups with justice to all. An unstreamed attempt at justice to all can mean justice to none.

It is realised that early streaming in the junior or even more the infant school could lessen equality of opportunity since the influence of the home is paramount on achievement in the early years of schooling. A pupil placed in a B or C stream at the age of eight or nine could accept this as his correct academic classification for life and could adjust his whole attitude to it. Thus in a streamed primary school care must be taken to ensure that the teachers of B and C streams encourage all pupils and are on the lookout for potential A stream children. The very fact that the primary school is too early to categorise pupils with high accuracy means that there was never an attempt to have a bipartite system in junior schools. Yet it is really to return to the practice of the cottage industry for one teacher to divide an unstreamed class of ten- to eleven-year-olds in a large school into two, three or four teaching groups so that the bright, the average and the dull all gained something from the lesson.

It is doubtful whether the new experimental teaching methods are as successful as the traditional methods in advancing knowledge of the basic subjects. Professor Cyril Burt wrote that the standards of ten-year-old children in London schools in reading comprehension, spelling, and problem arithmetic were lower in 1965 than they were in 1914 despite smaller classes and a huge increase in educational expenditure. My research into literacy in the Ashworth cotton mills near Bolton discovered a 98 per cent ability to read in 1833.[7] It was estimated that in 1870, when there were not enough schools for all, that national literacy had reached 90 per cent. Yet after a century of increasing state expenditure it is estimated that 7 per cent of adolescents are illiterate or near-illiterate and a further 13 per cent of school leavers are unable to read fluently. The 1972 and 1973 reports on literacy standards from the National Foundation for Educational Research indicate that standards are falling steadily.[8]

The National Bureau for Co-operation in Child Care which is following the lives of 11,000 children born in the same week of 1958 found to its obvious embarrassment that reading and arithmetical standards were, if anything, higher in primary schools with more than forty pupils in a class than in those with fewer than thirty. It would appear that smaller classes have simply been used for the introduction of informal ineffective teaching methods which the deprived home, unlike the cultured home, cannot balance by home instruction. A report on the progress of immigrant children in British infant schools lends support to this view by indicating that there was more progress in learning when the teacher used formal rather than informal methods.[9] This report makes special mention of the fact that the formal infants school gave an immigrant child greater security. It would appear that pupils experiencing home and neighbourhood forms of cultural deprivation might gain from the secure framework of a formal school and a formal classroom.

It seems obvious that it is the child from the deprived home background who will gain least from the new methods of informal teaching. The child from a privileged home will be interested in words and figures before he comes to school and books will already be to him a source of information and enjoyment. His vocabulary will be wider and he will be anxious to learn. Not so the child from a deprived home where words are used simply for commands and not for rational discussion. If the school gives freedom of approach to activities then the child from the privileged home will eagerly look at books and rapidly advance his reading ability while the one from the deprived home which

[7] C. Burt, 'Intelligence or Hereditary', *Irish J. of Education*, 1969, **3**, pp. 75–94; Rhodes Boyson, *The Ashworth Cotton Enterprise: The Rise and Fall of a Family Firm, 1818–80* (OUP), 1970, pp. 132–3.

[8] Start and Wells, *The Trend of Reading Standards* (NFER), 1972; T. R. Horton, *Reading Standards of Children in Wales* (NFER), 1973.

[9] *Immigrant Children in Infant Schools*, Schools Council Working Paper 31.

sees little point in books will be content to play boisterous games with lots of shouting. The traditional approach where teacher teaches and the pupil is expected to listen and to try his best seems far more likely to advance the cause of equal opportunity since without swift action to teach them basic literacy and numeracy children from culturally deficient homes will fall further behind their more fortunate fellows. It is as well to remember that some 10 to 20 per cent of parents cannot or do not read even a simple newspaper.

Mrs Betty Root, lecturer and tutor at the Centre for the Teaching of Reading at Reading University, said in November, 1970: 'Infant Schools no longer spend 90 per cent of their time on the three Rs because they are trying to do too many things'. Dr Joyce M. Morris wrote in 1968:

'We are reminded that reading is a product of civilisation not, like physical growth, a natural phenomenon. Hence, children generally will neither begin to learn to read nor proceed to acquire the necessary reading skills if left to their own devices no matter how rich the reading environment provided by their teachers. They must be given systematic instruction based on an accurate diagnosis of their individual needs throughout their school lives.'[10]

A report prepared in 1971 for the National Foundation for Educational Research showed that children who were taught to read immediately they entered infant school at five achieved far better results than those kept waiting until they showed 'reading readiness'. Firm teacher-control and systematic organisation of reading brought the best results.[11]

Yet we still have school advisors propagating the view that reading is one of the skills which is more or less picked up automatically and that there is no reading problem until a child is eight years old. If a child cannot read by the age of eight then he will probably always be behind his fellows and it is in the light of fashionable views and the neglect of school teaching that many dissatisfied parents are trying to teach their children to read at home, often with the Ladybird books. Parents are doing the teachers' work and it is obvious which sort of child falls behind in such a situation. Continually hearing children read from the same

[10] Introduction to Donald Moyle's *The Teaching of Reading*, (Ward Lock Educational), 1968, p. 9.
[11] Brian Cane, *The Roots of Reading: A Survey of Twelve Infant Schools* (NFER), 1971.

reading books is very boring and it is to ease their and not the child's boredom that many teachers, encouraged by the fashions of the age, have ceased to do their work properly. The new methods are not child-centred but teacher-centred education, where they can neglect effective if tedious methods for new approaches every year. It is also amazing that only one in eight primary school teachers are now trained to teach reading.

The widespread use of 'discovery' methods will probably bring a continued decline in learning. The amount that any person can discover in his own lifetime is so limited that the advocates of discovery methods are really attacking both learning and civilisation. How many Michael Faradays are alive to 'discover' the principles of the electric motor and should a class sit in an orchard in September until an apple falls upon everyone's head to enable them to 'discover' the law of gravity?

There is a sad paradox in that the more money is spent giving pupils better facilities and a wide and varied curriculum the less chance will they have of obtaining a sound, basic education in the subjects on which all their future progress will depend. The more modern and well-equipped the infant school the more time must be spent in justifying the enormous expense of a hall, gymnastic equipment, a large playing field, sand and water facilities, radios, television sets, tape recorders, etc., to the neglect of the three Rs.

The results of building open-plan primary and secondary schools where there are no separate classrooms must be carefully scrutinised since it is very likely that the standards of achievement of pupils in such schools will not be equal to those attained by pupils attending schools built on the traditional pattern. The new schools will simply encourage or compel the adoption of experimental methods of teaching, the noise and general movement will be distracting to pupils and irritating to teachers. It will be far more difficult to pin down responsibility for standards in such schools as compared with traditional organisation with a primary school teacher being responsible for a class for a whole year in almost all subjects. Diffused responsibilities mean that no one will be responsible for a pupil. Nor can each teacher work out his own classroom atmosphere and approach to find the methods by which he can teach best. Teachers will become prisoners of whims of fashion, in many of which they do not believe.

In a primary school in Eastergate, Sussex, opened in 1970, visitors have to talk to the headmistress above the noise of more than 100 children in the one big classroom and the 'staffroom' consists of four easy chairs in one corner of the main concourse. The headmistress takes telephone calls in the entrance lobby. The lack of a staffroom for peace and quiet and relaxation could be more wearing on teachers than the hated dinner duty of previous years and their functional efficiency could be seriously reduced. Such schools will probably continue to be built until the number of psychological breakdowns among staff causes medical officers to realise that these will be the Rowan Points of the school situation. At least the central-hall type schools of the mid-nineteenth century had strong headmasters in the middle to keep order.

The introduction of primary school French to pupils, many of whom cannot read English, is a further dispersal of effort and a decoy cover for continuing failure in the basic subjects. The lack of skilled French teachers in the primary schools has meant, according to heads of grammar schools, poor standards of reading and writing accuracy in the language, the rudiments of which have to be retaught in secondary schools.[12] Reteaching is always difficult and frustrating for a pupil. Primary school French was introduced in America with the intention of introducing a subject which demanded mental discipline into a flabby curriculum. Yet in England when we copied America we made it a play subject.

Mr R. C. Lyness, one of her Majesty's staff-inspectors, has also warned about the dangers of the new Mathematics:

> 'Mathematics for the abler half of our school population requires thoroughness, the learning of techniques, a proper challenge in problem-solving, and a firmer grasp of systematically developed areas of knowledge than can come from the fluttering over the surface which characterises many of today's courses.'[13]

It is a fascinating comment on social history that it was the Russian launching of the first Sputnik in 1957 which changed and probably dangerously diluted the teaching of mathematics in a Britain with no significant space programme.

The British eleven-plus examination for selection to academic schools was opposed not only because it separated children at that age into different types of schools but because it was considered to be a restrictive influence on the primary school curriculum. What is wrong with a restrictive influence if the restriction is a wise and proven one which gives full opportunity to all pupils and stresses the conventional linguistic and number skills necessary for a full life? Freedom for primary schools should not mean

[12] Clare Burstall, *French in the Primary School* (NFER), 1970.
[13] *Trends in Education* (HMSO), April 1969.

the freedom for every head's and teacher's whim to teach anything
or nothing, but their freedom to follow whatever method they wish
provided that, by a certain age, high standards are achieved in
certain specified subjects. It appears that the decline of the eleven-
plus examination is producing not liberty but disastrous licence,
as a result of which it will again be the deprived pupil who will be
disadvantaged further when compared with the pupil from the
cultured and concerned home. The Plowden Report includes
these amazing words:

> 'We have considered whether we can lay down standards that
> should be achieved by the end of the primary school but concluded
> that it is not possible to describe a standard of attainment that
> should be reached by all or most children.'

Thus the pupil who depends upon his school for all his
numeracy and literacy is put at risk to the whims of his teachers.

It is at the age of eleven, the year of normal transfer from
primary to secondary school in the British state system, that the
choice of comprehensive (common) schooling or selective
schooling arises. The Norwood Report of 1943 recommended a
great variety of provision of secondary education but the administrators finally produced three and then two types—the grammar,
technical and general secondary school, and then the grammar
and secondary modern school—with something like 20 per cent of
an age group being selected for the grammar school. The grammar
schools, with an academic curriculum, had from the early twentieth century taken one quarter of their intake as free places and
this number had increased by the 1930s to some half of their
intake. The rest were fee-payers, although the fees charged covered
only a part of the cost. Central schools or intermediate schools
between the grammar and modern schools were also introduced
by some authorities, all of whose intake were on free places.

For selection to the grammar schools there was an eleven-plus
examination usually based on intelligence, mathematical and
English tests taken on one morning in the late winter preceding
transfer to secondary school in the following autumn. It was
known as the scholarship examination. The intelligence tests
were introduced to provide a fairer assessment of working class
children attending poor schools with poor teachers. They were a
test of potential while the English and mathematical tests were
tests of achievement. When the Northumberland Education
Committee introduced intelligence tests in the middle twenties
the number of children receiving poor schooling in remote rural

schools who passed the scholarship test increased in number. Jean Floud and A. H. Halsey compared selection in Hertfordshire in 1952, when an intelligence test provided one-third of the selection marks, with selection in 1954, when, in response to attacks upon them, the intelligence tests were dropped. The percentage of working-class children selected fell between the two years from 14·9 per cent to 11·5 per cent and the percentage of children selected with professional and managerial class parents rose from 40 per cent to 64 per cent. Children can be effectively coached for intelligence tests and if there is a minimum of two to three hours' practice on intelligence tests given to all pupils then children from privileged homes providing their own coaching gain no advantage.

As long as (under the pre-1944 system) some 5 to 10 per cent of an age group were selected for free places in grammar schools, while another 5 to 10 per cent were subsidised fee-payers, there was no social stigma in non-selection. Once all the places in grammar schools were awarded on an examination which was introduced under the 1944 Act, however, the situation was different. The middle and artisan working-class parents who greatly valued education were unable to buy places for their children in grammar schools. The exclusion of such children created in their families a tension which eventually killed both the eleven-plus examination and a selective secondary system by providing the leaders and the ground troops of the comprehensive school lobby. The concern of such parents about the actual or possible exclusion of their children from the grammar schools was aggravated by the loosening of a tight class system during and after the Second World War, for it is at a time of the loosening of class barriers that class feelings and tensions are most acute. Parents saw success or failure of their children at the eleven-plus examination as a family class matter affecting the whole family: if their children entered the grammar schools then they were entering the ranks of the professional classes, if they failed, then the family itself was slighted.

The attack on the selective school system was, however, strategically made on practical grounds: at first the inefficiency of the eleven-plus selection and finally the evil of any system which divided children into two fairly permanent groups at the age of eleven. The fact that selection was shown to be some 10 per cent inefficient provided ammunition to attack the whole system, although such a low inefficiency rate would have been welcomed in practically every other sphere of human or indeed mechanical activity. Most or all authorities made provision for transfer between types of school, but parents did not welcome a child's demotion from a grammar school, and secondary modern school heads did not show any eagerness to transfer their best pupils to grammar schools. Professor H. J. Eysenck considers that it is not impossible to predict the late developers, in whom slowness to develop is apparently associated with certain personality traits of introversion, but the achievement of the late developer who failed the eleven-plus and then went on to university was continually quoted to throw doubt on the efficiency, and indeed the justice, of the system.

Nor was the maintenance of the selective system helped by the treatment of the modern schools by many local education authorities. The thesis was that grammar and modern schools were equal but different. Since the grammar schools had better qualified teachers and trained their pupils for university and well-esteemed careers they obviously enjoyed higher public standing than the modern schools. This should not however, have led many education authorities to give higher cash allowances for books and games to grammar schools than were given to modern schools for pupils of the same age. Such thoughtless action was much resented in the modern schools.

The abolition of the intermediate central schools meant that at the age of eleven pupils were divided on a simple in/out arrangement and there was a 20 per cent grammar school pupil and parents selection and an 80 per cent modern school pupil and parents rejection. There was no middle group which, as in society, buttressed and supported a class or hierarchical system. The difference in the percentage of grammar school selection between some 5 per cent for one English town to some 50 per cent in certain Welsh counties threw further doubt on the justice of the selection procedure. Nor could many parents take advantage of the benefit of a transfer system which gave a child who won a grammar school place in an area with 50 per cent selection an entitlement to a grammar school place in a district with a 5 per cent selection provided the parents moved house. Wise parents noticed that eleven-plus success was not against a standard set nationally but was simply fixed each year under each authority to fill the number of places vacant in local grammar schools.

The increased parental demand for education after the Second World War and the attempt of the secondary modern schools to win some parity of esteem meant that an increasing proportion of them, in areas where the percentage of grammar school selection was not too high, began, in the face of much official opposition, to enter their pupils for the GCE 'O' level examinations as sat at sixteen by the grammar schools. This they did with increasing success, although they generally entered their pupils for fewer subjects than were normally entered by grammar school pupils. It is possible that their success arose because their pupils were carefully graded and taught by teachers trained to teach a certain ability level who welcomed an examination which enhanced their personal stature. Yet critics of the eleven-plus selection procedure quickly pointed to the better 'O' level results achieved in 'A' stream secondary modern schools than in 'C' or 'D' streams of grammar schools.

The movement in favour of comprehensive secondary schools came from an alliance of two factions. These were firstly the professional teachers worried about the unfairness of the existing bipartite system and the waste of talent in many secondary modern schools whose aims were 'social' and not educational. I was then a Head of a secondary modern school introducing external examinations and extended courses, having myself seen as a teacher the waste of talent in the secondary modern schools whose only successes were those who moved elsewhere. As a meritocrat and as an eleven-plus failure myself, I then began to advocate comprehensive schools as part of the open society where movement of pupils could be easily made and where all pupils could share in the success of their more academic friends as they already rejoiced in the successes of their school football teams.

The second faction was basically a middle-class intellectual affair with overtones of egalitarianism. They used the weapons of unfair and wrong selection procedures as a stepping-stone to eventual abolition of all forms of selection and possibly even of academic excellence. Their particular ground was that if there was any error in selection then selection was wrong, but their emotional appeal was to middle-class parents who objected to any form of selection which could exclude their own children. The practical reason that a comprehensive rather than a bipartite system might increase educational opportunity for all, particularly the middle-band children about whom the professional teachers were increasingly worried, was rarely argued by the middle-class lobbyists.

Many of the members of this middle-class lobby recognised differences of ability but felt sympathy for the less able and wished to develop on emotional grounds a system which they believed would be less harmful to them. This was the same lobby which advocated greater equality of incomes. They believed and still believe that schools should be so arranged that inequalities between pupils should not show or could be neutralised. They desired to make of school life a handicap race so that no one would arrive at the tape before anyone else. It is doubtful, however, whether the dull will suffer more from their early protection from reality than will the clever from the lack of stimulation or recognition of their talents. Ultimately, of course, real social equality can be achieved only by denying the concept of academic values and the whole scholastic purpose of education.

Indeed many of these middle-class advocates of comprehensive schools have side-stepped completely the question of the maintenance of academic standards by claiming for British comprehensive schools the virtue of social cohesion. Yet American experience of the comprehensive school has shown that it has neither fostered social cohesion nor academic standards. Love and tolerance between social groups do not seem to be fostered by the common school. Adolescence is the age of discrimination when young people seek unconsciously for a mate and they may in the common school only become more aware of their differences from other social classes.

A situation was reached by the late 1960s when it was considered extremely reactionary to defend selective schools of any type. The Labour Party became committed to a rapid and wholesale move to comprehensive schools and the spokesmen for the Conservative Party largely agreed with the philosophical case for the comprehensive school but argued for new buildings before schools were combined.

There was no impartial investigation of the results of existing comprehensive schools before a national commitment was made by the Labour Party for their universal introduction. Many traditionally working-class Labour Party areas were slow to introduce comprehensive schooling because the local Party leaders were well aware of the advantages that grammar schools had given working-class children, but their voices were drowned in an alliance of middle-class intellectuals and of teachers who saw advantages for themselves in the comprehensive system in providing them both with greater prospects of promotion and a chance to teach more able children.

There are three tests against which the comprehensive schools in this country can be judged to decide whether they provide more, the same, or less equality of opportunity than did the bipartite school system. The first test is whether they bring a greater proportion of working-class pupils through to university, second, whether they encourage more pupils, particularly working-class pupils, to stay on at school and pass worthwhile examinations and train for worthwhile careers, and finally whether they will encourage both the very brightest pupils and the least able pupils to realise more of their potential. Future historians will judge the comprehensive experiment against these three tests of equality of opportunity.

One can, however, already attempt an interim judgement on these tests. It is doubtful whether a comprehensive secondary school system will achieve a higher percentage of intake to universities from the working-class. Britain already boasts the highest percentage of university intake coming from the working-class of any western country, a fact which was a source of pride to Mrs Shirley Williams when she addressed the European Ministers of Education in 1967. In 1961-2, 25 per cent of the British university entrants were from working-class backgrounds as was 35 per cent of the intake to other forms of advanced further education and some 40 per cent of entry to colleges of education. The percentage of university entry coming from the working-class has since increased to 27 per cent. By comparison the percentage of university intake from working-class backgrounds in 1961-2 in Sweden was only 14 per cent, in Denmark 10 per cent, in France 8·3 per cent, in West Germany 5·3 per cent and in Switzerland 4 per cent.

The high percentage of university intake drawn in Britain from the working-class probably arose from the system of secondary school organisation, the external examinations system and the generous university grants. There is little doubt that intelligence tests did take into grammar schools high ability working-class boys from deprived homes and deprived schools who would have been rejected if they had been judged solely on their mathematical and English standards. The scholarship examination undoubtedly transferred many of these working-class pupils into a school with an atmosphere of learning which was decisive in influencing their general attitude in a way that a neighbourhood school dominated by lower local standards would rarely achieve.

The higher average ability and even more the higher motivation of the middle-class means that there are whole neighbourhoods which take for granted the aim of higher education for all. There are very many working-class boys brighter than the average middle-class boy but their lower motivation needs compensation by early placement in the right school environment. This the grammar school did, but the new comprehensive schools, which are really neighbourhood schools, will reflect the educational and career expectations of their neighbourhoods and may fail to provide many bright working-class pupils with the opportunities they had under the bipartite system.

In a town with four areas, three working-class and one middle and upper-class there will not be four equal neighbourhood comprehensive schools but three secondary modern schools with GCE streams and one grammar school with a Certificate of Secondary Education stream, an examination of lower standard and esteem than the GCE. A headmaster of a 1,300-strong Newcastle comprehensive school pointed out in 1969 that since his school was serving a deprived area his school's annual intake of 240 pupils included only twenty boys with an intelligence quotient of 120 or above, that is of university potential, but included eighty-two boys with an intelligence quotient of below 89, of more or less C stream modern school ability. Yet a comprehensive school of the same size in the same city in a middle-class area enrolled in the same year eighty-five pupils with an intelligence quotient of 120 or above in its intake of 240 but only twenty-eight with intelligence quotients below 89. There is no doubt that in the following years, unless unpopular and restrictive movement of pupils were insisted upon by that authority, the advantaged school would gain an even better intake because middle-class parents would move into its catchment area and working-class parents with ambition for their children would struggle and save to do the same. The atmosphere of these two schools will be completely different—like a see-saw, the weight of pupils' average ability will be decisive on the norms and expectations of the schools. A bright working-class pupil will be less likely to develop to his full potential in the first school than in the second whereas on the bipartite system he would automatically have entered a school with academic pretensions. Boys particularly are very much beings of social groups and they are influenced by the attitude of their peers as to what is expected of them. Revolt against the dominant group can mean isolation and misery. J. W. B. Douglas wrote in 1963:

'Pupils of high ability leave comprehensive schools at an earlier age than those of similar ability in other maintained schools. . . . It is the boys and girls themselves who differ in their aspirations and they do so dramatically. Only 29 per cent of the comprehensive school pupils of high ability wish to continue with full-time higher education after leaving school, compared with 60 per cent of the pupils at other maintained schools.[14]

The study of neighbourhood so-called comprehensive schools and their effect upon house prices could become part of any course of study for estate agents. In Inner London, the old boroughs of Chelsea, Hampstead and Lewisham had a proportion of non-manual workers to manual workers six times as high as had Bermondsey and Bethnal Green and surveys carried out in the various boroughs showed that the proportion of children of grammar school ability to dull or backward children varied in roughly the same proportion. Neighbourhood comprehensive schools in these areas will be enormously different.

Inner London and other areas have attempted to equalise the intake to comprehensive schools by keeping the eleven-plus examination, by dividing, according to results, the children into several bands of ability, and allocating the same spread of ability intake to each school. If this were to be rigidly insisted upon, then all the schools in a town might have an intake of equal ability. But banding is unpopular with parents and teachers, as witnessed by the storm of opposition it brought at Haringey, and if ability is unevenly distributed within a town then banding could work only by obliging pupils to travel over considerable distances. Such 'bussing' would be very unpopular.

Other towns have divided the catchment area of comprehensive schools on a pie pattern with the neighbourhood areas being in the shape of a slice of the pie with the school placed in an intermediate position between the inner city slums and the outer suburbs. This is the system advocated by Harold Simmons, a Bristol head. To succeed it requires a town of reasonable size and bus routes in and out of the city centre in more or less straight lines. Manchester has drawn names by lot for oversubscribed schools, and Rotherham applied a similar system for one oversubscribed girls' school. One other authority claims to allocate by computer, but this means nothing unless we know the conditions fed into this machine.[15]

Whichever system of secondary school recruitment is adopted there is little doubt that middle-class parents will make every endeavour to get their children into a favoured school. They are

[14] J. W. B. Douglas, *All Our Future* (Peter Davies), 1968, p. 63.

[15] Bedfordshire may use a computer to fill state-aided places at four public and direct grant schools after parents have applied for their children and their teachers have vouchsafed their suitability. *TES*, 14 May 1971.

the parents most likely to understand, and if necessary frighten, the bureaucratic educational administrators, they mix with the officials who decide the marginal cases and they speak the same language as the senior officers.

Once a comprehensive school becomes favoured in intake or achievement it grows by feeding upon its own success. It will be able to attract and retain a higher calibre of graduate staff since the genuine academic teacher will wish to teach sixth-form pupils who are capable of high achievement and no system of financial allowances will encourage a self-respecting academic graduate to teach in a school of low attainment. The shortage of graduate staff is such that there are not enough graduates, never mind good graduates, to staff every secondary school, particularly in mathematical and scientific subjects. In 1968 there was only 0·82 of a chemistry graduate teacher available for every 1,000 pupils in comprehensive schools, and the shortage of mathematicians and physicists is even more acute. Such teachers will choose the most satisfactory neighbourhoods in which to live and teach, and the bright pupils in poor neighbourhood comprehensive schools will be further deprived of educational opportunities.

Thus the eleven-plus objective test may come to be looked back upon as the lost defence mechanism of the working-class pupil without which the bright pupils from poor homes will be handicapped if not destroyed by the low standards of the poor neighbourhood comprehensive schools. Meanwhile the middle-class parent will rejoice that his duller son or daughter who would have failed the eleven-plus examination can now go to a neighbourhood comprehensive school, and he can celebrate his good fortune by starting a campaign against streaming to ensure that his slower offspring may not suffer any social stigma because of their allocation to a C or D stream. Equality of opportunity will have declined further when residence, that is income, is used to select children for the better State schools.

The variation of standards between area schools reminds one that the search for full equality of opportunity is as unlikely to be successful as was the search for the holy grail even if its pursuit is equally enjoyed by the egalitarian knights of the present time. The variation of educational standards does not occur only within towns but may occur between towns, between town and country areas, and between the north and south of the country. In the past, the expectation that grammar school pupils should normally achieve a minimum of five 'O' levels at least acted as a determinant of grammar school standards.

Towns like Bournemouth have a much higher proportion of pupils staying on beyond the school leaving age and successfully sitting external examinations than have northern towns like Gateshead. Thus the prevailing ethos of schools in the two towns will be completely different. The 1969 survey on the reading ability of London's children commissioned by the Inner London Education Authority shows that inner London's pupils, despite the generosity of staffing allowed by the LEA, read much less well than the average for the country. Whether this arises from the concentration of first generation immigrants or the movement of the more affluent and ambitious parents to the suburbs is not known but it means that brighter pupils in central London, by virtue of the lower average expectations in their schools, could be deprived compared with brighter pupils attending outer London schools in areas of higher school expectations.

If under the second test, a comprehensive school system brought more pupils through to a pass standard in 'O' and 'A' level GCEs one could at least argue that through their philosophy and efficiency such schools had widened educational opportunity irrespective of which class of society the extra passes came from. Many such claims have been made by the supporters of comprehensive schools but they were effectively demolished by the late R. R. Pedley in 1969 and John Todd in 1970.[16] It will be interesting to see whether the full-scale investigation of the National Foundation for Educational Research, which is to be completed by 1974, will throw more light on the comparative successes of selective and non-selective secondary education.

Equality of opportunity applies not only to the average pupil but to the very brightest and to those most backward academically. 'Equality for all' must not mean 'average opportunity for all', if its claims are to be taken seriously. There are as many pupils with an intelligence quotient of 150 to 200 as there are below 50, and both need special care. If it is generally accepted that pupils with an IQ below 50 have no place in an ordinary school because they are basically ineducable then a similar case could be made out for children with an IQ over 150 who undoubtedly need a special school curriculum and speed of study. There has recently been more concern expressed for such pupils and it has been hinted that they often pass unnoticed in an ordinary school class where being so bright they buy peace with their teachers and their fellows by contracting out of their lessons and just drifting

[16] Black Paper 2, *Critical Quarterly*, 1969; Black Paper 3, *Critical Quarterly*, 1970.

M

along.[17] One wonders what happens these days to boys like J. S. Mill, Jeremy Bentham and Lord Macaulay who had the advantages of private tuition of a high order. Professor Cyril Burt described how he discovered in London schools half a dozen children with IQs of 180 or over, unrecognised by their teachers; nearly all of whom later rose to eminence in business, literature or science. There is every argument for removing such pupils after suitable testing from ordinary schools and placing them together under the most intelligent teachers. Unless such action is taken, equality of opportunity for such pupils will be nothing but a bitter farce.

There is every evidence that under the bipartite system in Britain the education given to the academically very able children was exceedingly good. In the postwar period, Britain has been awarded more Nobel Prizes for science and literature per head of population than any other major country. In the 1967 mathematical schools olympiad the British team came fourth out of the twelve participating countries. It is noteworthy that the boys were drawn from Edward VI's School, Stafford; Manchester Grammar School; Winchester; and Eton. The first three places in the olympiad were taken by Russia, East Germany and Hungary, all of which countries maintain highly selective schools for their more able children. The International Study of Achievement in Mathematics by Professor T. Hüsen of the University of Stockholm lists twelve countries in order of achievement according to the standards of those studying mathematics at sixth-form level, and only Israel was superior to this country. The Swedish mean score was only 80 per cent and the American mean score only 40 per cent of the British score. It does not appear that there was any lack of educational opportunity and achievement in Britain under the bipartite system, direct grant and public school system.

Concern for educational opportunity for the academically very dull is necessary under any system of justice and equal citizenship. Is it likely that in a comprehensive school the security and careful teaching offered to these pupils can equal that offered under the bipartite system? I have always been both impressed and humbled by the concern and the excellent teaching offered to such pupils in the best of our secondary modern schools. If staff in the comprehensive school are expected

[17] Professor Robert Green to MENSA members, 13 December 1970. In 1965 the National Association for Gifted Children was formed to cater for parents of the estimated 2 per cent of children with exceptional gifts. Also see M. L. Kellmer Pringle, *Able Misfits* (Longmans Studies in Child Development Series), 1970.

to teach at all levels of ability as well as all year groups then the duller pupil may easily lose out since the teaching of backward pupils is of as specialised a nature as is sixth-form teaching to the very bright. Neither must the backward pupils be rushed back and forth at lesson bells in a huge school. If, alternatively, the backward pupils in the comprehensive school are put under specialised teachers and have their own rooms what advantages are to be claimed for them from comprehensive education?

I think that these advantages are two. Those who quickly overcome their difficulties, following the skilled diagnosis of a specialised handicap, can be quickly moved into the main school and may even move on to advanced academic work with no need to change school. The second advantage is that by wearing the uniform of a school taking all types of pupils they can face the world proudly, and in many cases they will obtain a much better job when they leave school than they could have obtained if they had attended a specialised school for the less able. This is particularly true since most professions and employers tend to aim at recruiting entrants with educational qualifications higher than are really required for the work to be performed. The less able pupil recruited because of attending a respected comprehensive school will painstakingly and loyally hold down a job which because of boredom would be done less effectively by a more academically-gifted operative.

I have been struck by the fact that while I have often thought the level of education received by the less able pupil in the comprehensive school was inferior to that which they would have received in a specialised group in a secondary modern school with a poor intake yet the morale of these boys and their parents can be very much higher. What boy or girl would wish to go out at night, still less apply for a job, wearing the uniform of a school for remedials? It is because of the effect on the morale of the pupil that it is often a good move for children in educationally sub-normal schools to transfer into general comprehensive schools for the last year or so of their schooling, provided that the schools have special units in which to place them. Equality of educational opportunity is one aspect of their life but if they receive it in a specialised institution for educational sub-normals it may not confer equality of opportunity when they come to apply for employment in trades in which they could succeed. Thus the advantages of small specialised schools for educationally sub-normal pupils and small C streams in secondary modern schools for less able pupils must be weighed against the greater status and employment opportunities of attending a large comprehensive school.

The case for the comprehensive secondary school is on balance not proved in terms of educational opportunity. The range of types and intake and philosophy of comprehensive secondary schools in this country is so wide that it is difficult to generalise about them. Their intake depends upon whether the local education committee has a fully comprehensive policy, the number of local direct grant and voluntary aided grammar schools, and the particular catchment area of the school. The form of comprehensive organisation depends more upon administrative convenience than educational principle since the Labour Governments from 1964–70 pressed for comprehensive reorganisation without voting the money for the building programmes to make this effectively possible. Thus the ingenuity of chief education officers was taxed to devise systems of comprehensive education which would fit the school buildings they already had. Just as it was always amazing under the bipartite system to find that the number of pupils suitable for an academic education in any year filled exactly the number of grammar school places available so it was similarly amazing to see chief education officers advocating as the *ideal* comprehensive system that which could be made to fit their existing buildings. Circular 10/65 recognised six different types of comprehensive school, in 1968 the National Foundation's survey discovered twelve types and the Comprehensive Schools Committee claims to distinguish twenty-one types.

It is possible that the 5–9, 9–13, 13–18 school organisation has considerable merit provided that the 9–13 school is not too permeated by primary school play methods, but transfer of 14-year old pupils between one school and another seems to have severe disadvantages in that a maximum of two years only remain before pupils sit external examinations. If two or three schools with different teaching methods and indeed syllabi feed into one school at fourteen, then it will take the best part of a year to bring the pupils to the same level in the same classes and only one year will be left for the GCE 'O' or CSE course. Such pupils must be educationally disadvantaged compared with the rest of the country and pupils from a 11–14 school not following the same syllabi as the 14–18 school will be further disadvantaged compared with pupils in a 11–14 school with syllabi like that of the senior school. The only fair way of ensuring educational equality of opportunity between two or three 11–14 schools feeding into one 14–18 school is to make the head of the 14–18 school the overall head of the three or four schools, in full charge of organisation and syllabi, while his senior master remains in daily charge of the 14–18 school. The philosophies of different comprehensive schools vary far more than do those of grammar schools or modern schools. The grammar school has an established ethos aiming at five 'O' levels and two 'A' level GCE passes and wide internal and sporting activities. The modern school originally had a set ethos in that it provided basic literacy and numeracy, and trained people for ordinary working jobs. This was changed somewhat when certain modern schools began to aim at 'O' level and even 'A' level courses for their brighter pupils, and parents began to differentiate between schools accordingly. The comprehensive schools vary enormously between tightly-organised and streamed schools aiming at high academic success for the great majority of their pupils and with high standards of cultural activities and effective sports organisation to schools which are creatures of social engineers, where slogans like 'liberation' and 'life orientations' are used to hide their pathetic academic results and poor cultural standards from public view. These latter schools boast of values like 'good fellowship' and 'community concern' as if these were the exclusive products of non-academic schools rather than the ancillary virtues of all good schools. The significance to the pupil of attending a comprehensive school with one type of intake, organisation, and ethos instead of another differing from it in all respects, may become as important as success or failure in an eleven-plus examination with a 10 per cent error in selection or residence in an authority with a 5 or 50 per cent grammar school intake.

The future of secondary school organisation in Britain is still undetermined. Will some areas retain a full bipartite system with a 20 per cent selection rate for grammar schools? There may be a movement towards acceptance of a 5 per cent direct grant and state grammar school selection. This would be, perhaps, the best temporary solution for the country, since it would retain highly academic schools against which the results of comprehensive schools could be judged. Any move to retain any selection will be opposed by the egalitarian members of the comprehensive schools' lobby. They will declare that any selection which removes some of the most highly intelligent from the comprehensive schools will be seriously detrimental to the development of these schools, and that to succeed all these schools need their full share of top ability pupils. It is amazing that this argument should come from the very people who have rebutted any belief in hereditary intelligence and the eleven-plus system. All children are apparently equal until the comprehensive schools are deprived of their brightest pupils.

It is possible that there may be a move towards specialist comprehensive schools in mathematics, linguistics, science, art and music rather on the lines of those developing in Eastern Europe and Russia. It is perhaps symbolic that in 1970 the ILEA opened in the new Pimlico Comprehensive School a musical wing which will draw the most able musicians from all over the ILEA area. If one can recognise that at the age of eleven there are specific musical gifts then one cannot deny that there are pupils with pronounced mathematical, linguistic and even general academic qualities.

There may also be a move towards secondary school courses after the age of thirteen dividing between academic and craft-based subjects on a mixture of parental choice and examination. I should imagaine that some 50 per cent would then follow each course. If independent schools are not abolished there could be a great increase in their numbers as parents opted in large numbers out of the poorer city comprehensive schools.

Graham Savage, the Education Officer of the London County Council Education Committee (the precursor of ILEA) said in 1944: 'Put them [the children] altogether and stream like mad'. There was a period when certain large comprehensive schools with an intake of up to 400 pupils a year divided each teaching group by ability from A to N if there were fourteen teaching classes in the year. There has, however, over the last few years been a movement away from streaming until today even the assertion of Bertrand Russell that it is the height of cruelty to teach bright and dull pupils together would be disputed by some teachers and educational writers. This movement against tight streaming has influenced grammar and modern as well as comprehensive schools. It was indeed the fact that tight streaming showed up the failure of some grammar school 'C' and 'D' streams to achieve 'O' level results at all compatible with the targets of a grammar school education of 5 'O' level and 2 'A' level passes and the behaviour problems of the notorious 'C' stream secondary modern school pupils which first threw doubts on the wisdom of dividing children in any way. No one objected to the excellent results of the grammar school 'A' streams or the rising expectations and successes of the modern school 'A' streams.

Girls' grammar schools began to unstream first but since their pupils normally all had IQs of 110 upwards this was still equivalent to dividing a comprehensive school into three, four, or five bands of ability. Similarly, certain ILEA comprehensive schools which claimed to unstream received pupils only from what was effectively the bottom 50 per cent of the ability range, and even they maintained a backward stream or made special provision for backward pupils. In neither case did this mean having pupils from an IQ of 70, or below, to 140, or above, in one class. Now this ultimate aim of non-streaming pupils of all abilities is being advocated by the TUC and certain sections of the Labour Party. It is fascinating that trade unions with their clear divisions between skilled and unskilled workers and their tight apprenticeship regulations limiting entry to their crafts have the effrontery to talk about non-streaming on grounds of equality. It is also of interest that remedial groups for backward pupils are still advocated. One is permitted to go slower and be academically duller and receive special treatment, but no special provision is to be permitted for the bright who must presumably be slowed down to the average, since like the fast worker in industry, they are a threat to the slower pace and self-satisfaction of the average. It is also interesting that these small groups for backward pupils are called remedial groups. No one objects to the name remedial if by remedial action pupils can be helped to learn more quickly but many of the backward are backward because of low hereditary intelligence and no remedial action will quicken their pace. This misuse of words lends the present educational controversies a distinct 1984 flavour.

Most comprehensive schools still divide their intake into three bands of ability, an A band, a B band and a remedial or backward band. If each of these bands is not to function as a separate school it is essential that all bands cover the same subjects and syllabi but at different depths, otherwise transfer between bands will be difficult to make. Highbury Grove School transferred 17 per cent between bands between entry at the age of eleven and the end of the third year, a figure which exceeds the recognised error in the eleven-plus examination.

To band pupils as soon as they arrive in a comprehensive school on the recommendations of their primary schools could be most unfair. Both quality and stability of staffing and the type of intake vary greatly between primary schools. In one school a boy may have had a succession of different teachers, most of them incompetent. Heads' assessments of pupils' abilities are again conditioned by the average standard of their schools—a boy rated very highly from a school of poor-ability intake may have been considered only of average ability if he had attended a school half a mile away in a different housing area. Nor will achievement tests or examinations sat in the first week of entry to the new comprehensive school suffice, because these will often be more a reflection of the teaching competence of the contributory schools rather than the potential ability of the boys tested.

It would appear that before any banding is done, apart from the removal for special diagnostic tests and tuition of those unable to read or number, that there could be an introductory period of a term when the pupils are taught in unstreamed groups on common syllabi. They should then be examined in each subject on what has been taught with each head of department setting and marking for the whole year group. It should also be possible in English and mathematics to test the position progress of all boys against their position on tests in these two subjects sat on the day of entry. This more than the position in the term or year's test will be most useful in English and mathematics in testing potential. Teaching efficiency of teachers taking the unstreamed groups will vary but again, while one can only move towards equality of educational opportunity, it will never be fully achieved.

In this diagnostic term or year teachers will probably teach to the average ability of the groups, giving additional reading to the brighter and additional help to the duller pupils. After the first year or so of the comprehensive school, it is probably inevitable that some form of banding, streaming or setting is introduced if difficult subjects like Latin and Russian are to be taught, if the more difficult but academically more rewarding parts of each subject are to be covered and indeed if the brighter pupils are to be taught at their own speed instead of proceeding at the speed of a sea convoy.

There is really no reason why the very brightest pupils of approximately the same percentile of intake as those withdrawn for remedial and backward teaching, should not be separated for specialised teaching from the time of entry to the school. The enthusiasm of such pupils on joining a new school could then be immediately channelled into the mastery of difficult intellectual topics.

The alternative to some form of banding in the second year, however, is a common detailed curriculum (as against similar syllabi), which cuts out all difficult topics and could cause boredom and the contracting out from lessons of the brighter pupils who find they can keep up with the class while making a minimum effort. Whatever diagnostic method of assessment of potential is used for pupils at the age of eleven it is essential that on a two tier system, with transfer to the senior tier at 14+, there is not another long waiting period before pupils set off at their own pace.

The egalitarian teacher would claim, though with little statistical evidence in his favour, that the teacher of an unstreamed class will not teach to the average level of the class, or even divide the class into small groups working at different speeds, but that he will teach each child as an individual. This, were it possible, would seem a painfully slow and exhausting way of teaching, the very opposite to the economic division of labour. In each lesson of 30 minutes' effective teaching, in a class of thirty pupils each pupil will receive 1 minute's teaching. In a day of eight lessons he will then receive 8 minutes' actual teaching. It would appear that pupils would do better with correspondence courses and pupils from bright home backgrounds would opt for home tuition. Such individual unstreamed teaching certainly seems a method of teaching which will encourage the brighter pupils to rival the truancy figures of the duller pupils, for there would appear little point in regular school attendance. Again, even to teach a pupil effectively for 1 minute a lesson, a teacher must classify pupils in his mind according to their abilities and powers of concentration and how he can keep his information from his pupils is difficult to understand.

The only successful secondary school non-streaming I myself have investigated was limited to a small three-stream northern secondary modern school with a fairly good artisan working-class intake. Here the first year of entry to external examinations of pupils who had been unstreamed for five years brought an increase in the number of GCE 'O' entries and passes beyond the rise in the comparative national figures. There were probably special reasons at work to produce this result. First, there was no grammar school intake and there were no very bright pupils to be held back by non-streaming. Second, a new head was appointed who was a superb teacher and disciplinarian and understood fully the importance of external examination results to his pupils. Third, and most important, it was a small school in a small town where the boys (and in many cases their parents) were well-known to the staff and they could be taught as individuals in a way impossible in a large school in a large conurbation where the very size of school and the rapidity of staff changeover would make the teaching of pupils as known individuals impossible. The experience of this one school again shows that good teachers can work any system. It does not mean, after one localised success, that here is a system that can be transplanted to every part of the country.

Julienne Ford has suggested after studying two unidentified schools that streaming often reflects the class structure of the school.[18] This need not necessarily be so, if there is a diagnostic period, if there is a social structure different from the academic structure of the school, and if there is easy movement between bands or streams to allow for what are the varying performances and developments of individual pupils. Nor, if there is a strong House structure, need all friendships arise from the academic groups in which a pupil is taught, although many friendships will inevitably arise from shared intellectual interests. If pupils register in their Houses in unstreamed inter-year tutor groups and spend their leisure time in their Houses before school, in their breaks, eat lunch, and have clubs and games there in the evening, then they will see the academic bands simply as teaching units for a specialised task like soccer or cricket teams in sport. Reports and parental contacts should similarly come from the House. It is then very likely that friendships will arise in the House bridging year and teaching groups. I have often found in Highbury Grove that pupils could identify another person's House and tutor group but not his teaching band or class. Since in each of the second and third years of 240 boys each, there are three parallel A classes, four parallel B classes and two C classes it is little wonder that a boy does not know the teaching group of many of his acquaintances. Nor, to be successful, need each band have an equal share from each social class represented in the school. This would be the height of unfairness since genetic factors, even apart from environmental influences, would make it likely that a higher proportion of the middle- and professional-class children were in higher streams or bands. Strangely enough, we have in Highbury Grove a higher proportion of the middle- and professional-class children in the B than the A bands but this is due to the pattern of entry from middle-class areas where very bright children are sent distances to renowned direct grant and day public schools while their duller brothers apply for a highly respected comprehensive school.

It has been alleged that educational opportunity is lessened because children in the lower streams of comprehensive (and

[18] J. Ford, *Social Class and the Comprehensive School* (Routledge & Kegan Paul), 1969.

perhaps all types of schools) have the poorest teachers. If, by poorest teachers, one means those with least academic qualifications, this could easily be true, but academic teachers are not necessarily the best teachers by temperament, qualifications, or interest for the less able pupils. A good College of Education trained teacher or a man trained under the Emergency Training Scheme after service in the Second World War is often better equipped to understand the problems of the less able and help them to overcome their difficulties than is an academic teacher with a doctorate in Medieval English Literature or an obscure foreign language. Similarly a College of Education trained teacher who failed his 'A' levels is unlikely to be of great use in teaching sixth form work. The idea that all teachers, irrespective of training and qualifications, must take an equal share of all classes is rather like China's cultural revolution where intellectuals were put to field labour. If a highly qualified graduate were given against his will a timetable heavily weighted in favour of teaching the backward classes, then it would be likely that he would leave the teaching profession as would a poorly qualified College of Education trained teacher set to teach for Oxbridge opens.

In a comprehensive school and to a lesser extent in grammar and modern schools a decision will have to be made at the end of the third year (age 14+) as to the external examination a pupil will aim at and the subjects he should take. This need for a 14+ assessment has been severely criticised in recent years. The syllabi of the GCE 'O' levels and the CSE are often very different in content as well as in type of examination. This demands an assessment of a pupil's potential at fourteen as to what he or she is likely to achieve at sixteen. As long as the GCE 'O' was taken only by the top 20 per cent ability pupils and the CSE by the next 20 per cent this was not very serious, but now pupils in the top 40 per cent of the ability groups sit GCE 'O' and pupils in the second 20 per cent and the next 40 per cent ability groups sit CSE. This means that there is a great difficulty in the second 20 per cent ability group in choosing at the age of fourteen the examination to be sat at the age of sixteen.

This difficulty has caused the Socialist Education Association, the NUT and the Schools Council to advocate one examination at the age of sixteen. This would be disastrous as no one 16+ examination will be suitable to pupils whose ability varies from the potential Oxbridge scholar to those bordering on the ineducable. Any such examination paper must either be an insult to the very intelligent or the ultimate depressive to the non-academically gifted pupil. There should be more overlap of syllabi between the two examinations so that pupils could move from one to the other with little difficulty, and more overlapping grades between the two examinations so that it did not matter as much which was sat by a pupil. Some dozen grades of GCE 'O' pass, four of which overlapped with the top grades of the CSE, and a dozen grades in the CSE examination, four of which overlapped with the bottom grades of the GCE 'O' would make the position sufficiently flexible while preserving two different levels of examination.

The widening in the choice of subjects in the fourth and fifth year courses demands that a decision on subject options as well as level of examination has to be made at the end of the third year of the secondary school course. There was a time when all pupils were expected to take the same spread of subjects with minor options in art, craft and music. Now with additional subjects like commerce and economics and with pupils in a comprehensive school usually taking fewer subjects than in a grammar school, choices have to be made at the end of the third year. This requires not only examinations but interviews with parents and career officers, and frequent discussions with subject teachers and headmasters. A boy should not just be allowed to keep a rag-bag of subjects because he is good at them, as in the story of the boy who took 'A' level woodwork and religious education and had to become an undertaker. It is doubtful whether there are any advantages in a wide choice of subjects: they simply foster a growth industry of career and subject advisors. A balanced diet of English, mathematics, science (particularly physics), history, geography, art or crafts, and possibly a foreign language should be retained for all reasonably academic pupils so that choice of career is kept as wide as possible. A great variety of options simply encourages the ambitious staff of unscrupulous departments to introduce more fancy subjects and further limit the career choice and the balanced education of pupils.

In the fourth and fifth years it is possible to replace banding by setting, which could further enhance educational opportunity for many pupils. In banding and streaming, pupils are kept together for all or most subjects and go round as a class. In setting, all pupils of the same age go to one subject at the same time, and they are arranged in teaching groups according to their ability in this one subject. Thus all pupils work at their level and speed in every subject. The disadvantage of setting is that teaching groups must re-form at the end of every lesson. Thus regular checks have to be made at each lesson to see whether all pupils are present, and in a large school some pupils may arrive at their next teaching group 7 or 8 minutes after others either because of the distance of their last classroom or because the teacher has dismissed the class late. By the age of fourteen, however, there will be many double periods on the timetable, lesson dodgers will be more easily identifiable and it is likely that the advantages of setting outweigh the disadvantages.

It could be argued that a group of very bright pupils should be kept together in the fourth and fifth years because by virtue of very high intellectual morale they might obtain excellent examination results. It is possible that they could sit their 'O' levels after one year. One could also argue that a remedial or backward group should similarly be kept together and given a different course concentrating on social studies, the life of the area, and additional craft experience. This latter scheme seems to be a way of depriving academically less able boys of any further academic opportunities. To compel such boys to stay on at school instead of leaving and taking a well-paid job which they would prefer, and then to give them an 'outgoing course' in which they are removed from any structured body of knowledge is the ultimate insult, and is the very antithesis of equality of opportunity. Such boys do not require guidance to travel round their own towns, to help decorate rooms for old people, and to fill up sample forms. All this they can adequately manage for themselves: what they need is more not less academic work. The 1968 Schools Council Report on the *Young School Leavers* shows clearly that these pupils and their parents see school as a means of gaining mastery of the 3Rs and other knowledge which will give them a better job when they leave school. To offer less is the height of inequality and unfairness, and they are the first to realise this. After all a university education doubles a graduate's earning power over the rest of his life, CSE, 'O' and 'A' level GCE courses are passports to jobs and earning power and most subjects are studied with such prospects in mind. Michael Young summed up the situation when he wrote:

'These [School's Council Newsom-type] courses, which explicitly deny pupils access to the kinds of knowledge which are associated with rewards, prestige and power in our society are given a kind of legitimacy which masks the fact that educational success in terms of them would be defined as "failure".'

It is possible that the raising of the school leaving age depresses overall equality. Educational achievement is only part of life: 75 per cent of company directors are not university graduates. Many of the least intellectually bright or intellectually motivated who could achieve success and even fame in building up a business or in pop-singing will have these channels closed to them for another year by the raising of the school leaving age. Educationalists and administrators idealise education and think it is the only way of achievement for all men. This is an arrogant assumption for which they and indeed education will not be thanked by the reluctant fifteen to sixteen-year-old school conscript.

Any society concerned for equality of opportunity and standards of achievement must regularly test its pupils and adult trainees. These standards may be altered, there will be no examination which is perfect but to have no external tests or examinations would mean a collapse both of equality of opportunity and of standards. There is a movement afoot these days which opposes this view and neither believes in external examinations nor any restrictions on schools or teachers. This would mean that lady luck took charge completely inside schools since every pupil would depend upon the efficiency, ideals and purpose of each teacher. One teacher of English in one school may not believe in the teaching of formal rules of grammar and punctuation, he may simply believe in encouraging creative writing even if the result is misspelt, untidy, with little grammatical accuracy and centred upon ideas which themselves are not worth expressing. His pupils will be semi-literate. A second teacher of English may believe in the cult of the beautiful people, the Noble Savage and of primitivism and his pupils will be completely illiterate. A third teacher of English will be zealous in all forms of written instruction, realising with responsibility that he is turning his pupils out into a real world which usually demands certain standards before people are able to earn a good living, and his pupils will be literate and much sought after by employers.

Without external examinations, employers will seek employees from the highly respected schools and from families known to them—nepotism and the old boys' act will replace equality of opportunity. At the moment the bright boy from the deprived and ill-respected school can show his GCE or CSE certificate to prove his suitability for appointment, while the lack of such a certificate indicates the unsuitability of the dull boy attending a well-respected school. This defence of merit and opportunity would disappear if external examinations were withdrawn, and the bright working-class boy would be a prisoner of his school's reputation, unable to compete for appointment with the boy wearing the favoured school tie.

To the egalitarian, examinations, in so far as they show differences between pupils, are an evil force. There must be no academic élite. Indeed it has been suggested that there must be no sporting or any other form of élite—all appointments must be by structured random selection made by the ruling mandarins, themselves presumably chosen by balanced or random selection by some computer.[19]

The egalitarians are obviously not just in revolt against school organisation but are at war with the whole concept of modern competitive society and they are using the children in the schools as cannon fodder for their destructive purposes. Mr D. Marsden writes we 'must seek positive unstreaming, a common curriculum and teaching methods to promote a new co-operative atmosphere'.[20] Mr. Edward Short, late Secretary of State for Education and Science, has declared that schools were undemocratic and industry was undemocratic and that 'An élitist, class-ridden society needs an élitist class-ridden system'.[21] There is no reason why we should allow such people to determine the way our schools should be organised when it is to the obvious disadvantage of the pupils, of the schools, and of our society as a whole.

There is a move towards internal assessment externally moderated to replace the present pattern of external examinations. Our present experience with such methods gives reason for suspicion as to their effectiveness and validity. Under the Mode III of the CSE teachers may draw up their own syllabi which are then accepted by the CSE boards and the examinations are internally set and marked but externally moderated. The fact that in 1970 only 2·9 per cent of the total entries under the Metropolitan Examinations Board of the CSE were under this system points to the conclusion that practising teachers, as against those who spend their days sitting on regional and national committees, are opposed to such innovations.

Nor is the experience of the Joint Matriculation Board's experiment with a similar scheme of school assessment in English

[19] *See* Frances Stevens, *The New Inheritors* (Hutchinson Educational), 1970, pp. 119–20, 141–2.

[20] D. Marsden, 'How comprehensives missed the Tide' in D. Rubinstein and C. Stoneman, *Education for Democracy* (Penguin), 1970.

[21] Speech in House of Commons, 21 April 1971.

GCE 'O' level more auspicious. In co-operation with a group of schools in Yorkshire the Board provide for such ordinary level passes in English to be awarded without the evidence of formal examinations of any kind. The grades awarded under this scheme were based entirely on externally-moderated school assessments of written work made in the final year of the ordinary level course, and formal test results played no part at all. Since the pass rates of all such entrants averaged between 91·9 and 94 per cent in each year between 1965 and 1969, as against between 55·5 and 68·6 per cent in the formal set examinations in other schools, it is no wonder that the Board in its third report on the scheme published in August 1970 could write, 'it is pleasant to note from the high percentage of successful candidates' that the pupils 'seem for the most part to have thrived on it'.[22] One wonders whether outside employers and professional bodies would so freely accept these pupils' passes if they knew how they had been obtained. It seems that one's equality of opportunity is increased if one's school sits such examinations! In Western Germany with no national external examinations only 6 per cent of the working-class pupils pass the Abitur examination—this is a warning of the class bias which could enter our system of education if external examinations were removed.

In recent years there has been considerable discussion of the sixth form curriculum, and the arrival of the so-called non-academic sixth former in comprehensive sixth forms has been used as an excuse to try to upset the courses of study for the academic sixth former. The three 'A' level course with the variety of liberal studies available probably means that the standard of university entrants in this country is the highest in the world. Each suggestion for the alteration of this course has so far been rejected by the teaching profession. Another of these suggestions, for three 'normals' and two 'furthers' at the age of eighteen was suggested by a committee of the Schools Council in May, 1970. It was but another attempt to dilute the sixth form academic curriculum in an attempt to help the weaker candidates not destined for university courses. The academic sixth former wishes to specialise in the sixth and really master in depth certain fields of learning while the non-academic sixth former wishes either to resit CSE or 'O' levels, which he has failed in the fifth, or to study 'O' levels after reasonable success in the CSE examination. If some of these non-academic sixth formers see such examination successes as a

[22] Joint Matriculation Board, 'An Experimental Scheme of School Assessment in Ordinary Level English Language, 3rd Report', August 1970.

prelude to further school study and not as an immediate passport to some outside employment then they can commence the normal 'A' level two year course after they have passed at a satisfactory standard their CSE and 'O' levels. For many of them, however, the new Certificate of Extended Education would be more suitable and could probably well be sat at a College of Further Education. There have always been in the sixth form boys taking 'A' levels in some subject such as art in which they have a particular gift while they were picking up 'O' levels—the system has always been interpreted flexibly in most schools.

Any weakening of the academic excellence of the 'A' level course in pursuit of chimerical opportunities for the non-academic sixth former would be disastrous. The great rejoicings with which the non-academic sixth former has been received by education officials and spokesmen speaks more for the easing of a guilt complex about the privileged upbringing of men now concerned to worship at the shrine of equality than it does for their hard assessment of the value of the projected sixth form courses to the student or society. If the new sixth former is there not to take additional qualifications but because he cannot think of anything else to do, because he is afraid of the world of work, or because he thinks education is something that rubs off on him without effort after a number of years, then his greatest service to education will be in inflating the salaries of his headmaster and the senior staff. If for some strange reason new courses need to be evolved for such pupils then the place for them is probably in the Colleges of Further Education with their closer contact with the world of work.

The establishment of a number of sixth form colleges which have imposed a minimum academic standard on entry, generally of five 'O' levels, is itself a pointer that certain authorities have doubts about the place of the non-academic sixth former and are concerned for the maintenance of academic standards. Sixth form colleges, themselves a product of comprehensive reorganisation, have been supported as a means of furthering academic opportunities for the maximum of pupils by the careful husbanding of highly qualified specialist staff who are in short supply. There can be no equality of opportunity if pupils in one school lack specialised teachers, and comprehensive reorganisation by increasing the number of sixth forms has been instrumental in lessening equality of opportunity. Just as the standards of the eleven-plus intake reflected in many cases the standards of the primary schools and the calibre of their teaching staffs, so do

N

fifth and sixth form examination results. Equality of educational opportunity would be more helped by a better qualified teaching staff than by any scheme of comprehensive reorganisation, and the continuing shortage of highly qualified staff to teach sixth formers in science and mathematics may eventually force the spread of sixth form colleges.

It is concern with the standards of schools and the qualities of teaching staff that still cause parents to pay fees for the schooling of their children in an attempt to increase their opportunities in life. Of pupils in Britain $5\frac{1}{2}$ per cent are in private and public schools and another $1\frac{1}{2}$ per cent are educated in direct grant schools. Thus opportunities for some pupils are greater than for others. The bright pupil within reach of a direct grant school and the son or daughter of rich parents can opt out of their neighbourhood comprehensive school unlike duller and poorer boys who have no choice but to go to the nearest school. Thus British society is faced by a choice on how to further equality of opportunity: to increase choice for more parents or to lessen choice for the 7 per cent.

The Labour Party intends to move to restrict choice for the 7 per cent despite the fact that the rich can further evade the system by buying residences near the most respected day schools. The Donnison Commission recommended that all direct grant schools should join the state comprehensive system or go fully independent. Mr Edward Short has since confirmed that the Labour Party if returned to power in 1970 would have insisted on this choice being made by all direct grant schools by 1973. The Labour Party's educational programme published in 1973 moved further to abolish all independent schools and declared: 'Our aim is to abolish fee-paying schools and to bring all children of compulsory school age under the national education system'. It called for the winding up of the small, highly privileged, independent sector', whose influence it quotes from the Newsom Report as being 'divisive'.Three years earlier Miss Alice Bacon had told the 1970 Labour Party Conference that the 1966–70 Labour Government had been considering a licensing system for independent schools under which licences would have been granted only where a school fulfilled an educational need which could not be met by the maintained system. No school, whether recognised as efficient or not, would have been permitted to exist without a licence granted by the Secretary of State, and this would run for only a few years.

If a future British Government prohibited private school fees it would be the first non-totalitarian country to have adopted such a measure. As I have written elsewhere:

'Effective egalitarianism will not be achieved however, until all parents are prohibited from all forms of additional educational help to their children, for example buying gramophone records, books, tutors, correspondence courses, television sets with BBC-2, or even talking to their offspring. Perhaps there will be 20th century 'tutor holes' to rival the 'priest holes' of the 16th and 17th centuries with police and troops searching them out.'[23]

Thus the Labour Party gave notice that freedom of choice of parents not to have a foreign holiday, not to run one or two cars, but instead to buy private education for their children because they considered this would be a more worthwhile expenditure, would be curtailed. The fall of the first selective grammar school before an egalitarian onslaught was the beginning of the end for Eton. R. H. S. Crossman made this clear years ago when he said, 'The grammar school cap is a more potent emblem of privilege than the public school tie ever was'. The attempt to prohibit private education is an outcome of a levelling-down not a levelling-up philosophy, of the destroyers not the builders. It would not only lessen educational opportunities and bring a decline in standards but it would further increase the power of the state and the ruling bureaucracy.

Dr James Kay told Gladstone in 1838 that when instruction was given gratuitously

'the parent surrenders the right of interfering as to the quality and extent of the instruction which shall be given to his child, and that in point of fact he places himself in that respect in the position of a pauper, who is to be treated according to the will of others, and not his own.'

Since that time state education, now costing in 1973 some £3,000,000,000 a year, has come to be truly organised by the will of others, not the parents, but it is not gratuitous since it is paid for by these same parents in direct and indirect taxation. The real alternative, both to the Labour Party's projected state monopoly of education and the limited choice of the present time, is to pass choice back to many more parents so that they, through their free choice, can ensure that their children obtain full educational opportunities, which is certainly not the case when, as now, 37 per

[23] *Education. A Framework for Choice*, 2nd ed. (The Institute of Economic Affairs), 1970, pp. xiii–xiv.

cent of secondary school mathematical instruction is given by teachers who are without either a degree or a College of Education qualification in mathematics or physics![24]

The answer is simple. For each son or daughter of school age the state should give parents a voucher exchangeable only for their education either in the state or private system. The voucher would be equal to the average cost of primary or secondary school places in the previous year—in 1972 this was £110 for primary school pupils, £205 for secondary school pupils and £300 for sixth formers. Parents could, where they wished, add money to these vouchers to buy private education. The results of such a voucher system would be dramatic: hundreds of thousands of parents could operate choice and buy for their children the education that they desired, and the state schools would have to respond to parents' demands for the maximum opportunity for their children or they would empty—no longer would they be a prey to every whim of fashion of the so-called experts.

The combination of fee-paying and scholarship pupils in the pre-1944 grammar school system and in the existing direct grant system is an ideal combination of those who come from environments concerned with improvement and of brilliant boys from all backgrounds. Ultimate equality of opportunity is impossible to achieve and the stability and security of society is equally important. This country has been a strange but potent mixture of aristocracy, plutocracy, and meritocracy. Standards of excellence must be retained within maximum equality of opportunity for improvement. There is no reason why through the voucher system there should not develop a large private sector of grammar-type schools made up of scholarship winners at the voucher cost and fee payers who paid additionally to the voucher some £50 per annum for day schools or much more for boarding schools. This £50 could be afforded by some 80 per cent of our families.

The threat to standards and true equality of education has now moved to the sixteen-plus examination, to the eighteen-plus, and to university entry. If all pupils are to go to the same institution at eleven-plus because selection is held to be a bad principle, why should not all pupils enter the sixth form, or indeed go on to university, without any form of selection? If streaming or selection within the comprehensive school is wrong why can it be right at sixth form level or indeed at university? This principle that previous results and potential ability tests are all equally

[24] Statement of Department of Education and Science in reply to the Institute of Mathematics and Its Application, 1970.

unimportant is now enshrined in the arrangements for the Open University. Not only is the amount of study required for an Open University degree at 20 hours a week over three years one-half of that expected on a full-time university course but entrants for courses are not chosen on academic qualifications, suitability for study, and 'stickability' but simply because they are the first who apply within a quota of geographical area and occupation.

Christopher Price, Labour MP and educational correspondent of the *New Statesman*, expressed such views clearly at the 1970 Labour Party Conference:

'If the 11-plus examination was wrong so was the 14-plus, the 16-plus, the 18-plus and the filtering and selection mechanism for university and higher level education.

Miss Jennie Lee had produced the right idea by starting the Open University with no entry qualifications. The principle of the Open University should be applied to the whole of the higher education system and the Labour Party should adopt the slogan of higher education for all. This would be a good policy for the next 10 to 20 years.'

It would be interesting to ask Mr Price what policy he would follow after 10–20 years. If no longer in education brick was to be placed upon brick, if existing qualifications and judged potential no longer mattered and all people of a set age could join a course, then the complete collapse of our educational standards and our culture would follow. Presumably no one need be able to write his name before he joined an honours degree course in classics or mathematics or history. This is not equality of educational opportunity but an equal opportunity for all to join in the destruction of our learned civilisation.

Mr Dick Scorer, a Labour Parliamentary candidate and a Professor of Mathematics at London University, at the same Labour Conference, followed this philosophy to its conclusion by condemning degree examinations when he said, 'The 18-plus examinations were just as bad as the 11-plus and so were the degree examinations'. With no qualifications for course entry and no examinations at their end, anyone might set up as a doctor, a veterinary surgeon, an accountant, or an engineer.

It is against such a background that Lord Bowden, Principal of the Manchester Institute of Science and Technology wrote:

'As far as we are concerned, the rigour of the scientific disciplines has been unimpaired by 'progressive education.' If a man wants to learn how to design a suspension bridge or to remove an appendix, he has to accept traditional discipline and submit himself to formal examination, before he can be let loose in the world.'

At the very time that supporters of comprehensive schools are becoming suspicious of their size which brings a lack of contact and tends to turn many teachers into bureaucrats, Jack Straw, then President of the National Union of Students, advocated at the Annual NUS Conference in 1970 the amalgamation of universities, polytechnics and colleges of education into vast new 'polyversities'. He attacked the existing system of higher education which gave prestige to the universities, and 'prestige reduction' to the technical colleges as suicidal for a nation which lived by its wits.

There is no doubt that the actual capital investment in university education per student is higher than it is in polytechnics, which again is higher than in colleges of education, and this has brought Edward Short to compare their structure to the secondary school tripartite system. But universities fulfil a special role in our society producing the finest scholars and élite intellectual leaders rather than sandwich course engineers and managers, as do polytechnics, or teachers, as do colleges of education. There is no reason why the cost per place in each institution should be the same if they require different equipment and facilities to fulfil their aims. Combining three very different types of institutions into giant polyversities will not make them better at their tasks but will simply create bureaucratic mediocrity. The education originally intended for 5 per cent of our pupils is not necessarily the right form of education for some 20 or 25 per cent who move on to higher education.

The Labour Party programme of 1973 withdrew from the precipice and accepted the binary system of higher education provided there was rationalisation of sporting, recreational and library facilities.

There could, however, be another dangerous and completely anti-intellectual suggestion which would destroy our universities: the allocation of a percentage of entry to each immigrant group or social class without any test. This has already happened in certain institutions in America where final degree results are also suspect as lecturers and professors buy peace by refusing to fail anyone for fear of being accused of discrimination.

If real equality of educational opportunity is to be realised or maintained in higher education then we must study the lessons of what happened in secondary schools. Higher education must be open not only to those who are most suited to it but also to those who most want it and are prepared to pay for it since the motivation of such students will probably bring them success. Free higher education with student grants as at present provided will lead to inevitable disaster. This education is financed by the general tax and ratepayer and all will demand it as of right irrespective of motivation rather as they would demand holidays in Corsica if they were offered free to a selected percentage of the age group.

The present system is that universities choose their own students with standards differing from university to university and subject to subject. Advising students applying for university entrance is rather like backing horses by using last year's racing results. Headmasters' and headmistress' reports vary as do the assessments of university lecturers. A student who is rejected for his four university choices and yet sees a colleague accepted in the same subject with the same or lower examination grades has a justified grievance against the system.

There is no reason why full scholarships and generous living grants should not be made available each year to the 10,000 students who gain the highest 'A' level grades and another 10,000 exhibitions on half fees and half grants to those who gain the next best results. These scholarship and exhibition holders could then choose any institution or any course which accepted them for three years. All the remaining entrants to higher education should pay full fees varying from £1,200 a year for some university courses to £600 at polytechnics and £772 at colleges of education. Loan systems would be arranged to allow them to cover these fees. Thus the finest scholars would be given every assistance to enter higher education, and all who really wished to enter university and were suitably qualified and prepared to make sacrifices could also enter as fee payers. This seems just: the very brightest can always be identified, it is far more difficult to identify those in the average plus ratings at every stage.

The present system of entry to higher education whereby some enter free and receive living grants while others are rejected does not foster equality of opportunity. Many who do enter do so because it is an accepted fashion, because they can think of nothing better to do, and because in the case of girls three years in a college of education studying infant education or home economics is a splendid preparation, at the taxpayers' expense, for marriage. If applicants could enter higher education provided they paid full fees, including capital costs, then they would finance the extra investment, if expansion was required, or there would be a decline in applications which would make further expansion unnecessary.

There is one final aspect of equality of opportunity which cannot be ignored. This is the early leaver who, disillusioned by education or his own lack of ability, leaves at fifteen or sixteen and whose taxes then help to maintain the heavy cost of education. Everything must be done to encourage such leavers to return to full-time education later in life if they so desire. The number of mature scholarships is at a couple of dozen a year far too small and a larger number of scholarships and exhibitions must be offered to early leavers who wish to study for degrees. They should first, however, have to obtain good 'O' and 'A' level qualifications—there should be no decline of accepted standards as in the Open University. Equality of opportunity affects age, as well as sex and social class.

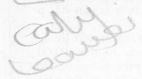

Index of Subjects

Index of Names